Birnbaum's 96

Bahamas and Turks & Caicos

A BIRNBAUM TRAVEL GUIDE

Alexandra Mayes Birnbaum
EDITORIAL CONSULTANT

Lois Spritzer
Editorial Director

Laura L. Brengelman
Managing Editor

Mary Callahan
Beth Schlau
Senior Editors

Jill Kadetsky
Editor

Patricia Canole
Gene Gold
Susan McClung
Associate Editors

Marcy Pritchard
Map Coordinator

Susan Cutter Snyder
Editorial Assistant

HarperPerennial
A *Division* of HarperCollins*Publishers*

For Stephen, who merely made all this possible.

BIRNBAUM'S BAHAMAS AND TURKS & CAICOS 96. Copyright © 1995 by
HarperCollins*Publishers*. All rights reserved. Printed in the United States of
America. No part of this book may be used or reproduced in any manner
whatsoever without written permission except in the case of brief quotations
embodied in critical articles and reviews. For information, address
HarperCollins*Publishers*, 10 East 53rd Street, New York, NY 10022.

FIRST EDITION

ISSN 0749-2561 (Birnbaum Travel Guides)
ISSN 1055-5625 (Bahamas and Turks & Caicos)
ISBN 0-06-278217-7 (pbk.)

95 96 97 98 ❖/RRD 5 4 3 2 1

Cover design © Drenttel Doyle Partners
Cover photograph © Bob Krist

BIRNBAUM TRAVEL GUIDES

Bahamas, and Turks & Caicos
Bermuda
Canada
Cancun, Cozumel & Isla Mujeres
Caribbean
Country Inns and Back Roads
Disneyland
Hawaii
Mexico
Miami & Ft. Lauderdale
United States
Walt Disney World
Walt Disney World for Kids, By Kids
Walt Disney World Without Kids

Contributing Editors

Samuel E. Bleecker
Susan Kelly
Julie Ann Sipos

Maps

B. Andrew Mudryk

Contents

Getting Ready to Go

Practical information for planning your trip.

The Islands

Thorough, qualitative guides to the Bahamas and the Turks and Caicos. Each section offers a comprehensive report on the islands' most compelling attractions and amenities—highlighting our top choices in every category.

Bahamas

Bahamas At-a-Glance

Diversions

*A selective guide to a variety of unexpected
pleasures, pinpointing the best places to pursue them.*

Exceptional Pleasures and Treasures

Directions

*The most delightful walks and drives through
the Bahamas and the Turks and Caicos.*

Foreword

To tell the truth, neither my husband Steve Birnbaum nor I started out as fans of the Bahamas. Our first Bahamian travel experience took place a couple of decades ago on Grand Bahama Island, arguably the least attractive of all the 700 or so Bahamian islands. It wasn't so much that Grand Bahama was any less attractive physically than its sister islands, but that it was cursed by the kind of cynical development that had no regard for Bahamas culture or island values—the island looked like a poor man's Las Vegas with the emphasis on bad taste and indifferent management.

Much in the Bahamas has changed significantly over the last generation, and while Grand Bahama Island hasn't improved much, it is no more representative of the broad scope of the Bahamas than New York City is an example of the United States as a whole. Happily, travelers have discovered that such popular stops as Nassau/Paradise Island and Grand Bahama are not the real lure of the Bahamas. The Bahamian places where the appeal of authentic island life is most often discovered are on Eleuthera and Spanish Wells, on Great Abaco and the Exumas, and on the Berry Islands and the Turks and Caicos. And at a time when true get-away-from-it-all escapes are harder and harder to find in our modern world, the Bahamas represent a nearby destination that can produce serenity and solitude in abundance. Though all members of the same island group, the individual atolls that make up the Bahamas have very different flavors and atmospheres, and we have attempted to isolate and explain the very varied attitudes that prevail within a single nation.

That's why we've tried to create a guide to the Bahamas that's specifically organized, written, and edited for today's demanding modern traveler, one for whom qualitative information is infinitely more desirable than mere quantities of unappraised data. We realize that it's impossible for any single travel writer to visit hundreds of restaurants (and nearly as many hotels) in any given year and provide accurate appraisals of each. And even if it were physically possible for one human being to survive such an itinerary, it would of necessity have to be done at a dead sprint, and the perceptions derived therefrom would probably be less valid than those of any other intelligent individual visiting the same establishments. It is, therefore, both impractical and undesirable (especially in an annually revised and updated guidebook series such as we offer) to have only one person provide all the data on the entire world. Instead, we have chosen what we like to describe as the "thee and me" approach to restaurant and hotel evaluation and, to a more limited degree, to the sites and sights we have included in our text. This reflects a personal sampling tempered by intelligent counsel from informed local sources.

This guidebook is directed to the "visitor," and such elements as restaurants have been specifically picked to provide the visitor with a representative, enlightening, and above all pleasant experience. Since so many extraneous considerations can affect the reception and service accorded a regular restaurant patron, our choices can in no way be construed as an exhaustive guide to resident dining. We think we've listed all the best places, in various price ranges, but they were chosen with a visitor's enjoyment in mind.

Other evidence of how we've tried to tailor our text to reflect modern travel habits is apparent in the section we call DIVERSIONS. Where once it was common for tourists to spend an island visit nailed to a single spot, today's traveler is more likely to want to pursue a special interest or to venture off the beaten path. In response to this trend, we have collected a series of exceptional experiences so that it is no longer necessary to wade through a pound or two of superfluous prose just to find exceptional pleasures and treasures.

Finally, I also should point out that every good travel guide is a living enterprise; that is, no part of this text is carved in stone. In our annual revisions, we refine, expand, and further hone all our material to serve your travel needs better. To this end, no contribution is of greater value to us than your personal reaction to what we have written, as well as information reflecting your own experiences while using the book. Please write to us at 10 E. 53rd St., New York, NY 10022.

We sincerely hope to hear from you.

Alexandra Mayes Birnbaum

ALEXANDRA MAYES BIRNBAUM, editorial consultant to the *Birnbaum Travel Guides,* worked with her late husband, Stephen Birnbaum, as co-editor of the series. She has been a world traveler since childhood and is known for her travel reports on radio on what's hot and what's not.

Bahamas and Turks & Caicos

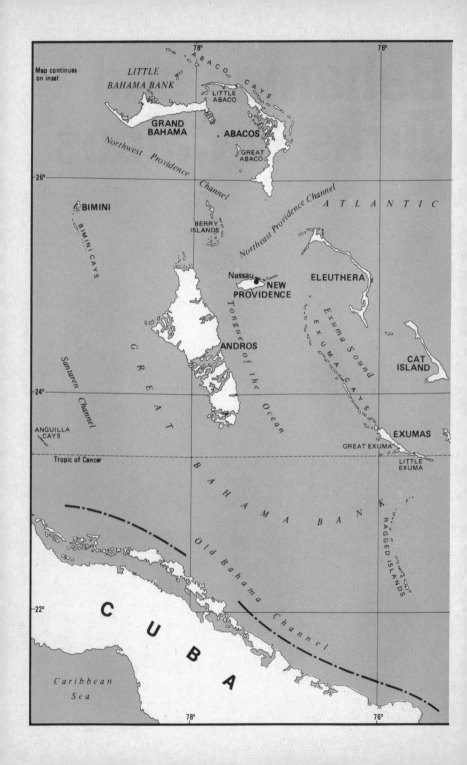

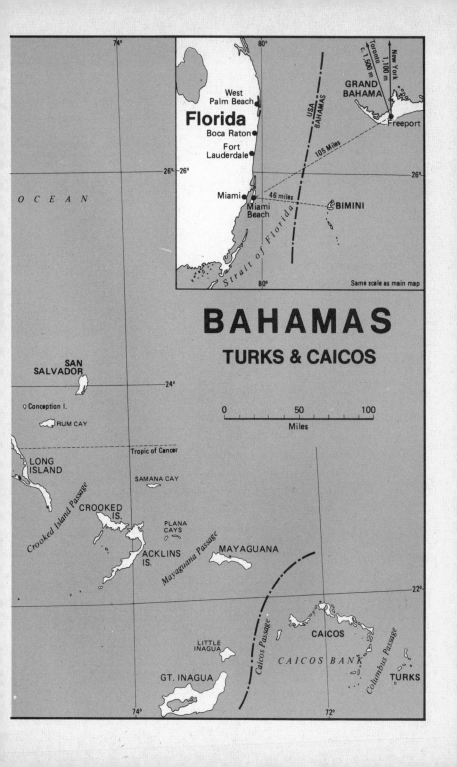

OCEAN

West
Palm Beach
Florida
Boca Raton
Fort
Lauderdale

GRAND
BAHAMA

Toronto
c. 1,500 m

New York
1,100 m

Freeport

USA
BAHAMAS

105 Miles

Miami
46 miles

BIMINI

Miami
Beach

Strait of Florida

Same scale as main map

BAHAMAS
TURKS & CAICOS

SAN
SALVADOR

◇ Conception I.

🝊 RUM CAY

24°

0	50	100

Miles

Tropic of Cancer

LONG
ISLAND

SAMANA CAY

Crooked Island Passage

CROOKED
IS.

PLANA
CAYS

Mayaguana Passage

MAYAGUANA

ACKLINS
IS.

Mayaguana Passage

22°

Caicos Passage

CAICOS

Columbus Passage

CAICOS BANK

LITTLE
INAGUA

TURKS

GT. INAGUA

74°

72°

How to Use This Guide

A great deal of care has gone into the special organization of this guide-book, and we believe it represents a real breakthrough in the presentation of travel material.

Our text is divided into four basic sections, in order to present information in the best way on every possible aspect of a Bahamas vacation. Our aim is to highlight what's where and to provide basic information—how, when, where, how much, and what's best—to assist you in making the most intelligent choices possible.

Here is a brief summary of what you can expect to find in each section. We believe that you will find both your travel planning and on-island enjoyment enhanced by having this book at your side.

GETTING READY TO GO

A mini-encyclopedia of practical travel facts with all the precise data necessary to create a successful Bahamas holiday. Here you will find how to get where you're going, currency information and exchange rates, plus selected resources—including useful publications, and companies and organizations specializing in discount and special-interest travel—providing a wealth of information and assistance useful both before and during your trip.

THE ISLANDS

Our individual reports on the Bahamas and the Turks and Caicos offer a short-stay guide, including an essay introducing the islands as a contemporary place to visit. *At-a-Glance* contains a site-by-site survey of the most important, interesting, and sometimes most eclectic sights to see and things to do. *Sources and Resources* is a concise listing of pertinent tourist information, such as the address of the local tourism office, which sightseeing tours to take, where to find the best nightspot, to play golf, to rent scuba equipment, to find the best beach, or to get a taxi. *Best on the Islands* lists our choices of the best places to eat and sleep on a variety of budgets.

DIVERSIONS

This section is designed to help travelers find the best places to engage in a variety of exceptional experiences for the mind and body, without having to wade through endless pages of unrelated text. In every case, our particular suggestions are intended to guide you to that special place where the quality of experience is likely to be highest.

DIRECTIONS

Here are 12 itineraries that follow the most beautiful routes and roads, past the most spectacular diving spots, and through the most serene and quaint little towns. DIRECTIONS is the only section of this book that is organized geographically; walks, bike tours, and drives can be connected for longer trips or used individually for short, intensive explorations.

Each entry includes a guide to sightseeing highlights, a qualitative guide to food along the road, and suggestions for activities.

To use this book to full advantage, take a few minutes to read the table of contents and random entries in each section to get a firsthand feel for how it all fits together. You will find that the sections of this book are building blocks designed to help you put together the best possible trip. Use them selectively as a tool, a source of ideas, a reference work for accurate facts, and a guidebook to the best buys, the most exciting sights, the most pleasant accommodations, and the tastiest foods—*the best travel experience* that you can possibly have.

Getting
Ready to Go

Getting Ready to Go

When to Go

The climate of the Bahamas and Turks and Caicos is warm and pleasant year-round, although temperatures and humidity can be uncomfortably high in the summer. The best weather is during the peak winter travel season (December through April). Hurricanes may occur any time from June through October, but are most common in September. Travel during the off-season and shoulder seasons (the months immediately before and after the peak months) offers relatively fair weather and smaller crowds, and often is less expensive.

If you have a touch-tone phone, you can call *The Weather Channel Connection* (phone: 900-WEATHER) for current worldwide weather forecasts. This service, available from *The Weather Channel* (2600 Cumberland Pkwy., Atlanta, GA 30339), costs 95¢ per minute; the charge will appear on your phone bill.

Traveling by Plane

SCHEDULED FLIGHTS

Airlines offering flights between the US and the Bahamas, as well as flights to the outlying islands, include *American, American Eagle, American Trans Air (ATA), Bahamasair, Carnival Air Lines, Chalk's International, Delta, Delta Connection, Laker Airways, Paradise Island Airlines, USAir,* and *USAir Express.* Flights to the Turks and Caicos are offered by *American* and *Turks and Caicos Airways (TCA). Turks and Caicos Airways* also provides inter-island connections throughout the Bahamas and Turks and Caicos.

FARES The great variety of airfares can be reduced to the following basic categories: first class, business class (not usually available on flights to the Bahamas), coach (also called economy or tourist class), excursion or discount, and standby, as well as various promotional fares. For information on applicable fares and restrictions, contact the airlines listed above or ask your travel agent. Most airfares are offered for a limited time; once you've found the lowest fare for which you can qualify, purchase your ticket as soon as possible.

RESERVATIONS Reconfirmation is strongly recommended for all international flights. It is essential that you confirm your round-trip reservations—*especially the return leg*—as well as any inter-island flights.

SEATING Airline seats usually are assigned on a first-come, first-served basis at check-in, although you may be able to reserve a seat when purchasing your ticket. Seating charts may be available from airlines and are included in the *Desktop Flight Guide* (Official Airline Guides, 2000 Clearwater Dr., Oak Brook, IL 60521; phone: 800-342-5624 or 708-574-6000; fax: 708-574-6565).

SMOKING US law prohibits smoking on flights scheduled for six hours or less within the US and its territories on both US and foreign carriers. These restrictions do not apply to nonstop flights between the US and international destinations; however, the US and the Bahamas have an agreement prohibiting smoking on all flights between the two countries. Although this agreement does not apply to the Turks and Caicos, at press time, *Delta* had independently banned smoking on all flights to the Turks and Caicos. A free wallet-size guide that describes the rights of nonsmokers under current regulations is available from *ASH* (*Action on Smoking and Health;* DOT Card, 2013 H St. NW, Washington, DC 20006; phone: 202-659-4310).

SPECIAL MEALS When making your reservation, you can request one of the airline's alternate menu choices for no additional charge. Though not always required, it is a good idea to call and reconfirm your request the day before departure.

BAGGAGE On major international airlines, passengers usually are allowed to carry on board one bag that will fit under a seat or in an overhead bin and to check two bags in the cargo hold. Specific regulations regarding dimensions and weight restrictions vary among airlines, but a checked bag usually cannot exceed 62 inches in combined dimensions (length, width, and depth) or weigh more than 70 pounds. There may be charges for additional, oversize, or overweight luggage, and for special equipment or sporting gear. Note that baggage allowances may be more limited on inter-island flights. Check that the tags the airline attaches are correctly coded for your destination.

CHARTER FLIGHTS

By booking a block of seats on a specially arranged flight, charter operators frequently can offer travelers bargain airfares. If you do fly on a charter, however, read the contract's fine print carefully. Federal regulations permit charter operators to cancel a flight or assess surcharges of as much as 10% of the airfare up to 10 days before departure. You usually must book in advance, and once booked, no changes are permitted, so buy trip cancellation insurance. Also, make your check out to the company's escrow account, which provides some protection for your investment in the event that the charter operator fails. For further information, consult the publication *Jax Fax* (397 Post Rd., Darien, CT 06820; phone: 203-655-8746; fax: 203-655-6257).

DISCOUNTS ON SCHEDULED FLIGHTS

COURIER TRAVEL In return for arranging to accompany some kind of freight, a traveler pays only a portion of the total airfare (and sometimes a small registration fee). One agency that matches would-be couriers with courier companies is *Now Voyager* (74 Varick St., Suite 307, New York, NY 10013; phone: 212-431-1616; fax: 212-219-1753).

Courier Companies

Discount Travel International (169 W. 81st St., New York, NY 10024; phone: 212-362-3636; fax: 212-362-3236).

F.B. On Board Courier Club (10225 Ryan Ave., Suite 103, Dorval, Quebec H9P 1A2, Canada; phone: 514-633-0740; fax: 514-633-0735).

Halbart Express (147-05 176th St., Jamaica, NY 11434; phone: 718-656-5000; fax: 718-917-0708).

Midnite Express (925 W. Hyde Park Blvd., Inglewood, CA 90302; phone: 310-672-1100; fax: 310-671-0107).

Way to Go Travel (6679 Sunset Blvd., Hollywood, CA 90028; phone: 213-466-1126; fax: 800-700-8359).

Publications

Insiders Guide to Air Courier Bargains, by Kelly Monaghan (The Intrepid Traveler, PO Box 438, New York, NY 10034; phone: 800-356-9315 for orders; 212-569-1081 for information; fax: 212-942-6687).

Travel Unlimited (PO Box 1058, Allston, MA 02134-1058; no phone).

CONSOLIDATORS AND BUCKET SHOPS These companies buy blocks of tickets from airlines and sell them at a discount to travel agents or directly to consumers. Since many bucket shops operate on a thin margin, be sure to check a company's record with the *Better Business Bureau*—before parting with any money.

Council Charter (205 E. 42nd St., New York, NY 10017; phone: 800-800-8222 or 212-661-0311; fax: 212-972-0194).

Fare Deals Travel (9350 E. Arapahoe Rd., Suite 330, Englewood, CO 80112; phone: 800-878-2929 or 303-792-2929; fax: 303-792-2954).

Omniglobe Travel (690 Market St., Suite 510, San Francisco, CA 94104; phone: 800-894-9942 or 415-433-9312; fax: 415-433-9315).

Southwest Travel Systems (1001 N. Central Ave., Suite 575, Phoenix, AZ 85004; phone: 800-STS-TRAVEL or 602-255-0234; fax: 602-255-0220).

STT Worldwide Travel (9880 SW Beaverton Hillsdale Hwy., Beaverton, OR 97005; phone: 800-348-0886 or 503-641-8866; fax: 503-641-2171).

Travac Tours and Charters (989 Ave. of the Americas, New York, NY 10018; phone: 800-872-8800 or 212-563-3303; fax: 212-563-3631).

Unitravel (1177 N. Warson Rd., St. Louis, MO 63132; phone: 800-325-2222 or 314-569-0900; fax: 314-569-2503).

LAST-MINUTE TRAVEL CLUBS Members of such clubs receive information on imminent trips and other bargain travel opportunities. Some clubs charge an annual fee; others offer free membership. Despite the names of some of the clubs listed below, you don't have to wait until literally the last minute to make travel plans.

> *Discount Travel International* (169 W. 81st St., New York, NY 10024; phone: 212-362-3636; fax: 212-362-3236).
>
> *FLY ASAP* (PO Box 9808, Scottsdale, AZ 85252-3808; phone: 800-FLY-ASAP or 602-956-1987; fax: 602-956-6414).
>
> *Last Minute Travel* (1249 Boylston St., Boston, MA 02215; phone: 800-LAST-MIN or 617-267-9800; fax: 617-424-1943).
>
> *Moment's Notice* (425 Madison Ave., New York, NY 10017; phone: 212-486-0500/1/2/3; fax: 212-486-0783).
>
> *Spur of the Moment Cruises* (411 N. Harbor Blvd., Suite 302, San Pedro, CA 90731; phone: 800-4-CRUISES or 310-521-1070 in California; 800-343-1991 elsewhere in the US; 24-hour hotline: 310-521-1060; fax: 310-521-1061).
>
> *Traveler's Advantage* (3033 S. Parker Rd., Suite 900, Aurora, CO 80014; phone: 800-548-1116 for membership services; 800-835-8747 for reservations; fax: 303-368-3985).
>
> *Vacations to Go* (1502 Augusta Dr., Suite 415, Houston, TX 77057; phone: 713-974-2121 in Texas; 800-338-4962 elsewhere in the US; fax: 713-974-0445).
>
> *Worldwide Discount Travel Club* (1674 Meridian Ave., Miami Beach, FL 33139; phone: 305-534-2082).

GENERIC AIR TRAVEL These organizations operate much like an ordinary airline standby service, except that they offer seats on not one but several scheduled and charter airlines. One pioneer of generic flights is *Airhitch* (2472 Broadway, Suite 200, New York, NY 10025; phone: 212-864-2000; fax: 212-864-5489).

BARTERED TRAVEL SOURCES Barter—the exchange of commodities or services in lieu of cash payment—is a common practice among travel suppliers. Companies that have obtained travel services through barter may sell these services at substantial discounts to travel clubs, who pass along the savings to members. One organization offering bartered travel opportunities is *Travel World Leisure Club* (225 W. 34th St., Suite 909, New York, NY 10122; phone: 800-444-TWLC or 212-239-4855; fax: 212-564-5158).

CONSUMER PROTECTION

Passengers whose complaints have not been satisfactorily addressed by the airline can contact the *US Department of Transportation* (*DOT;* Consumer Affairs Division, 400 Seventh St. SW, Room 10405, Washington, DC 20590; phone: 202-366-2220). Also see *Fly Rights* (*Consumer Information Center,*

Dept. 133B, Pueblo, CO 81009; phone: 719-948-3334; fax: 719-948-9724). If you have safety-related questions or concerns, write to the *Federal Aviation Administration* (*FAA;* 800 Independence Ave. SW, Washington, DC 20591) or call the *FAA Consumer Hotline* (phone: 800-322-7873). If you have a complaint against a local travel service in the Bahamas, contact the *Ministry of Tourism* (Visitor Relations Dept., PO Box N3701, Nassau, Bahamas; phone: 809-322-7500; fax: 809-328-0945). In the Turks and Caicos, contact the *Turks and Caicos Tourist Board* (PO Box 128, Pond St., Grand Turk, Turks and Caicos Islands, British West Indies; phone: 809-946-2321; fax: 809-946-2733) or the *Ministry of Tourism* (Chief Minister's Office, Grand Turk, Turks and Caicos Islands, British West Indies; phone: 809-946-1113; fax: 809-946-1120).

Traveling by Ship

Your cruise fare usually includes all meals, recreational activities, and entertainment. Shore excursions are available at extra cost, and can be booked in advance or once you're on board. An important factor in the price of a cruise is the location (and sometimes the size) of your cabin. Charts issued by the *Cruise Lines International Association* (*CLIA;* 500 Fifth Ave., Suite 1407, New York, NY 10110; phone: 212-921-0066; fax: 212-921-0549) provide information on ship layouts and facilities, and are available at some *CLIA*-affiliated travel agencies.

The *US Public Health Service* (*PHS*) inspects all passenger vessels calling at US ports; for the most recent summary or a particular inspection report, write to the *National Center for Environmental Health* (Attention: Chief, Vessel Sanitation Program, 1015 N. America Way, Room 107, Miami, FL 33132; phone: 305-536-4307). Most cruise ships have a doctor on board, plus medical facilities.

For further information on cruises and cruise lines, consult *Ocean and Cruise News* (PO Box 92, Stamford, CT 06904; phone/fax: 203-329-2787). And for a free list of travel agencies specializing in cruises, contact the *National Association of Cruise Only Agencies* (*NACOA;* 3191 Coral Way, Suite 630, Miami, FL 33145; phone: 305-446-7732; fax: 305-446-9732).

A number of major cruise lines offer sailings to the Bahamas. Shorter excursions are available through companies such as *Island Vacations* (1200 NW 78th Ave., Suite 211, Miami, FL 33126; phone: 800-900-4242 or 305-477-7667; fax: 305-477-9665) and *SeaEscape* (8751 W. Broward Blvd., Suite 400, Plantation, FL 33324; phone: 800-327-7400, 800-327-2005, or 305-379-0000; fax: 305-476-9921). Other options include crewed or uncrewed (called "bareboat") charters.

International Cruise Lines

American Canadian Caribbean Line (PO Box 368, Warren, RI 02885; phone: 401-247-0955 in Rhode Island; 800-556-7450 elsewhere in the US; fax: 401-245-8303).

Carnival Cruise Lines (3655 NW 87th Ave., Miami, FL 33178-2428; phone: 800-327-9501 or 305-599-2600; fax: 305-471-4740).

Celebrity Cruises and *Fantasy Cruises* (5200 Blue Lagoon Dr., Miami, FL 33126; phone: 800-437-3111 or 305-262-6677; fax: 800-437-9111 or 305-267-3505).

Costa Cruises (80 SW Eighth St., Miami, FL 33130; phone: 800-462-6782; fax: 305-375-0676).

Cunard (555 Fifth Ave., New York, NY 10017; phone: 800-5-CUNARD, 800-221-4770, or 212-880-7300; fax: 718-786-2353).

Dolphin Cruise Line (901 South America Way, Miami, FL 33132-2073; phone: 800-222-1003 or 305-358-2111; fax: 305-358-4807).

Majesty Cruise Line (c/o *Dolphin Cruise Line,* address above; phone: 800-532-7788 or 305-536-0000; fax: 305-358-4807).

Norwegian Cruise Line (95 Merrick Way, Coral Gables, FL 33134; phone: 800-327-7030 or 305-445-0866; fax: 305-448-6406).

P&O Cruises (c/o *Golden Bear Travel,* 16 Digital Dr., Suite 100, Novato, CA 94948; phone: 800-551-1000 or 415-382-8900; fax: 415-382-9086).

Premier Cruise Lines (PO Box 656, Cape Canaveral, FL 32920; phone: 800-327-7113 or 407-783-5061; fax: 407-784-0954).

Princess Cruises (10100 Santa Monica Blvd., Los Angeles, CA 90067; phone: 800-421-0522 or 310-553-1770; fax: 310-284-2844).

Royal Caribbean Cruise Lines (1050 Caribbean Way, Miami, FL 33132; phone: 800-327-6700 or 305-539-6000; fax: 800-722-5329).

SSC Radisson Diamond Cruise (11340 Blondo St., Omaha, NE 68164; phone: 800-333-3333 or 402-498-5072; fax: 402-498-5055).

Sun Line Cruises (1 Rockefeller Plaza, Suite 315, New York, NY 10020; phone: 800-872-6400 or 212-397-6400; fax: 212-765-9685).

Windjammer Barefoot Cruises, Ltd. (PO Box 190120, Miami, FL 33119-0120; phone: 800-327-2601 or 305-534-7447; fax: 305-674-1219).

Chartered Boat Companies

Lynn Jachney Charters (PO Box 302, Marblehead, MA 01945; phone: 617-639-0787 in Massachusetts; 800-223-2050 elsewhere in the US; fax: 617-639-0216).

SailAway Yacht Charter Consultants (15605 SW 92nd Ave., Miami, FL 33157; phone: 305-253-7245 in Dade County, Florida; 800-724-5292 elsewhere in the US; fax: 305-251-4408).

Sunsail (115 E. Broward Blvd., Ft. Lauderdale, FL 33301; phone: 800-327-2276 or 305-524-7553; fax: 305-524-6312).

Whitney Yacht Charters (4065 Crocker's Lake Blvd., Suite 2722, Sarasota, FL 34238; phone: 800-223-1426 or 813-927-0108; fax: 813-922-7819).

Touring by Car

Driving is an enjoyable way to explore much of the Bahamas and Turks and Caicos. Although some of the islands in the Bahamas are too small to accommodate cars, you may be able to rent an all-terrain or four-wheel-drive vehicle, motorbike, moped, or bicycle. Driving is on the left side of the road; the steering wheel may be on either side of the car (although in rental cars it usually is on the left). Gasoline is sold by the gallon, and road signs and speed limits are in miles and miles per hour (mph).

RENTING A CAR

You can rent a car through a travel agent or international rental firm before leaving home, or from a local company once in the islands. Reserve in advance.

To rent a car in the Bahamas, a traveler from the US must have a valid US driver's license. Most car rental companies require a credit card, although some will accept a substantial cash deposit. The minimum age to rent a car is set by the company; some also may impose special conditions on drivers above a certain age. Electing to pay for collision damage waiver (CDW) protection will add to the cost of renting a car, but releases you from financial liability for the vehicle. Additional costs include drop-off charges or one-way service fees.

Car Rental Companies

Avis (phone: 800-331-1084).
Budget (phone: 800-472-3325).
Dollar Rent A Car (phone: 800-800-4000).
European Car Reservations (phone: 800-535-3303).
Hertz (phone: 800-654-3001).

Package Tours

A package is a collection of travel services that can be purchased in a single transaction. Its principal advantages are convenience and economy—the cost usually is lower than that of the same services purchased separately. Tour programs generally can be divided into two categories: escorted or locally hosted (with a set itinerary) and independent (which usually are more flexible).

When considering a package tour, read the brochure *carefully* to determine exactly what is included and any conditions that may apply, and check the company's record with the *Better Business Bureau*. The *United States Tour Operators Association* (*USTOA;* 211 E. 51st St., Suite 12B, New York, NY 10022; phone: 212-750-7371; fax: 212-421-1285) also can be helpful in determining a package tour operator's reliability. As with charter flights, to safeguard your funds, always make your check out to the company's escrow account.

Many tour operators offer packages focused on special interests such as the arts, nature study, or sports. *All Adventure Travel* (5589 Arapahoe, Suite 208, Boulder, CO 80303; phone: 800-537-4025 or 303-440-7924; fax: 303-440-4160) represents such specialized packagers. Many also are listed in the *Specialty Travel Index* (305 San Anselmo Ave., Suite 313, San Anselmo, CA 94960; phone: 415-459-4900 in California; 800-442-4922 elsewhere in the US; fax: 415-459-4974). In addition, a variety of package tours to the Bahamas and Turks and Caicos are listed in the *Island Vacation Catalog,* issued by *TourScan* (PO Box 2367, Darien, CT 06820; phone: 800-962-2080 or 203-655-8091; fax: 203-655-6689).

Below is a list of companies offering package tours to the Bahamas and/or the Turks and Caicos. Note that those companies described as wholesalers accept bookings only through travel agents.

Package Tour Operators

Adventure Tours (10612 Beaver Dam Rd., Hunt Valley, MD 21030-2205; phone: 410-785-3500 in the Baltimore area; 800-638-9040 elsewhere in the US; fax: 410-584-2771). Wholesaler.

American Airlines FlyAAway Vacations (offices throughout the US; phone: 800-321-2121).

Angling Travel and Tours (c/o *John Eustice & Associates,* 1445 SW 84th Ave., Portland, OR 97225; phone: 800-288-0886 or 503-297-2468; fax: 503-297-3048).

Apple Vacations East (7 Campus Blvd., Newtown Sq., PA 19073; phone: 800-727-3400 or 610-359-6500; fax: 610-359-6524). Wholesaler.

Backcountry (PO Box 4029, Bozeman, MT 59772; phone: 406-586-3556; fax: 406-586-4288).

Certified Vacations (110 E. Broward Blvd., Ft. Lauderdale, FL 33302; phone: 800-233-7260 or 305-522-1440; fax: 305-357-4687).

Delta's Dream Vacations (PO Box 1525, Ft. Lauderdale, FL 33302; phone: 800-872-7786).

Ecosummer Expeditions (936 Peace Portal Dr., PO Box 8014-240, Blaine, WA 98231; and 1516 Duranleau St., Vancouver, British Columbia V6H 3S4, Canada; phone: 800-688-8605 or 604-669-7741; fax: 604-669-3244).

Fishing International (PO Box 2132, Santa Rosa, CA 95405; phone: 800-950-4242 or 707-539-3366; fax: 707-539-1320).

Frontiers International (PO Box 959, Wexford, PA 15090-0959; phone: 412-935-1577 in Pennsylvania; 800-245-1950 elsewhere in the US; fax: 412-935-5388). Wholesaler.

Gadabout Tours (700 E. Tahquitz Canyon Way, Palm Springs, CA 92262; phone: 800-952-5068 or 619-325-5556; fax: 619-325-5127).

GOGO Tours (69 Spring St., Ramsey, NJ 07446-0507; phone: 201-934-3759). Wholesaler.

Kerrville Tours (PO Box 79, Shreveport, LA 71161-0079; phone: 800-442-8705 or 318-227-2882; fax: 318-227-2486).

Liberty Travel (for the nearest location, contact the central office: 69 Spring St., Ramsey, NJ 07446; phone: 201-934-3500; fax: 201-934-3888).

Marathon Tours (108 Main St., Boston, MA 02129; phone: 800-444-4097 or 617-242-7845; fax: 617-242-7686).

Oceanic Society Expeditions (Ft. Mason Center, Building E, San Francisco, CA 94123; phone: 800-326-7491 or 415-441-1106; fax: 415-474-3395).

PanAngling Travel Service (180 N. Michigan Ave., Room 303, Chicago, IL 60601; phone: 800-533-4353 or 312-263-0328; fax: 312-263-5246).

Steve Currey Expeditions (PO Box 1574, Provo, UT 84603; phone: 800-937-7238; phone/fax: 801-224-5715).

Thomas Cook Vacations (headquarters: 45 Berkeley St., Piccadilly, London W1A 1EB, England; phone: 44-171-499-4000; fax: 44-171-408-4299; main US office: 100 Cambridge Park Dr., Cambridge, MA 02140; phone: 800-846-6272 or 617-868-2666; fax: 617-349-1094).

Tours and Travel Odyssey (230 E. McClellan Ave., Livingston, NJ 07039; phone: 800-527-2989 or 201-992-5459; fax: 201-994-1618).

Trans National Travel (2 Charlesgate W., Boston, MA 02215; phone: 800-262-0123 or 617-762-9200; fax: 617-638-3445). Wholesaler.

Travel Impressions (465 Smith St., Farmingdale, NY 11735; phone: 800-284-0077, 800-284-0044, or 516-845-8000; fax: 516-845-8095). Wholesaler.

Tropical Adventures Travel (111 Second Ave. N., Seattle, WA 98109; phone: 800-247-3483 or 206-441-3483; fax: 206-441-5431).

Uniworld (16000 Ventura Blvd., Suite 210, Encino, CA 91436; phone: 800-366-7831 or 818-382-7830; fax: 818-981-5524). Wholesaler.

Insurance

The first person with whom you should discuss travel insurance is your own insurance broker. You may discover that the insurance you already carry protects you adequately while traveling and that you need little additional coverage. If you charge travel services, the credit card company also may provide some insurance coverage (and other safeguards). Below is a list of the basic types of travel insurance and companies specializing in such policies.

Types of Travel Insurance

Automobile insurance: Provides collision, theft, property damage, and personal liability protection while driving.

Baggage and personal effects insurance: Protects your bags and their contents in case of damage or theft at any point during your travels.

Default and/or bankruptcy insurance: Provides coverage in the event of default and/or bankruptcy on the part of the tour operator, airline, or other travel supplier.

Flight insurance: Covers accidental injury or death while flying.

Personal accident and sickness insurance: Covers cases of illness, injury, or death in an accident while traveling.

Trip cancellation and interruption insurance: Guarantees a refund if you must cancel a trip; may reimburse you for additional travel costs incurred in catching up with a tour or traveling home early.

Combination policies: Include any or all of the above.

Travel Insurance Providers

Access America International (PO Box 90315, Richmond, VA 23230; phone: 800-284-8300 or 804-285-3300; fax: 804-673-1491).

Carefree (c/o *Berkely Care,* Arm Coverage, PO Box 310, Mineola, NY 11501; phone: 800-645-2424 or 516-294-0220; fax: 516-294-0258).

NEAR Services (PO Box 1339, Calumet City, IL 60409; phone: 708-868-6700 in the Chicago area; 800-654-6700 elsewhere in the US; fax: 708-868-6706).

Tele-Trip (3201 Farnam St., Omaha, NE 68131; phone: 800-228-9792 or 402-345-2400; fax: 402-978-2456).

Travel Assistance International (c/o *Worldwide Assistance Services,* 1133 15th St. NW, Suite 400, Washington, DC 20005; phone: 800-821-2828 or 202-331-1609; fax: 202-331-1530).

Travel Guard International (1145 Clark St., Stevens Point, WI 54481; phone: 800-826-1300 or 715-345-0505; fax: 800-955-8785).

Travel Insurance PAK Worldwide Coverage (c/o *Travel Insured International,* PO Box 280568, East Hartford, CT 06128-0568; phone: 800-243-3174 or 203-528-7663; fax: 203-528-8005).

Disabled Travelers

Make travel arrangements well in advance. Specify to all services involved the nature of your disability to determine if there are accommodations and facilities that meet your needs. For information about accessibility and services for the disabled in the Bahamas, contact the *Bahamas Association for the Physically Disabled* (PO Box N4252, Nassau, Bahamas; phone: 809-322-2393; fax: 809-322-7984).

International Organizations

ACCENT on Living (PO Box 700, Bloomington, IL 61702; phone: 800-787-8444 or 309-378-2961; fax: 309-378-4420).

Access: The Foundation for Accessibility by the Disabled (PO Box 356, Malverne, NY 11565; phone/fax: 516-568-2715).

American Foundation for the Blind (15 W. 16th St., New York, NY 10011; phone: 800-232-5463 or 212-620-2147; fax: 212-727-7418).

Information Center for Individuals with Disabilities (Ft. Point Pl., 27-43 Wormwood St., Boston, MA 02210; phone: 800-462-5015 in Massachusetts; 617-727-5540 elsewhere in the US; TDD: 617-345-9743; fax: 617-345-5318).

Mobility International (main office: 25 Rue de Manchester, Brussels B-1070, Belgium; phone: 32-2-410-6297; fax: 32-2-410-6874; US office: *MIUSA,* PO Box 10767, Eugene, OR 97440; phone/TDD: 503-343-1284; fax: 503-343-6812).

Moss Rehabilitation Hospital Travel Information Service (telephone referrals only; phone: 215-456-9600; TDD: 215-456-9602).

National Rehabilitation Information Center (8455 Colesville Rd., Suite 935, Silver Spring, MD 20910-3319; phone: 301-588-9284; fax: 301-587-1967).

Paralyzed Veterans of America (*PVA;* PVA/Access to the Skies Program, 801 18th St. NW, Washington, DC 20006-3585; phone: 202-872-1300 in Washington, DC; 800-424-8200 elsewhere in the US; fax: 202-785-4452).

Royal Association for Disability and Rehabilitation (*RADAR;* 12 City Forum, 250 City Rd., London EC1V 8AF, England; phone: 44-171-250-3222; fax: 44-171-250-0212).

Society for the Advancement of Travel for the Handicapped (*SATH;* 347 Fifth Ave., Suite 610, New York, NY 10016; phone: 212-447-7284; fax: 212-725-8253).

Travel Industry and Disabled Exchange (*TIDE;* Attention: Yvonne Nau, 5435 Donna Ave., Tarzana, CA 91356; phone: 818-344-3640; fax: 818-344-0078).

Publications

Access Travel: A Guide to the Accessibility of Airport Terminals (Consumer Information Center, Dept. 575A, Pueblo, CO 81009; phone: 719-948-3334; fax: 719-948-9724).

Air Transportation of Handicapped Persons (Publication #AC-120-32; *US Department of Transportation,* Distribution Unit, Utilization and Storage Section, M-45.3, 400 Seventh St. SW, Washington, DC 20590; phone: 202-366-0039; fax: 202-366-2795).

The Diabetic Traveler (PO Box 8223 RW, Stamford, CT 06905; phone: 203-327-5832; fax: 203-975-1748).

Directory of Travel Agencies for the Disabled and *Travel for the Disabled,* both by Helen Hecker (Twin Peaks Press, PO Box 129, Vancouver,

WA 98666; phone: 800-637-CALM for orders; 206-694-2462 for information; fax: 206-696-3210).

The Disabled Driver's Mobility Guide (*American Automobile Association,* Traffic Safety Dept., 1000 AAA Dr., Heathrow, FL 32746-5063; phone: 407-444-7961; fax: 407-444-7956).

Guide to Traveling with Arthritis (*Upjohn Company,* 7000 Portage Rd., Kalamazoo, MI 49001; phone: 800-253-9860).

Handicapped Travel Newsletter (PO Box 269, Athens, TX 75751; phone/fax: 903-677-1260).

Handi-Travel: A Resource Book for Disabled and Elderly Travellers, by Cinnie Noble (*Canadian Rehabilitation Council for the Disabled,* 45 Sheppard Ave. E., Suite 801, Toronto, Ontario M2N 5W9, Canada; phone/TDD: 416-250-7490; fax: 416-229-1371).

Holidays and Travel Abroad, edited by John Stanford (*Royal Association for Disability and Rehabilitation,* address above).

On the Go, Go Safely, Plan Ahead (*American Diabetes Association,* 1660 Duke St., Alexandria, VA 22314; phone: 800-232-3472 or 703-549-1500; fax: 703-863-7439).

Travel for the Patient with Chronic Obstructive Pulmonary Disease (Dr. Harold Silver, 1601 18th St. NW, Washington, DC 20009; phone: 202-667-0134; fax: 202-667-0148).

Travel Tips for Hearing-Impaired People (*American Academy of Otolaryngology,* 1 Prince St., Alexandria, VA 22314; phone: 703-836-4444; fax: 703-683-5100).

Travel Tips for People with Arthritis (*Arthritis Foundation,* 1314 Spring St. NW, Atlanta, GA 30309; phone: 800-283-7800 or 404-872-7100; fax: 404-872-0457).

Traveling Like Everybody Else: A Practical Guide for Disabled Travelers, by Jacqueline Freedman and Susan Gersten (Modan Publishing, PO Box 1202, Bellmore, NY 11710; phone: 516-679-1380; fax: 516-679-1448).

Package Tour Operators

Accessible Journeys (35 W. Sellers Ave., Ridley Park, PA 19078; phone: 800-846-4537 or 610-521-0339; fax: 610-521-6959).

Accessible Tours/Directions Unlimited (Attention: Lois Bonanni, 720 N. Bedford Rd., Bedford Hills, NY 10507; phone: 800-533-5343 or 914-241-1700; fax: 914-241-0243).

Classic Travel Service (8 W. 40th St., New York, NY 10018; phone: 212-869-2560 in New York State; 800-247-0909 elsewhere in the US; fax: 212-944-4493).

CTM Beehive Travel (77 W. 200 S., Suite 500, Salt Lake City, UT 84101; phone: 800-777-5727 or 801-578-9000; fax: 801-297-2828).

Dahl's Good Neighbor Travel Service (124 S. Main St., Viroqua, WI 54665; phone: 800-338-3245 or 608-637-2128; fax: 608-637-3030).

Dialysis at Sea Cruises (PO Box 218, Indian Rocks Beach, FL 34635; phone: 800-544-7604 or 813-596-4614; fax: 813-596-0203).

Flying Wheels Travel (PO Box 382, Owatonna, MN 55060; phone: 800-535-6790 or 507-451-1966; fax: 507-451-1685).

The Guided Tour (7900 Old York Rd., Suite 114B, Elkins Park, PA 19027-2339; phone: 800-783-5841 or 215-782-1370; fax: 215-635-2637).

Hinsdale Travel (201 E. Ogden Ave., Hinsdale, IL 60521; phone: 708-325-1335 or 708-469-7349; fax: 708-325-1342).

MedEscort International (*Lehigh Valley International Airport,* PO Box 8766, Allentown, PA 18105-8766; phone: 800-255-7182 or 215-791-3111; fax: 215-791-9189).

Prestige World Travel (5710-X High Point Rd., Greensboro, NC 27407; phone: 800-476-7737 or 910-292-6690; fax: 910-632-9404).

Sprout (893 Amsterdam Ave., New York, NY 10025; phone: 212-222-9575; fax: 212-222-9768).

Weston Travel Agency (134 N. Cass Ave., Westmont, IL 60559; phone: 708-968-2513 in Illinois; 800-633-3725 elsewhere in the US; fax: 708-968-2539).

Single Travelers

The travel industry is not very fair to people who vacation by themselves—they often end up paying more than those traveling in pairs. There are services catering to single travelers, however, that match travel companions, offer travel arrangements with shared accommodations, and provide information and discounts. Useful publications include *Going Solo* (Doerfer Communications, PO Box 123, Apalachicola, FL 32329; phone/fax: 904-653-8848) and *Traveling on Your Own,* by Eleanor Berman (Random House, Order Dept., 400 Hahn Rd., Westminster, MD 21157; phone: 800-733-3000; fax: 800-659-2436).

Organizations and Companies

Gallivanting (515 E. 79th St., Suite 20F, New York, NY 10021; phone: 800-933-9699 or 212-988-0617; fax: 212-988-0144).

Globus and Cosmos (5301 S. Federal Circle, Littleton, CO 80123; phone: 800-221-0090, 800-338-7092, or 303-797-2800; fax: 303-798-5441).

Jane's International Travel and Sophisticated Women Travelers (2603 Bath Ave., Brooklyn, NY 11214; phone: 800-613-9226 or 718-266-2045; fax: 718-266-4062).

Marion Smith Singles (611 Prescott Pl., N. Woodmere, NY 11581; phone: 800-698-TRIP, 516-791-4852, 516-791-4865, or 212-944-2112; fax: 516-791-4879).

Partners-in-Travel (11660 Chenault St., Suite 119, Los Angeles, CA 90049; phone: 310-476-4869).

Singleworld (401 Theodore Fremd Ave., Rye, NY 10580; phone: 800-223-6490 or 914-967-3334; fax: 914-967-7395).

Solo Flights (612 Penfield Rd., Fairfield, CT 06430; phone: 800-266-1566 or 203-256-1235).

Suddenly Singles Tours (161 Dreiser Loop, Bronx, NY 10475; phone: 718-379-8800 in New York City; 800-859-8396 elsewhere in the US; fax: 718-379-8858).

Travel Companion Exchange (PO Box 833, Amityville, NY 11701; phone: 516-454-0880; fax: 516-454-0170).

Travel Companions (Atrium Financial Center, 1515 N. Federal Hwy., Suite 300, Boca Raton, FL 33432; phone: 800-383-7211 or 407-393-6448; fax: 407-451-8560 or 407-393-6448).

Travel in Two's (239 N. Broadway, Suite 3, N. Tarrytown, NY 10591; phone: 914-631-8301 in New York State; 800-692-5252 elsewhere in the US).

Umbrella Singles (PO Box 157, Woodbourne, NY 12788; phone: 800-537-2797 or 914-434-6871; fax: 914-434-3532).

Older Travelers

Special discounts and more free time are just two factors that have given older travelers a chance to see the world at affordable prices. Many travel suppliers offer senior discounts—sometimes only to members of certain senior citizens organizations (which provide benefits of their own). When considering a particular package, make sure the facilities—and the pace of the tour—match your needs and physical condition.

Publications

Going Abroad: 101 Tips for Mature Travelers (*Grand Circle Travel,* 347 Congress St., Boston, MA 02210; phone: 800-221-2610 or 617-350-7500; fax: 617-423-0445).

The Mature Traveler (PO Box 50820, Reno, NV 89513-0820; phone: 702-786-7419).

Take a Camel to Lunch and Other Adventures for Mature Travelers, by Nancy O'Connell (Bristol Publishing Enterprises, PO Box 1737, San Leandro, CA 94577; phone: 510-895-4461 in California; 800-346-4889 elsewhere in the US; fax: 510-895-4459).

Unbelievably Good Deals & Great Adventures That You Absolutely Can't Get Unless You're Over 50, by Joan Rattner Heilman (Contemporary Books, 180 N. Stetson Ave., Suite 1200, Chicago, IL 60601; phone: 312-782-9181; fax: 312-540-4687).

Organizations

American Association of Retired Persons (*AARP;* 601 E St. NW, Washington, DC 20049; phone: 202-434-2277).

Golden Companions (PO Box 754, Pullman, WA 99163-0754; phone: 208-858-2183).

Mature Outlook (Customer Service Center, 6001 N. Clark St., Chicago, IL 60660; phone: 800-336-6330; fax: 312-764-5036).

National Council of Senior Citizens (1331 F St. NW, Washington, DC 20004; phone: 202-347-8800; fax: 202-624-9595).

Package Tour Operators

Elderhostel (75 Federal St., Boston, MA 02110-1941; phone: 617-426-7788; fax: 617-426-8351).

Gadabout Tours (700 E. Tahquitz Canyon Way, Palm Springs, CA 92262; phone: 800-952-5068 or 619-325-5556; fax: 619-325-5127).

Grand Circle Travel (347 Congress St., Boston, MA 02210; phone: 800-221-2610 or 617-350-7500; fax: 617-542-2887).

Grandtravel (6900 Wisconsin Ave., Suite 706, Chevy Chase, MD 20815; phone: 800-247-7651 or 301-986-0790; fax: 301-913-0166).

Interhostel (*University of New Hampshire,* Division of Continuing Education, 6 Garrison Ave., Durham, NH 03824; phone: 800-733-9753 or 603-862-1147; fax: 603-862-1113).

Mature Tours (c/o *Solo Flights,* 612 Penfield Rd., Fairfield, CT 06340; phone: 800-266-1566 or 203-256-1235).

OmniTours (104 Wilmot Rd., Deerfield, IL 60015; phone: 800-962-0060 or 708-374-0088; fax: 708-374-9515).

Saga International Holidays (222 Berkeley St., Boston, MA 02116; phone: 800-343-0273 or 617-262-2262; fax: 617-375-5950).

Money Matters

CURRENCY

The Bahamian dollar has parity with the US dollar, and both currencies are accepted throughout the islands. In the Turks and Caicos, the US dollar is legal tender.

CREDIT CARDS AND TRAVELER'S CHECKS

Most major credit cards enjoy wide domestic and international acceptance; however, not every hotel, restaurant, or shop in the Bahamas and Turks and Caicos accepts all (or in some cases any) credit cards. When making purchases with a credit card, note that most credit card companies charge a 1% fee for converting foreign currency charges to dollars. It's also wise to carry traveler's checks while on the road, since they are replaceable if stolen or lost and are widely accepted throughout the islands. You can buy traveler's checks at banks and some are available by mail or phone. Keep a separate list of all traveler's checks (noting those that you have cashed) and the names and numbers of your credit cards. Both traveler's check and credit card companies have international numbers to call for information or in the event of loss or theft.

CASH MACHINES

Automated teller machines (ATMs) are increasingly common worldwide, and most banks participate in international ATM networks such as *MasterCard/Cirrus* (phone: 800-4-CIRRUS) and *Visa/PLUS* (phone: 800-THE-PLUS). Using a card—with an assigned Personal Identification Number (PIN)—from an affiliated bank or credit card company, you can withdraw cash from any machine in the same network. The *MasterCard/Cirrus ATM Travel Directory* and the *Visa/PLUS International ATM Locator Guide 1996* provide locations of network ATMs worldwide and are available from banks and other financial institutions.

SENDING MONEY ABROAD

Should the need arise, you may be able to have money sent to you in the Bahamas and Turks and Caicos via the services provided by *American Express MoneyGram* (phone: 800-926-9400 for information; 800-866-8800 for money transfers) or *Western Union Financial Services* (phone: 800-325-6000 or 800-325-4176). At press time, however, only *Western Union* served the Bahamas, and neither company provided service in the Turks and Caicos. Call for current information when planning your trip. You also can have money wired to you in the Bahamas and Turks and Caicos via a direct bank-to-bank transfer from the US; arrangements can be made with the participating institutions. If you are down to your last cent and have no other way to obtain cash, the nearest *US Consulate* (see *Consular Services* for addresses) will let you call home to set matters in motion.

Accommodations

For specific information on hotels, resorts, and other selected accommodations, see *Best on the Islands* in THE ISLANDS. Also consult *Nassau–Cable Beach–Paradise Island Tourist News* (Star Publishers, PO Box N4855, Nassau, Bahamas; phone: 809-322-3724; fax: 809-322-4527), which is available from *Bahamas Tourist Offices* in the US. In addition, a *Hotel and Marina Guide* is available from the *Bahama Out Islands Promotion Board* (1100 Lee Wagener Blvd., Suite 204, Ft. Lauderdale, FL 33315; phone: 800-OUT-ISLANDS or 305-359-8099; fax: 305-359-8098).

RENTAL OPTIONS

An attractive accommodations alternative for the visitor content to stay in one spot is a vacation rental. For a family or group, the per-person cost can be reasonable. To have your pick of the properties available, make inquiries at least six months in advance.

The *Worldwide Home Rental Guide* (3501 Indian School Rd. NE, Suite 303, Albuquerque, NM 87106; phone/fax: 505-255-4271) lists rental properties and managing agencies. In addition, *Rental Directories International* (*RDI;* 2044 Rittenhouse Sq., Philadelphia, PA 19103; phone: 215-985-4001; fax: 215-985-0323) publishes national and regional directories listing vacation properties that can be rented directly from the owners. Their "Islands and Mexico" guide covers properties in the Bahamas.

Condo World (4230 Orchard Lake Rd., Suite 3, Orchard Lake, MI 48323; phone: 800-521-2980 or 810-683-0202; fax: 810-683-5076).

Europa-Let (92 N. Main St., Ashland, OR 97520; phone: 800-462-4486 or 503-482-5806; fax: 503-482-0660).

Hideaways International (767 Islington St., Portsmouth, NH 03801; phone: 800-843-4433 or 603-430-4433; fax: 603-430-4444).

Property Rentals International (1 Park W. Circle, Suite 108, Midlothian, VA 23113; phone: 800-220-3332 or 804-378-6054; fax: 804-379-2073).

Rent a Home International (7200 34th Ave. NW, Seattle, WA 98117; phone: 206-789-9377; fax: 206-789-9379).

Rent a Vacation Everywhere (*RAVE;* 135 Meigs St., Rochester, NY 14607; phone: 716-256-0760; fax: 716-256-2676).

VHR Worldwide (235 Kensington Ave., Norwood, NJ 07648; phone: 201-767-9393 in New Jersey; 800-633-3284 elsewhere in the US; fax: 201-767-5510).

Villas International (605 Market St., Suite 510, San Francisco, CA 94105; phone: 800-221-2260 or 415-281-0910; fax: 415-281-0919).

ACCOMMODATIONS DISCOUNTS

The following organizations offer discounts of up to 50% on accommodations in the Bahamas:

Encore Marketing International (4501 Forbes Blvd., Lanham, MD 20706; phone: 800-638-0930 or 301-459-8020).

Entertainment Publications (2125 Butterfield Rd., Troy, MI 48084; phone: 800-477-3234 or 810-637-8400; fax: 810-637-9779).

Hotel Express International (International Concepts Group, 707 E. Arapaho Rd., Richardson, TX 75081-2260; phone: 800-866-2015, 800-770-2015, or 214-497-9792; fax: 214-994-2298).

International Travel Card (6001 N. Clark St., Chicago, IL 60660; phone: 800-342-0558 or 312-465-8891; fax: 312-764-8066).

Privilege Card (3391 Peachtree Rd. NE, Suite 110, Atlanta, GA 30326; phone: 800-236-9732 or 404-262-0255; fax: 404-262-0235).

Quest International (402 E. Yakima Ave., Suite 1200, Yakima, WA 98901; phone: 800-325-2400 or 509-248-7512; fax: 509-457-8399).

Time Zones

The Bahamas and Turks and Caicos observe eastern standard time. As in the US, daylight saving time is observed from the first Sunday in April to the last Sunday in October. Thus, the time in the islands is the same as in East Coast US cities throughout the year.

Business and Shopping Hours

Most businesses in the Bahamas and Turks and Caicos are open weekdays from 9 AM to between 5 and 6 PM; stores also often are open for a full day on Saturdays. Banks in the Bahamas are open Mondays through Thursdays from 9 AM to 3 PM, and Fridays from 9 AM to 5 PM. In the Turks and Caicos, banking hours generally are Mondays through Thursdays from 8:30 AM to 2:30 PM, and Fridays from 8:30 AM to noon, and 2:30 PM to 4:30 PM.

Holidays

Below is a list of the public holidays in the Bahamas and Turks and Caicos and the dates they will be observed this year. (Note that the dates of some holidays vary from year to year; others occur on the same day every year.)

In the Bahamas

New Year's Day (January 1)
Good Friday (April 5)
Easter Monday (April 8)
Whitmonday (May 20)
Labour Day (June 3)
Independence Day (July 10)
Emancipation Day (August 5)
Discovery Day (October 12)
Christmas (December 25)
Boxing Day (December 26)

In the Turks and Caicos

New Year's Day (January 1)
Commonwealth Day (March 14)
Good Friday (April 5)
Easter Monday (April 8)
National Heroes Day (May 30)
Her Majesty the Queen's Official Birthday (observed on June 8 and 10)
Emancipation Day (August 1)
National Youth Day (September 30)
Columbus Day (October 12)
International Human Rights Day (October 24)

Christmas (December 25)
Boxing Day (December 26)

Mail

Post offices in the Bahamas are open Mondays through Fridays from 8:30 AM to 5:30 PM, and Saturdays from 8:30 AM to 12:30 PM. Post offices in the Turks and Caicos are open weekdays from 8 AM to 12:30 PM and from 2 to 4 PM (no Saturday hours). In the Bahamas and Turks and Caicos, stamps generally are available only at post offices, although a few hotels and stores also may sell them.

When sending mail between the US and the Bahamas and Turks and Caicos, always use airmail and allow at least 10 days for delivery. If your correspondence is especially important, you may want to send it via an international courier service, such as *FEDEX* (*Federal Express;* phone: 800-238-5355 in the US; 809-322-5656 in the Bahamas; 809-946-4682 in the Turks and Caicos) or *DHL Worldwide Express* (phone: 800-225-5345 in the US; 809-352-6415 or 809-325-8420 in the Bahamas; 809-325-8266 in the Turks and Caicos).

You can have mail sent to you care of your hotel (marked "Guest Mail, Hold for Arrival") or to a post office (the address should include "c/o General Delivery"). *American Express* offices also will hold mail for customers ("c/o Client Letter Service"); information is provided in their pamphlet *Travelers' Companion.* Note that *US Embassies* and *Consulates* abroad will hold mail for US citizens *only* in emergency situations.

Telephone

Direct dialing is possible both to and from the Bahamas and the Turks and Caicos and the US, as well as between the islands. Phone numbers in the Bahamas are either six or seven digits in length; all Turks and Caicos phone numbers are five digits in length.

To call a number in the Bahamas from the US: Dial 1 + 809 (the general area code for the Bahamas and Turks and Caicos) + the local number (no country code).

To call a number in the Turks and Caicos from the US: Dial 1 + 809 (the area code) + 94 (the country code for the Turks and Caicos Islands) + the local number.

To call a number in the US from the Bahamas: Dial 1 + the area code + the local number.

To call a number in the US from the Turks and Caicos: Dial 01 + the area code + the local number.

To make a call between islands in the Bahamas or between the Bahamas and the Turks and Caicos: Dial 1 + 809 + the local number.

To call a number on the same island in the Bahamas: Dial the local number.

To make a call between islands _or_ on the same island in the Turks and Caicos: Dial the local number.

Although most public telephones in the Bahamas still take coins, pay phones that accept special phone debit cards have been introduced in Nassau. These cards can be purchased at offices of the phone company, _Bahamas Telecommunications Corp._ (_BATELCO;_ main office: Mall at Marathon, Nassau, Bahamas; phone: 809-394-4000; fax: 809-393-4965).

In the Turks and Caicos, most public telephones on the street accept only phone cards, although pay phones in most hotels and restaurants still take coins. Phone cards can be purchased at offices of _West Indies Cable & Wireless, Ltd._ (main office: Queen St., Grand Turk, Turks and Caicos Islands, British West Indies; phone: 809-946-2222; fax: 809-946-2497), the islands' phone company, as well as from licensed agents at the airports and in some hotels and shops.

You can use a telephone company calling card number on any phone, and some pay phones take major credit cards (_American Express, MasterCard, Visa,_ and so on). Also available are combined telephone calling/bank credit cards, such as the _AT&T Universal Card_ (PO Box 44167, Jacksonville, FL 32231-4167; phone: 800-423-4343). Similarly, _Sprint_ (8140 Ward Pkwy., Kansas City, MO 64114; phone: 800-669-8585) offers _VisaPhone,_ through which you can add phone card privileges to your existing _Visa_ card. Companies offering long-distance phone cards without additional credit card privileges include _AT&T_ (phone: 800-CALL-ATT), _Executive Telecard International_ (4260 E. Evans Ave., Suite 6, Denver, CO 80222; phone: 800-950-3800), _MCI_ (323 Third St. SE, Cedar Rapids, IA 52401; phone: 800-444-4444; and 12790 Merit Dr., Dallas, TX 75251; phone: 800-444-3333), and _Sprint_ (address above; phone: 800-THE-MOST).

Hotels routinely add surcharges to the cost of phone calls made from their rooms. Long-distance telephone services that may help you avoid this added expense are provided by a number of companies, including _AT&T_ (International Information Service, 635 Grant St., Pittsburgh, PA 15219; phone: 800-874-4000), _MCI_ (address above), and _Sprint_ (address above). Note that some of these services can be accessed only with the companies' long-distance calling cards (see above). In addition, even when you use such long-distance services, some hotels still may charge a fee for line usage.

Useful telephone directories for travelers include the _AT&T Toll-Free 800 National Shopper's Guide_ and the _AT&T Toll-Free 800 National Business Guide_ (phone: 800-426-8686 for orders), the _Toll-Free Travel & Vacation Information Directory_ (Pilot Books, 103 Cooper St., Babylon, NY 11702; phone: 516-422-2225; fax: 516-422-2227), and _The Phone Booklet_ (Scott American Corporation, PO Box 88, W. Redding, CT 06896; no phone).

Important Phone Numbers
In the Bahamas
Emergency assistance: 322-2221 for an ambulance; 919 for the police
Local or international operator: 0
Local information: 916

In the Turks and Caicos
Emergency assistance: 999
Local operator: 110
Local information: 118
International operator: 115

Electricity

As in the US, 110-volt, 60-cycle, alternating current (AC) is used in the Bahamas and Turks and Caicos. Appliances running on standard current can be used throughout the islands without adapters or converters.

Staying Healthy

For up-to-date information on current health conditions, call the Centers for Disease Control's *International Travelers' Hotline:* 404-332-4559. The Centers for Disease Control also publishes *Health Information for International Travel, 1996* which provides worldwide information on health risks and vaccination requirements. It can be ordered from the Superintendent of Documents (*US Government Printing Office,* PO Box 371954, Pittsburgh, PA 15250-7954; phone: 202-512-1800; fax: 202-512-2250).

Travelers to the Bahamas and Turks and Caicos face few serious health risks. Tap water generally is clean and potable throughout the islands. Milk is pasteurized, and dairy products are safe to eat, as are fruit, vegetables, meat, poultry, and fish.

The most common health problem experienced by travelers to the Bahamas and Turks and Caicos probably is sunburn. When spending any length of time outdoors, take appropriate precautions—including the use of a sunscreen with a Sun Protection Factor (SPF) of 15 or higher.

In addition, when swimming in the ocean, be careful of the undertow (the water running back down the beach after a wave has washed ashore), which can knock you off your feet, and riptides (currents running against the tide), which can pull you out to sea. Sharks are found in local waters, but rarely come close to shore. Jellyfish—including Portuguese men-of-war—are common, as are eels and sea urchins. And note that coral reefs, while beautiful, can be razor sharp.

Tourist areas in the Bahamas and Turks and Caicos are well supplied with doctors, hospitals, clinics, and pharmacies (which carry most of the drugs available in the US). Note that pharmacies are not open around the clock; if you need a prescription filled during off-hours, go directly to a local hospital.

Should you need non-emergency medical attention, ask at your hotel for the house physician or for help in reaching a doctor. A list of doctors and dentists in the Bahamas also is available from the *US Embassy and Consulate* in Nassau; the Turks and Caicos list can be obtained from the *US Embassy* in Kingston, Jamaica (for the addresses of the US consular offices in the islands, see *Consular Services,* below.) **In an emergency: Go to the emergency room of the nearest hospital or dial the applicable emergency number provided in** *Telephone,* **above, or call a local operator for assistance.**

Be extremely cautious about injections when traveling abroad because reusable syringes and needles may be used, and sterilization procedures sometimes are inadequate. If you have a condition that requires periodic injections, bring a supply of syringes with you. To avoid any potential problems with customs authorities, bring along a note from your doctor confirming that they are required for treatment of a medical condition. You also can buy disposable syringes at local pharmacies in the islands.

Additional Resources

Global Emergency Services (2720 Enterprise Pkwy., Suite 106, Richmond, VA 23294; phone: 804-527-1094; fax: 804-527-1941).

Health Care Abroad/Global (c/o *Wallach and Co.,* PO Box 480, Middleburg, VA 22117-0480; phone: 800-237-6615 or 703-687-3166; fax: 703-687-3172).

International Association for Medical Assistance to Travelers (*IAMAT;* 417 Center St., Lewiston, NY 14092; phone: 716-754-4883; and 40 Regal Rd., Guelph, Ontario N1K 1B5, Canada; phone: 519-836-0102; fax: 519-836-3412).

International Health Care Service (440 E. 69th St., New York, NY 10021; phone: 212-746-1601).

International SOS Assistance (PO Box 11568, Philadelphia, PA 19116; phone: 800-523-8930 or 215-244-1500; fax: 215-244-2227).

Medic Alert Foundation (2323 Colorado Ave., Turlock, CA 95382; phone: 800-ID-ALERT or 209-668-3333; fax: 209-669-2495).

Travel Care International (*Eagle River Airport,* PO Box 846, Eagle River, WI 54521; phone: 800-5-AIR-MED or 715-479-8881; fax: 715-479-8178).

Traveler's Emergency Network (*TEN;* PO Box 238, Hyattsville, MD 20797-8108; phone: 800-ASK-4-TEN; fax: 301-559-5167).

TravMed (PO Box 10623, Baltimore, MD 21285-0623; phone: 800-732-5309 or 410-296-5225; fax: 410-825-7523).

Consular Services

The American Services section of the *US Consulate* is a vital source of assistance and advice for US citizens abroad. If you are injured or become seriously ill, the consulate can direct you to sources of medical attention and notify your relatives. If you become involved in a dispute that could lead to legal action, the consulate can provide a list of local attorneys. In cases of natural disasters or civil unrest, consulates handle the evacuation of US citizens if necessary.

The *US Embassy and Consulate* for the Bahamas is located at Queen St., Nassau, Bahamas (phone: 809-322-1181/2 or 809-322-4753; fax: 809-328-7838). The *US Embassy* in Jamaica has jurisdiction over the Turks and Caicos Islands. It is located at the *Jamaica Mutual Life Center,* 2 Oxford Rd., Third Floor, Kingston, Jamaica (phone: 809-929-4850; fax: 809-926-6743).

The *US State Department* operates an automated 24-hour *Citizens' Emergency Center* travel advisory hotline (phone: 202-647-5225). You also can reach a duty officer at this number from 5:15 PM to 10 PM, eastern standard time, seven days a week; at other times, call 202-647-4000. For faxed travel advisories and other consular information, call 202-647-3000 using the handset on your fax machine; instructions will be provided. Using a personal computer with a modem, you can access the consular affairs electronic bulletin board (phone: 202-647-9225).

Entry Requirements and Customs Regulations

ENTERING THE BAHAMAS AND TURKS AND CAICOS

To visit the Bahamas for a period of up to eight months, or the Turks and Caicos for a period of up to three months, a US citizen needs proof of citizenship (passport or birth certificate) and an official photo ID (a passport fulfills both these requirements), as well as an ongoing or return ticket. For longer stays in the Bahamas, contact the *Immigration Department* (PO Box N3008, Nassau, Bahamas; phone: 809-322-7530; fax: 809-326-0977); in the Turks and Caicos, contact the *Turks and Caicos Immigration Department* (South Base, Grand Turk, Turks and Caicos Islands, British West Indies; phone: 809-946-2700; fax: 809-946-2924).

DUTY-FREE SHOPS

Located in international airports, duty-free shops provide bargains on the purchase of goods imported to the Bahamas or Turks and Caicos from other countries. But beware: Not all foreign goods are automatically less expensive. You *can* get a good deal on some items, but know what they cost elsewhere. Also note that although these goods are free of the duty that customs authorities in the Bahamas or Turks and Caicos normally would assess, they will be subject to US import duty upon your return to the US (see below).

RETURNING TO THE US

US citizens leaving the Bahamas can clear *US Customs* at Nassau or Freeport international airports. Passengers departing from the Turks and Caicos must pass through customs at their point of entry into the US.

You must declare to *US Customs* everything you have acquired in the islands. The duty-free allowance for US citizens returning from the Bahamas is $600; the standard duty-free allowance of $400 applies to travelers returning from the Turks and Caicos. If your trip is shorter than 48 continuous hours, or if you have been outside the US within 30 days of your current trip, the duty-free allowance is reduced to $25. Families traveling together may make a joint customs declaration. To avoid paying duty unnecessarily on expensive items (such as computer equipment) that you plan to take with you on your trip, register these items with *US Customs* before you depart.

A flat 10% duty is assessed on the next $1,000 worth of merchandise; additional items are taxed at a variety of rates (see *Tariff Schedules of the United States* in a library or any *US Customs Service* office). Some articles are duty-free only up to certain limits. The $400 and $600 allowances include one carton of (200) cigarettes, 100 cigars, and one liter of liquor or wine; the $25 allowance includes 10 cigars, 50 cigarettes, and four ounces of perfume. Antiques (at least 100 years old) and paintings or drawings done entirely by hand also are duty-free. In addition, the Generalized System of Preferences (GSP), which allows US citizens to bring certain goods into the US duty-free, applies to the Bahamas and the Turks and Caicos. Each day you are abroad, you also can ship up to $200 in gifts (excluding alcohol, perfume, and tobacco) to the US duty-free.

FORBIDDEN IMPORTS

US regulations prohibit the import of some goods sold abroad, such as fresh fruits and vegetables, most meat products (except certain canned goods), and dairy products (except fully cured cheeses). Also prohibited are articles made from plants or animals on the endangered species list.

FOR ADDITIONAL INFORMATION Consult one of the following publications, available from the *US Customs Service* (PO Box 7407, Washington, DC 20044): *Currency Reporting; International Mail Imports; Know Before You Go; Pets, Wildlife, US Customs;* and *Pocket Hints. Travelers' Tips on Bringing Food, Plant, and Animal Products into the United States* is available from the *United States Department of Agriculture, Animal and Plant Health Inspection Service* (*USDA-APHIS;* 6505 Belcrest Rd., Room 613-FB, Hyattsville, MD 20782;

phone: 301-436-7799; fax: 301-436-5221). For tape-recorded information on customs-related topics, call 202-927-2095 from any touch-tone phone.

For Further Information

Branches of the *Bahamas Tourist Office* and the *Turks and Caicos Tourist Board* in the US are the best sources of travel information. Offices generally are open on weekdays during normal business hours. Additional information on the Bahamas is available from the *Bahama Out Islands Promotion Board* (1100 Lee Wagener Blvd., Suite 204, Ft. Lauderdale, FL 33315; phone: 800-OUT-ISLANDS or 305-359-8099; fax: 305-359-8098), which publishes *Getaway* magazine, a *Hotel & Marina Guide,* and a *Travel & Map Guide.* Additional information on the Turks and Caicos is available from the *Turks & Caicos Reservations Center* (4197 Braganza Ave., Coconut Grove, FL 33133; phone: 305-667-0966; fax: 305-667-2494), which also can make hotel reservations for visitors.

For information on entry requirements and customs regulations in the Bahamas, contact the islands' consular offices in the US. For information on the Turks and Caicos, contact a *British Consulate* or the *Consular Section* of the *British Embassy.*

Bahamas Tourist Offices

For information nationwide, phone: 800-4-BAHAMA (800-422-4262).

California: 3450 Wilshire Blvd., Suite 208, Los Angeles, CA 90010 (phone: 213-385-0033; fax: 213-383-3966).

Florida: 19495 Biscayne Blvd., Suite 809, Aventura, FL 33180 (phone: 305-932-0051; fax: 305-682-8758).

Georgia: 2957 Clairmont Rd., Suite 150, Atlanta, GA 30329 (phone: 404-633-1793; fax: 404-633-1575).

Illinois: 8600 W. Bryn Mawr St., Suite 820, Chicago, IL 60631 (phone: 312-693-1500; fax: 312-693-1114).

New York: 150 E. 52nd St., 28th Floor, New York, NY 10022 (phone: 212-758-2777; fax: 212-753-6531).

Pennsylvania: mail inquiries only: PO Box 16328, Philadelphia, PA 19114.

Texas: World Trade Center, Suite 116, Stemmons Frwy., Dallas, TX 75258-1408 (phone: 214-742-1886; fax: 214-741-4118).

Turks and Caicos Tourist Board

Florida: mail and phone inquiries only: PO Box 594023, Miami, FL 33159 (phone: 800-241-0824).

New York: c/o *Caribbean Tourism Organization,* 20 E. 46th St., New York, NY 10017 (phone: 212-682-0435; fax: 212-697-4258).

Embassy and Consulates of the Commonwealth of the Bahamas
Embassy
Washington, DC: 2220 Massachusetts Ave. NW, Washington, DC 20008 (phone: 202-319-2660; fax: 202-319-2668).

Consulates
Florida: *Consulate General,* Ingraham Building, 25 SE Second Ave., Suite 818, Miami, FL 33131 (phone: 305-373-6295; fax: 305-373-6312).

New York: *Consulate General,* 231 E. 46th St., New York, NY 10017 (phone: 212-421-6420; fax: 212-668-5926).

British Embassy and Consulates
Embassy
Washington, DC: 3100 Massachusetts Ave. NW, Washington DC 20008-3600 (phone: 202-462-1340; fax: 202-898-4255); *Consular Section:* 19 Observatory Circle, Washington, DC 20008-3600 (phone: 202-986-0205; fax: 202-797-2929).

Consulates
California: *Consulate General,* 11766 Wilshire Blvd., Suite 400, Los Angeles, CA 90025 (phone: 310-477-3322; fax: 310-575-1450); *Consulate General,* 1 Sansome St., Suite 850, San Francisco, CA 94109 (phone: 415-981-3030; fax: 415-434-2018).

Georgia: *Consulate General,* Marquis One Tower, 245 Peachtree Center Ave., Suite 2700, Atlanta, GA 30303 (phone: 404-524-5856; fax: 404-524-3153).

Illinois: 33 N. Dearborn St., Ninth Floor, Chicago, IL 60602 (phone: 312-346-1810; fax: 312-346-7021).

Massachusetts: *Consulate General,* Federal Reserve Plaza, 600 Atlantic Ave., 25th Floor, Boston, MA 02210 (phone: 617-248-9555; fax: 617-248-9578).

New York: *Consulate General,* 845 Third Ave., Ninth Floor, New York, NY 10022 (phone: 212-745-0200; fax: 212-754-3062).

Texas: *Consulate General,* 1000 Louisiana St., Suite 1900, Houston, TX 77002 (phone: 713-659-6270; fax: 713-659-7094).

The Islands

Bahamas

The Bahamas are in a class of their own. They're not Caribbean, for the archipelago lies just a bit farther north, in the Atlantic. They're not Bermuda, though many Bermudians settled there early on. And they're definitely not the US, though Bimini is closer to Florida than Miami is to Palm Beach.

It's easy to classify the Bahamas as a generic tropical resort, the sort of place where you sit, rum cocktail in hand, looking out over a perfect stretch of white sand to an endless expanse of turquoise blue ocean. In fact, there *are* great beaches here, and balmy breezes, potent punches, swaying palms, and all the other tropical clichés. But that's not all. If you don't mind the occasional bumpy road or desultory ferry schedule, or islands where goats outnumber TV sets, the Bahamas can be very much worth exploring. And the culture, with its *junkanoo* dances, rake-and-scrape bands, *goombay* music, and flavorful island cooking, is lively and unique.

Tourists discovered the Bahamas just before World War II, but the crowds didn't start arriving for another 20 or 30 years. Initially, British society frequented the islands, but then brash North Americans found the Bahamas, and the tourist industry really took off. Sir Harry Oakes, who had made a fortune in Canadian gold mines, set about building hotels in Nassau, the capital city on New Providence Island, and Florida real-estate developer Henry Flagler launched several projects here.

Early on, tourists generally came to the Bahamas only in the winter, and the hotels in Nassau were shuttered for the rest of the year. When the big resorts were built here in the 1950s, the pattern started to change. The Bahamas, like Florida, finally discovered summer. Of the 3.5 million or so tourists who now visit the islands each year, a good number come in the off-season—even during the hottest days of July and August. Cable Beach, just west of Nassau, attracts half a million visitors a year, as does tiny Paradise Island, across the bridge from downtown Nassau. With the exception of New Providence and Grand Bahama and their neighboring cays (pronounced *keys*), all the rest of the Bahamas come under the rubric of the Out Islands. Once known to titans, tycoons, and God alone, these isles now are being discovered by adventuresome tourists.

The quest to build a tourist's paradise here hasn't always been easy. In the early days of self-government, back in the mid-1960s, many visitors to Nassau, and Freeport on Grand Bahama Island, were met with a distinctly chilly reception (although most of the Out Islanders remained as gracious as ever). But time and persistent efforts by both the government and local hoteliers have had some positive effect, and island hospitality is once again being emphasized. If you haven't returned to the Bahamas recently, you're in for a pleasant surprise: Some of the dowager hotels have been spiffed up, a multimillion-dollar harbor expansion of the Port of Nassau was completed in 1993, and a $60-million expansion and upgrading of *Nassau Airport* was finished in 1994.

Hubert A. Ingraham, the Bahamas' charismatic prime minister, is working toward even more change. Ingraham's goals include healing the islands' ailing economy, combating government corruption, improving the tourist industry, and encouraging foreign investment in the Bahamas. A native of Great Abaco Island, Ingraham has a particular interest in making the Out Islands more attractive to visitors. All of which means that the Bahamas will continue to be an attractive destination for travelers looking for an exotic getaway in their own backyards.

Bahamas At-a-Glance

FROM THE AIR

Counting every reef, rock, and bump, there are some 700 islands and 2,000 cays in the Bahamas, scattered over 100,000 square miles of the Atlantic Ocean. The city of Nassau, the Bahamas' capital and chief port of entry, is on the island of New Providence, near the middle of the group. The Bahamas' other major resort center—also with an international airport— is Freeport/Lucaya on Grand Bahama Island, less than 60 miles east of Florida. The flight from Miami to Nassau or Freeport takes less than 45 minutes; from New York the flight is two and a half hours; and Toronto is a three-hour flight away.

SPECIAL PLACES

The most populous of the Bahamas and the most popular with tourists are New Providence (and adjacent Paradise Island) and Grand Bahama. The Out Islands that attract sunseekers, anglers, and other visitors include the Abacos, Andros, the Berry Islands, Bimini, Cat Island, Eleuthera, the Exumas, and San Salvador. For additional details on each of the main islands and island groups, see DIRECTIONS.

NEW PROVIDENCE and PARADISE ISLAND The favored destination for tourists since rumrunners came here to squander their fortunes in Prohibition days, New Providence is still worth a visit. Although the casino in Cable Beach, the island's prime strip since the postwar boom, may seem empty except for weekends and major holidays, there is still plenty of genuine excitement and charm to be found here. Nassau, the islands' capital and chief port, has more historic buildings and museums than any other town in the Bahamas, and Lyford Cay, the super-exclusive residential neighborhood on the west end of New Providence Island, is all that remains of the island's days as a chic retreat for the rich and famous. (Hire a guide to find the hideaways of various luminaries, from former Prime Minister Lynden Pindling to pop singer Julio Iglesias.) Paradise Island, a small cay in Nassau Harbour, is connected to New Providence by a bridge. This resort development has gotten a bit threadbare, but the huge recent investment in the island by Sun International, which has bought and completely overhauled three hotels here, including the sprawling former *Paradise Island Resort & Casino,* may spark something of a renaissance.

GRAND BAHAMA The big draws here are the twin resort developments of Freeport and Lucaya. They offer little of historical interest, but if baccarat is your game and pristine white beaches your passion, you won't be disappointed.

OUT ISLANDS Colonial traditions are stronger on these islands than they are on New Providence and Grand Bahama, and some towns—Harbour Island just off Eleuthera, Hope Town just off Great Abaco—look like Cape Cod with palm trees. While some of the Out Islands are relatively undeveloped, a few were discovered by adventuresome tourists some time ago and have complete resorts, marinas, and dive facilities. Accommodations and amenities on some islands range from good to rustic to primitive, but that doesn't mean they should be passed by. For example, the lodgings on Cat Island and historic San Salvador (allegedly the site of Columbus's first landing in the New World) tend to be comfortable but basic (with the notable exception of the luxurious *Club Med–Columbus Isle* on San Salvador), but both islands have terrific beaches and diving spots. The natural attributes of several islands attract sports enthusiasts: The giant reef off the east coast of Andros is a must for serious divers; blue-water sailors head for the secluded anchorages in the Abacos and the Exumas; and game fishermen set their compasses straight for Alice Town on North Bimini, an angler's paradise. But the islands aren't just for athletes. A visitor also can stroll on a rose-tinted beach and search for sand dollars, watch a regatta, visit a historic hermitage or a tropical garden, or dine on barbecued spiny lobster in a deserted cove.

EXTRA SPECIAL

The Bahamian government's free *People-to-People Programme* has a roster of more than 500 islanders lined up to entertain interested visitors with a "truly Bahamian experience." Hosts and guests are matched according to mutual interests and hobbies. To participate, contact the *People-to-People* coordinator in Nassau (phone: 328-7810) or in Freeport (phone: 326-5371). You also can ask your hotel's social desk or call the nearest Bahamas tourist information bureau.

Sources and Resources

TOURIST INFORMATION

In Nassau, the *Bahamas Ministry of Tourism* offers information on special events, sightseeing advice, arrangements for the above-mentioned *People-to-People Programme,* and answers to any questions. There are two *Tourist*

Information Centres at the airport—one in the arrivals area (phone: 377-6806) and the other in the departure area (phone: 377-6782)—and two downtown—in Rawson Square (phone: 327-7810/1) and at Market Square on Bay Street, where the *Ministry of Tourism*'s main offices are also located (phone: 322-7500). The main Market Square office is closed weekends; the others are open daily.

On Grand Bahama, the main tourist office is located at the *International Bazaar* in Freeport; it's closed weekends and holidays (phone: 352-8044). There's also a *Visitors' Information Centre* at the *International Bazaar* (closed Sundays and holidays; phone: 352-6909) as well as at Port Lucaya (closed Sundays and holidays; phone: 373-8988); at the airport (open daily; phone: 352-2052); and at Freeport Harbour (open daily; no phone).

At present, there are three tourist offices on the Out Islands, all closed weekends: at Marsh Harbour, Abacos (phone: 367-3067); at Governor's Harbour, Eleuthera (phone: 332-2142/3); and at George Town, Great Exuma (Queen's Highway; phone: 336-2430).

LOCAL COVERAGE Several digest-size guides, free to visitors and available locally, provide information on shopping, sightseeing, restaurants, nightspots, and island food and lore. These include *What-to-Do: Nassau, Cable Beach & Paradise Island; What-to-Do: Freeport-Lucaya; Pocket Guide to the Bahamas; Dining and Entertainment Guide: Nassau, Cable Beach, Paradise Island;* and *Best Buys in the Bahamas. What's On* is a monthly tabloid-size newspaper geared toward tourists in Nassau and Paradise Island. The quarterly *Bahamas* magazine carries features on island destinations and tourism industry news.

The *Out Islands Travel and Map Guide* and the annual *Getaways* magazine are available at no charge through the *Bahama Out Islands Promotion Board* (1100 Lee Wagener Blvd., Suite 204, Ft. Lauderdale, FL 33315; phone: 800-OUT-ISLANDS; 305-359-8099 in Florida; fax: 305-359-8098). *Abaco Life,* available free at the *Abaco Chamber of Commerce* (Marsh Harbour; phone: 367-2663), provides current information about the island.

Two daily newspapers are published in Nassau: the *Tribune* and the *Nassau Guardian.* The *Freeport News,* a daily, is published in Freeport. *The New York Times, Wall Street Journal, USA Today,* and *Miami Herald* are available on newsstands on the day of publication; other major North American newspapers also are flown in daily.

TELEPHONE The area code for the Bahamas is 809.

GETTING AROUND

BUS Minibuses (called jitneys) run from outlying sections of New Providence to downtown Nassau from 6 AM until 6:30 PM at rates starting at $1. In addition there are two free shuttles to the casinos on Paradise Island and Cable Beach; ask at your hotel for the schedule. On Grand Bahama, bus rides between Freeport and Lucaya cost $1. They're fast, inexpensive, and reasonably comfortable.

CAR RENTAL In addition to international companies (see GETTING READY TO GO), a number of local agencies operate in the Nassau–Cable Beach–Paradise Island area, including *Poinciana* (at the *Poinciana Inn,* Bernard Rd.; phone: 393-1720); *Red Kap/Hertz* (*Nassau Airport;* phone: 327-8684); *Teglo* (Mt. Pleasant; phone: 362-4361); and *Wallace* (Marathon Rd., off Wulff Rd.; phone: 393-0650). In Freeport on Grand Bahama, try *Courtesy* (at the *Holiday Inn;* phone: 352-5212); *Safari Kar* (4 Peach Tree; phone: 351-3223 or 352-6721, ext. 4297); or *Sears Rent-a-Car* (at the airport; phone: 352-8844; and at the *Clarion Atlantik Beach* hotel, Lucayan Beach; phone: 373-4938).

You also can rent a car on some outlying islands, but it won't be a recent model, and chances are it will have traveled some pretty rough roads before it gets to you. So be sure to check its tires (including the spare) and general condition, and listen to the motor before accepting delivery. There isn't always a phone handy in case of a breakdown. On Great Abaco, try *H & L Car Rentals* (Marsh Harbour; phone: 367-2840; fax: 367-2854) or *A & A* (*Marsh Harbour International Airport;* phone: 367-2148); on Andros, contact *Amklco* (Main St., Fresh Creek; phone: 368-2056) or *Berth Rent-a-Car* (Calabash Bay; phone: 368-2102); on Eleuthera, try *Burrows* (Governor's Harbour; phone: 332-2138), *David Carey's* (Tarpum Bay; phone: 334-4122), or *Dingle Motors Service* (Rock Sound; phone: 334-2031); on Harbour Island, there's *Baretta Taxi & Rent-A-Car* (New Dunmore subdivision; phone: 333-2361); on Great Exuma, *Exuma Transport* (George Town; phone: 336-2101).

US and Canadian driver's licenses are valid, but remember: *Drive on the left.*

INTER-ISLAND FLIGHTS Regularly scheduled commuter flights to the Out Islands from both Nassau and Freeport are available from *Bahamasair* (phone: 327-8451) and *Taino Air Service* (phone: 352-8885 or 352-8886). *Out Island Safari Seaplane* (phone: 393-2522) is a popular concession offering round-trip service from *Paradise Island Airport* to Great Exuma, either as a day trip or by arrangement for longer stays. A Bahamas fixture, *Chalk's International Airlines* (phone: 363-2845 on Paradise Island; 347-3024 on Bimini; 800-4-CHALKS) has offered daily seaplane service between Miami, Ft. Lauderdale, Paradise Island, and Bimini for over 70 years. There are no other pre-packaged local air tours, but Nassau's *Pinders Charters* (phone: 327-7320), *Sky Unlimited* (phone: 327-8993), *Trans Island Airways* (phone: 327-5979), and Freeport's *Major's Air Service* (phone: 352-5778) are available for island-hopping charter trips; rates are based on mileage and size of aircraft.

More than 45,000 private planes fly into the Bahamas each year. Pilots can get up-to-date information by calling the *Bahamas Pilot Briefing Center* (phone: 800-327-7678).

MOTOR SCOOTERS Motor scooter rentals are becoming increasingly popular in Nassau and at Cable Beach on New Providence, on Paradise Island, and in Freeport/Lucaya on Grand Bahama; they're also available on Eleuthera and in George Town, Great Exuma. Most scooters have an extra seat behind the driver. Hotels have their own stands or will direct you to the nearest outlet.

SEA EXCURSIONS Half-day and full-day snorkeling, sightseeing, and beach excursions are plentiful—particularly in the Nassau area of New Providence. The *Calypso I* and *II* (phone: 363-3577) leave from Hurricane Hole for a day at Blue Lagoon Island; the catamaran *Flying Cloud* (phone: 393-1957) offers half-day snorkeling trips and sunset and dinner cruises from West Dock on Paradise Island; and *United Cruises* (Woodes Rogers Wharf, Nassau; phone: 322-4941) operates three-hour cruises with live music by a *goombay* band and a chance to swim at a remote beach. *Booze & Cruise Co.* (phone: 393-3722) operates the glass-bottom boat *Lucayan Queen,* which leaves from the *Nassau Yacht Haven* dock on East Bay Street daily except Mondays for a four-hour snorkel, lunch, and beach cruise; and *Sea Island Adventure* (phone: 325-3910 or 328-2581) offers trips from *Nassau Yacht Haven* on the same days. *Majestic Lady,* operated by *Robinson Crusoe Shipwreck Cruises* (Hurricane Hole; phone: 322-2606), offers snorkeling trips during the day and harbor cruises Tuesday and Friday evenings.

Numerous excursions also depart from Freeport/Lucaya on Grand Bahama. The *Seaworld Explorer* (phone: 373-7863), which calls itself a "semi-submarine" (its glass-bottom hull sits five feet below sea level), leaves Lucaya Harbour three times daily for tours of the reefs off the coast. *Reef Tours* (at the *Port Lucaya MarketPlace and Marina;* phone: 373-5880 or 373-5891) offers glass-bottom boat tours, snorkel and sail cruises, and lunch and party cruises. Dinner cruises are offered on the *Fantasy* (*Port Lucaya MarketPlace and Marina;* phone: 373-4336).

Prices for sea excursions generally include unlimited rum and soft drinks. On all of the islands, your hotel tour desk can provide information on other picnic and cocktail sails.

Mail boats that connect the outlying islands with Nassau and Freeport and with each other can provide offbeat, inexpensive travel; however, departures are infrequent and can be unpredictable. For more information, call 322-2049. Another option is to take the *Sealink* (phone: 327-5444), a 200-foot cargo vessel that takes passengers to Eleuthera from *Nassau Shipyard* every Friday and Sunday.

SIGHTSEEING TOURS Local operators offer a wide variety of sightseeing tours on both New Providence and Grand Bahama—though it's more fun to explore Nassau on your own (walking, driving, on a motor scooter, or with a taxi driver; for further information, see *Nassau* in DIRECTIONS). On New Providence, *Majestic Tours* (*Hillside Manor,* Cumberland St.; phone: 322-2606) runs a nightclub tour of Nassau and Paradise Island. *Island Ranger Helitours* (phone: 363-1040) offers inexpensive helicopter tours from *Paradise Island Airport.* Other companies offering half- and full-day tours of Nassau and the surrounding countryside, as well as nightclub and native-show tours, are *Happy Tours* (Nassau St.; phone: 323-4555), and *Tropical Tours* (Palmdale Ave. at Mackey St.; phone: 322-5791). At least once—maybe as part of a Nassau tour—take your pick of the fringe-topped surreys lined up at Rawson Square (at the intersection of Parliament and Bay Sts.) and clip-clop around town for a while. Often a horse with a hat you admire has a driver you'll like, too. Rates are negotiable and usually quite reasonable.

The *Great Bahama Taxi Union* (at the airport taxi stand; phone: 352-7858 or 352-7101) offers three-hour taxi tours to groups or limo tours for two people. Both *Executive Tours* (*Grand Bahama Airport;* phone: 352-8858) and *Bahamas Travel* (14-15 Merport Bldg., Freeport; phone: 352-3141) offer half- and full-day tours. Your hotel travel desk is the best place to find out the full range of what's offered.

TAXI Readily available at airports and hotels in Nassau and Freeport, cabs are metered at rates fixed by law. On the Out Islands, taxis are available at the individual island airports. There, the unmetered rates may run slightly higher but are negotiable. The usual tip is 15% of the fare. Many taxi drivers are good, knowledgeable, and/or amusing guides to their particular islands. Ask your hotel to recommend one.

SPECIAL EVENTS

Among the most famous sporting events on the islands are the more than 30 annual sportfishing tournaments, including the prestigious six-tournament *Bahamas Billfish Championship,* which runs from March through June. The many regattas held throughout the year are always well attended; the most popular is the *Out Island Regatta* held in George Town, Great Exuma, in April (for more information, see *Sports*). A newer event, held during the summer, is the *Bahamas Boating Fling,* a government-sponsored program that draws boats together in a flotilla that travels from Florida to six different islands. *Goombay,* the ongoing summer celebration, offers visitors a variety of musical and cultural events, such as quadrille dancing, *junkanoo* parades, the maypole dance, and performances by the *Royal Bahamas Police Force Band* and rake-and-scrape bands. Both *Boxing Day* (December 26) and *New Year's Day* are occasions for *junkanoo* parades; beginning at 3 or 4 AM, masked celebrants in fantastic crêpe-paper costumes march to the rhythm of cowbells, goatskin drums, and whistles.

SHOPPING

Special island-made souvenirs are generally limited to Thompson Bros. pineapple rum (ask at their store in Gregory Town, Eleuthera; phone: 335-5009); the splendid straw hats worn by lobstermen on Spanish Wells off Eleuthera (ask any man wearing one where they're sold); the great canvas sail bags and totes Norman Albury makes (look for *Albury's Sail Loft* on Man-O-War Cay, off Great Abaco; no phone); and the crafts sold at straw markets. In New Providence, the *Straw Market* (the largest on the island) is housed in its own big building (at the foot of Market St., on Bay St.); smaller markets can be found on Cable Beach across from the *Radisson* and *Marriott* hotels. On Grand Bahama, there are straw markets at both the *Port Lucaya MarketPlace and Marina* and at the *International Bazaar*. On the Out Islands, look for the occasional straw market under a sheltering tree (as in George Town on Great Exuma). Baskets, hats, mats, totes, and the like, woven in traditional designs and often brightly colored, are predominant. Look carefully for authentic pieces (some baskets are woven outside the Bahamas and hand-finished on the islands), and don't be afraid to bargain—it's accepted and expected.

Hunting for bargains on *international* goods is the sport on New Providence and Grand Bahama. Nassau's Bay Street and Freeport's *International Bazaar* and *Port Lucaya MarketPlace and Marina* (the latter with 85 specialty shops and restaurants) are the most popular shopping areas. Many Bay Street merchants also have branches on Paradise Island.

The best buys throughout the Bahamas include British china, crystal, fabrics, and liquor, Scandinavian glass and silverware, Irish lace, Swiss watches, and French perfume. However, not all imported goods cost less in the Bahamas than in the US. A department store catalogue brought along for on-the-spot price comparisons will be a big help; otherwise, do some pre-trip browsing at home and take notes. Be sure to check prices in stateside discount outlets, particularly if you intend to shop for cameras or electronic equipment, because Bahamian savings on these items are usually quoted as X percent below a "manufacturer's suggested list price"—which is normally higher than you'd have to pay at home. And don't buy an unfamiliar brand of watch, camera, radio, tape recorder, or anything else that might need repairs without making sure there's a stateside service shop that will honor its warranty. Some final advice: Check a local source like *Best Buys in the Bahamas, What-to-Do,* or the *Pocket Guide* to find out which stores specialize in the things you're looking for.

Most shops are open Mondays through Saturdays from 9 AM to 5 PM (sometimes until 6 PM in Freeport); a few close one afternoon a week (usually Thursday, Friday, or Saturday).

NASSAU

Barry's Big on everything British—woolen sweaters, suits, men's furnishings; also guayabera shirts, dashikis, and gold, silver, and jade jewelry. Bay and George Sts. (phone: 322-3118).

Brass and Leather Shop Imported English and European riding gear, teapots, bookends, and lots of other gift items; plus good-looking belts, wallets, and luggage from Gucci and Bottega Veneta. Charlotte St. just off Bay St. (phone: 322-3806).

Cartier Jewelry, watches, scarves, pens, sunglasses, perfume, wallets, and other items from this exclusive French house. Bay St., opposite *Nassau Shop* (phone: 322-4391).

Cellar Wine Shop Just as the name suggests: a large stock of wines. Two locations: Bay and Charlotte Sts. (phone: 322-4164) and *British Colonial Beach Resort Arcade,* 1 Bay St. (phone: 322-8911).

Coin of the Realm Maps, stamps, coins, and numismatic souvenirs, as well as fine jewelry and watches. Charlotte St. off Bay St. (phone: 322-4862 or 322-4497).

Cole's of Nassau Designer swimwear and sports clothes for women. Parliament St. just off Rawson Sq. (phone: 322-8393).

Colombian Emeralds International This well-regarded shop features an extensive selection of emeralds and other precious and semi-precious stones set in every conceivable manner. Bay St. (phone: 322-1484; 800-524-2083).

Fendi All sorts of accessories—handbags, jewelry, watches, shoes, belts, brief-cases—and fragrances from the famous design house. Charlotte and Bay Sts. (phone: 322-6300).

Girls from Brazil Exclusive swimwear from Brazil, plus some sportswear and cock-tail attire, and Italian-design jewelry. Upstairs at 328 Bay St. between Charlotte and Parliament Sts. (phone: 323-5966).

Gucci Luggage, gift items, and accessories—watches, men's ties, women's scarves—from the Italian design house. Bay St. and Bank La. (phone: 325-0561).

Island Book Store Scores of books: novels, mysteries, best sellers, and all kinds of information on the Bahamas; also film and camera supplies. Frederick and Bay Sts. (phone: 322-1011).

John Bull The town's best selection of cameras and accessories, plus Rolex and Seiko watches, Ray-Ban sunglasses, perfume, cosmetics, and jewelry. Bay St. between East St. and Elizabeth Ave. (phone: 322-4542).

Leather Shop Handbags, belts, and accessories by Ted Lapidus, Lanvin, and others. Two locations: Saffey Sq. on Bank La. (phone: 322-7597) and Parliament St., two blocks from Bay St. (phone: 325-1454).

Lightbourn's Biggest perfume selection in town, at even bigger savings. Bay and George Sts. (phone: 322-2095).

Linen and Lace All sorts of lavish table and bed linen, including hibiscus-embroi-dered tea cozies and printed linen tea towels attractive enough to be wall hangings. Bay St. between Charlotte and Frederick Sts. (phone: 322-4266).

Little Switzerland China, crystal, figurines, silver, jewelry, watches, coins, antiques, and perfume. Three locations: 6065 Bay St., opposite the Royal Bank of

Canada (phone: 322-2201); 21 Bay St., at the corner of Charlotte St. (phone: 325-7554); and 61 Bay St., opposite the *Straw Market* (phone: 322-1239).

Marlborough Antiques Maps and prints, limited-edition artwork, and Georgian, Victorian, and Edwardian furniture, bric-a-brac, and collectibles from the UK. Corner of Marlborough and Queen Sts. (phone: 328-0502).

Nassau Shop The town's largest department store, it has good buys on French perfume, watches, jewelry, and British lambswool, shetland, and cashmere knitwear for men and women. 284 Bay St., between Frederick and Charlotte Sts. (phone: 322-8405/6).

Perfume Shop Fragrances for women and men at 20% to 40% off US prices. Bay and Frederick Sts. (phone: 322-2375).

Pipes of Peace Pipes, Cuban cigars, cigarettes, lighters, plus island souvenirs. Bay St. between Charlotte and Parliament Sts. (phone: 325-2022).

Pyfrom's The town's biggest stock of out-and-out souvenirs—dolls, steel drums, Nassau T-shirts and sweatshirts, you name it. Bay St. between Frederick and Charlotte Sts. (phone: 322-2603).

Scottish Shop Tams, clan jewelry, tartan ties, scarves, and kilts. Charlotte St. off Bay St. (phone: 322-4720).

Solomon's Mines A suitably dazzling collection of bone china, Waterford and Swedish crystal, figurines, and jewelry. On Woodes Rogers Walk at Rawson Sq. (phone: 322-8502).

Treasure Box Nicely done conch and coral jewelry, as well as West Indian silver bangles. Bay St. near Market St. (phone: 322-1662).

Tropical Fine Art Gallery Works by Bahamian artists such as watercolorist Darman Stubbs. In the *Nassau International Bazaar,* Woodes Rogers Walk at Charlotte St. (phone: 325-7492).

FREEPORT/LUCAYA

The 10-acre *International Bazaar* showcases imports from Europe, the Far East, and the Middle East, and is so full of so many things that it can get quite confusing. Don't try to sort it out without a map (pick one up at the *Tourist Information Centre* near the Scandinavian section) and your list of comparative prices. The other major shopping complex on Grand Bahama is *Port Lucaya MarketPlace and Marina* (phone: 373-8446), with 85 boutiques, 40 straw vendors, 11 arts and crafts shops, several restaurants, and a marina, all across the street from the *Clarion Atlantik Beach and Golf Resort* on Lucaya Beach. Several Nassau stores have outlet branches at both the *International Bazaar* and *Port Lucaya MarketPlace and Marina,* including *Pipes of Peace, John Bull, Fendi, Colombian Emeralds International, Gucci, Leather Shop,* and *Little Switzerland* (see "Nassau" listings for details on these shops).

Bahamas Perfume Factory Take a free tour of this factory to watch the process of making island-inspired perfumes, colognes, and aftershaves, and then sample and buy the fragrances. You can even mix and bottle your own original scent. In a plum-colored mansion behind the *International Bazaar* (phone: 352-5580).

Butler & Sands Duty- and tax-free liquor, Bahamian Kalik beer, and wines at much lower prices than in the US. On E. Sunrise Hwy., just in front of *Port Lucaya MarketPlace and Marina* (phone: 322-3785).

CariBah Original island batik clothing, as well as straw dolls and T-shirts. *International Bazaar* (phone: 352-5946).

Freeport Jewelers The main lures are 18-karat gold chains and other fine jewelry. *International Bazaar* (phone: 352-2004).

Island Galleria Handsome jewelry (especially coral), crystal, china, and watches. Also Far East lace tablecloths, linen, brocaded pajamas, and silk robes. *International Bazaar* (phone: 352-8194) and *Port Lucaya MarketPlace and Marina* (phone: 373-8400).

Midnight Sun Stocks all the best Scandinavian names in housewares, most at 25% or more below US prices. *International Bazaar* (phone: 352-9515) and *Port Lucaya MarketPlace and Marina* (phone: 373-8446).

Les Parisiens Perfumes and colognes from France and the US, all at reasonable prices. In the French section of the *International Bazaar* (phone: 352-5380) and *Port Lucaya Marketplace and Marina* (phone: 373-8396).

SPORTS

Due to the popularity of the Bahamas' first-rate golf, tennis, and water sports, there's a toll-free hotline to handle queries on sporting events and facilities throughout the islands: Dial 800-32-SPORT. You'll find the following on the islands:

BOATING There are lots of possibilities on both a large and small scale. Most island hotels rent Sailfish, Sunfish, and sometimes Hobie Cats. Island resorts often have Boston Whalers or other outboards available, at widely varying rental rates (they're sometimes free to guests). In Grand Bahama, *Reef Tours* (see *Sea Excursions,* above) rents 18-foot motorboats.

For yachting enthusiasts, the Bahamas' calm, open waters, safe bays, and vast number of anchorages (not to mention the swimming and diving waters found in and near them) make this an exceptionally fine cruising area. All sizes and types of boats (crewed and bareboat) are available for charter to both experienced skippers and neophytes. Arrangements can be made through a travel agent, your hotel, or specialists like *Nassau Yacht Haven* (phone: 393-8173).

On the outlying islands, *Abaco Bahamas Charters* (Hope Town, Elbow Cay; phone: 800-626-5690; 502-245-9428 in Kentucky) has a fleet of bareboat sailing vessels; *Marsh Harbour Marina* (Marsh Harbour, Great Abaco; phone: 367-2700) also charters boats. Bareboat and crewed charters in the Abacos are a specialty of *Sunsail* (Marsh Harbour, Great Abaco; phone: 367-2214; 800-327-2276). *Regency International Charters* (phone: 809-776-5950; 800-524-7676) and *Avery's Marine* (phone: 809-776-0113), both based in St. Thomas, US Virgin Islands, also charter vessels in the Bahamas. To sail or cruise the Berry Islands, contact *Tropical Diversions Yacht Charters* in Great Harbour Cay (phone: 367-8123; 800-343-7256; 305-921-9084 in Florida).

Well-equipped marinas on a number of islands provide water, fuel, food, ice, showers, and sometimes a bed for the night. In the Nassau/Paradise Island and Cable Beach areas, they include *Hurricane Hole Marina* (phone: 363-3600); *Nassau Yacht Haven* (phone: 393-8173); *Nassau Harbour Club* (phone: 393-0771); and *Paradise Harbour Club and Marina* (phone: 363-2992). On Grand Bahama, there are the *Port Lucaya MarketPlace and Marina* (phone: 373-9090); *Running Mon Marina* (see *Checking In*); and *Xanadu Marina* (phone: 352-6782, ext. 1333).

Marinas on the outlying islands include the following (for phone numbers not given here, see *Checking In*): in the Abacos, *Boat Harbour Marina* (phone: 367-2736), *Conch Inn Marina, Green Turtle Marina,* and *Hope Town Marina* (phone: 366-0254), *Marsh Harbour Marina* (phone: 367-2700), *Spanish Cay Marina, Treasure Cay Marina,* and *Walker's Cay Marina;* on Andros, *Andros Beach Hotel Marina* (phone: 329-2582); in the Berry Islands, *Chub Cay Marina* at the *Chub Cay Club* and *Great Harbour Cay Marina* (phone: 367-8123); on North Bimini, *Bimini Big Game Fishing Club, Bimini Blue Water,* and *Weech's Docks* (phone: 347-3028); on Eleuthera, *Davis Harbour Marina* (phone: 334-6303); on Harbour Island, off Eleuthera, *Romora Bay Club* and *Valentine's Yacht Club;* on Spanish Wells, off Eleuthera, *Spanish Wells Yacht Haven* (phone: 333-4255); in the Exumas, on Staniel Cay, *Happy People Marina* (phone: 355-2008); and on Long Island, *Stella Maris Marina & Yacht Club.*

For complete cruising information—including small charts, landfall sketches, anchorages, and approach descriptions—*The Yachtsman's Guide to the Bahamas* is invaluable. It's $28.95, plus postage, from Tropic Isle Publishers (PO Box 610938, N. Miami, FL 33261-0938; phone: 305-893-4277).

For those who prefer to tour the Bahamas aboard a small cruise ship, the *New Shoreham II,* a 70-passenger vessel run by *American/Canadian/Caribbean Cruise Line* (phone: 800-556-7450; 401-247-0955 in Rhode Island) offers cruises from Nassau to the Out Islands.

CRICKET A popular spectator sport in the Bahamas, this cousin of US baseball is played every other weekend from mid-March through the end of November at *Haynes Oval* near Fort Charlotte in Nassau, New Providence. Matches are held weekends at 1 PM (phone: 322-1875 or 322-3622). Look for other matches on pitches (fields) in Freeport on Grand Bahama and throughout the islands. For schedules, check with the tourist board of the island you plan to visit, or consult the sports section of the island newspaper.

GOLF Despite their essentially flat terrain, the Bahamas offer enough first-rate courses—both 18-hole and nine-hole layouts—to satisfy most golfers. Within the islands are examples of the course craft of many of golf's premier architects, including Robert Trent Jones Sr. and Jr., Pete Dye, Dick Wilson, and Joe Lee. We begin with our favorites.

TOP TEE-OFF SPOTS

Paradise Island Golf Club, Paradise Island This picturesque, Dick Wilson–designed, par 72 course is surrounded by the Atlantic Ocean and water hazards on three sides. The par 3 14th hole, affectionately dubbed "cocoa plum," affords golfers a breathtaking ocean view. Paradise Island Dr. (phone: 363-3925; 800-722-7466).

Sofitel Cotton Bay Club, Eleuthera At press time, this venerable resort was closed, but it's expected to reopen under new management. Designed by Robert Trent Jones Sr., the par 72, 7,068-yard course has been rated one of the world's top 33 by *Golf Magazine.* It boasts 129 sand traps and 13 water hazards—not counting the Atlantic Ocean. However, the course does get a bit brown during the dry months; the greens are most green from September through January. Rock Sound (phone: 334-6101; 800-221-4542 or 800-334-3523).

South Ocean Golf and Beach Resort, New Providence By far the best course on New Providence Island, this former Ramada resort has been taken over by new management. It occupies high ground that provides a striking view of the area called Tongue of the Ocean. The course, designed by Joe Lee, is highlighted by four challenging water holes, and the use of the unusually rolling terrain sets the layout of this 18-hole championship golf course apart from its peers. At the southwestern tip of the island (phone: 362-4391).

In addition to the above, fairway facilities on New Providence include the *Cable Beach Golf Club* (phone: 327-6000). Grand Bahama has four golf courses, all in the Freeport/Lucaya area: *The Ruby* and *The Emerald* courses, affiliated with the *Bahamas Princess* resort (see *Checking In*); the *Lucaya Golf & Country Club,* owned by the *Clarion Atlantik Beach & Golf Resort* (phone: 373-1006); and the *Fortune Hills Golf and Country Club* (phone: 373-4500). All 18-hole courses have complete facilities, including carts and clubs for rent and resident pros. Most also offer golf clinics and private lessons.

There's also a nine-hole course on Great Harbour Cay, one of the Berry Islands (phone: 367-8838; 800-343-7256), and an 18-hole course on Great Abaco at the *Treasure Cay* resort (see *Checking In*).

HORSEBACK RIDING Riding along lanes of casuarinas and sea grape–lined beaches is a beautiful way to tour the islands—especially in the early morning. Try *Happy Trails* stables (phone: 362-1820) at Coral Harbour on New Providence or *Pinetree Stables* (N. Beachway Dr.; phone: 373-3600) in Freeport, Grand Bahama.

KAYAKING An ideal way to explore hard-to-reach areas, kayaking is fast becoming a popular activity in the Bahamas. Kayaks are almost impossible to capsize, move faster than canoes, are relatively easy to maneuver, and can even be equipped with sail rigs. *Ibis Tours* (7040 W. Palmetto Park Rd., Suite 2-119, Boca Raton, FL 33433; phone: 800-525-9411) offers eight-day kayaking expeditions through the Exuma cays; the outfit provides 17-foot-long kayaks, life jackets, tents, sleeping bags, mattress pads, food, wine with meals, and even pillows. Novices are welcome. On Grand Bahama, Erica Moultric (phone: 373-2485) offers day-long kayak trips (including lunch) from Hawksbill Creek, Queen's Cove, to a deserted cay. Reservations are necessary, and there is a minimum of four people per tour. No experience is necessary; bring sunscreen and a hat.

REGATTAS They're held all year long, for both sail and power boats. Among the major annual events: *Regatta Time in Abaco* and *Green Turtle Yacht Club Regatta Week,* both held in the Abacos in early July; *Cat Island Regatta* in early August; the *Bahamas Boating Fling,* held during the summer; *Discovery Day Regatta* in October in San Salvador and Andros; and the *Miami-Nassau Powerboat Race* in December. Most fun: the *Out Island Regatta* (sometimes pronounced Re-*gret*-ta), a fierce competition for island workboats held every April in George Town, Great Exuma. Every vessel that can goes to George Town to race or watch, making this one of the all-time great parties afloat and ashore. There are only two rules at this event: Don't bump, and throw no one overboard.

SNORKELING AND SCUBA Incredible visibility, scores of reefs and drop-offs close to shore, and the rich variety of Bahamian marine life make a number of these islands great sites for underwater exploration. First-rate guides and scuba instruction are available at many island sites, and snorkeling is casual fun at any hotel beach, where masks and flippers can usually be borrowed or rented.

Be aware that though you can buy the gear you need at any dive shop, shops will only refill tanks for and rent scuba equipment to certified divers. You can get your certification during your stay by taking a course at a qualified scuba instruction center over a period of five days, with classes taking place in a classroom, a swimming pool, and the ocean. On-island courses are offered by the *Underwater Explorers Society* (*UNEXSO;* phone: 373-

1250 or 373-1244; 800-992-DIVE) and other accredited dive centers (call 800-327-7678 for a complete listing). For information about diving instruction, contact the *National Association of Underwater Instructors* (*NAUI;* PO Box 14650, 4650 Arrow Hwy., Suite F1, Montclair, CA 91763; phone: 714-621-5801); the *Professional Association of Diving Instructors* (*PADI;* 1251 E. Dyer Rd., Suite 100, Santa Ana, CA 92705; phone: 714-540-7234); or your local *YMCA*.

BEST DEPTHS

Andros The Andros Barrier Reef, the world's third largest, is the best diving spot here, with dives ranging from 15 to 185 feet. The only dive operator currently on Andros is affiliated with *Small Hope Bay Lodge* (see *Checking In*); the company arranges diving trips and offers both *NAUI* and *PADI* certification courses. More experienced divers can explore the reef's deep outside drop-off and blue holes.

Bimini Although better known for its fishing, the island offers a number of spectacular dive opportunities, including a 15-foot dive through the wreck of the *Sapona,* a huge vessel built by Henry Ford that sank off these shores in 1929. The waters around Bimini not only teem with grouper, grunts, and snapper, but the 3 miles of coral reef along the Bimini Wall are also home to lobsters, moray eels, and hogfish. Tours can be arranged through *Bimini Undersea Adventures* (phone: 347-3089; 800-327-8150).

Eleuthera Off the northern tip of the island are a number of excellent dive sites, including—for experienced divers only—the Current Cut. The current whooshes divers along the length of this narrow tidal channel, and a boat picks them up at the end of the thrilling 10-minute ride. Less intrepid divers may head for the Devil's Backbone to explore 8 miles of shallow coral gardens and four wrecks—all in less than 40 feet of water. One of the wrecks is of a locomotive engine that went down on a barge in 1865; it was being transported to be sold to raise cash for the Confederacy during the American Civil War. There are also good sites for novice divers to view grouper, angelfish, triggerfish, and other tropical marine life. Contact *Valentine's Dives* (Harbour Island; phone: 333-2309; 800-383-6480) for information on dive sites or *Scuba Schools International (SSI)* certification courses.

Grand Bahama Great dive sites here include the shallow Treasure Reef, the Wall, the Caves, and Theo's Wreck. Probably the best scuba instruction anywhere is offered at the *Underwater Explorers Society* (*UNEXSO;* phone: 373-1250 or 373-1244; 800-992-DIVE), a world class dive facility across from the *Lucayan Beach* hotel. Here scuba divers, snorkelers, and landlubbers who want to learn can take advantage of a variety of courses, ranging from one- or two-day specialty classes to week-long full-certification programs.

Even more unusual and memorable are *UNEXSO's* special programs. The "Dolphin Experience" allows divers to frolic in the open ocean with tame bottlenose dolphins (the organization also offers a program for non-divers in which participants view the dolphins from a boat and may pet and play with them from a wading platform); participants in the "Shark Junction Dive" sit 50 feet below the sea and watch as reef sharks are fed by a mesh-steel-gloved handler only a few feet away. Videotapes of your experience are available. These programs are popular, so make reservations early.

Long Island In addition to the shallow snorkeling available around the island, underwater enthusiasts shouldn't miss the shark dive offered by the *Stella Maris Resort Club* (see *Checking In*), a day-long outing during which you get to watch dive masters feed Caribbean reef, mako, and bull sharks—and possibly a barracuda or two. *PADI, NAUI,* and *SSI* certification courses are offered.

New Providence and Paradise Island There are numerous reefs, wrecks, and coral strands off these two adjoining islands. Among the best sites are Rose Island Reefs close to Nassau Harbour, a good place for novices to try their fins; the wreck of the *Mahoney* (a steel-hulled ship sunk in 30 feet of water just outside the harbor); Goulding Cay Reefs at the far western end of New Providence; Gambier Deep Reef off Gambier Village, New Providence; the elkhorn coral gardens off Green Cay; Booby Rock Channel, with its large fish population; the tiny, isolated South Side reefs; and Clifton Pier Drop-Off (for experienced divers only), near the south shore of New Providence, a gently sloping reef that culminates in a sheer drop of 110 feet.

Equipment and certified instruction can be obtained at most hotels. Most dive operators not affiliated with a hotel provide transportation to and from hotels as part of the packages they offer. *Bahama Divers* (phone: 393-5644; 800-398-DIVE) in Nassau near the Paradise Island Bridge offers certified instruction, dive trips, and free round-trip transportation from most major hotels. Other dive operations in the Nassau/Paradise Island vicinity include *Dive Dive Dive* (Coral Harbour; phone: 362-1143; 800-368-3483); *Sun Divers* (*Best Western British Colonial* hotel, 1 Bay St.; phone: 325-8927); *Divers' Haven* (E. Bay St., near the *Pilot House* hotel; phone: 393-0869); *Stuart Cove's Dive South Ocean* (*South Ocean* resort; phone: 362-4171), where three guided "Dive with the Sharks" programs are offered; and *Nassau Scuba Centre* (Coral Harbour; phone: 362-1964).

San Salvador There are nearly 80 marked sites here, most of them on the leeward side of the island. The walls begin in about 40 to 50 feet of water and vary from gentle sloping reefs to vertigo-inducing 170-foot drops. There are also good shore and wreck dives. Divers see lots of curious groupers and other fish, as well as the occasional turtle, ray, and shark. Snapshot Reef—named by the underwater photography school affiliated with *Guanahani Divers* (contact the *Riding Rock Inn;* see *Checking In*)—is a shallow site where a number of scuba magazine covers have been photographed. *Club Med* (see *Checking In*) has a complete dive center, with accredited certification instruction, an underwater photography lab with rentals and instruction, and the island's only decompression chamber.

There are also good dive spots on the outlying islands. In the Abacos, rentals and dive trips can be arranged at *Dive Abaco* (Marsh Harbour; phone: 367-2787) and *Walker's Cay Dive Shop* (Walker's Cay; phone: 359-1400 or 352-5252; 800-432-2092). The best diving spots are coral-lined Devil's Hole; 2,000-acre *Pelican Cay National Park* (between Lynyard and Tilloo Cays south of Marsh Harbour); Scotland, Spanish, and Deep Water Cays; and the wreck of the Union warship USS *Adirondack.* In the Exumas, *Exuma Fantasea* (George Town; phone: 336-3483) has dive boats and equipment. The *Exuma National Land and Sea Park* features beautiful sea gardens three to 10 feet below the water's surface, and the best dive sites are Thunderball Grotto (at Staniel Cay), Mystery Cave (off Stocking Island near George Town), and the wreck of a 1560 privateer (off Highborne Cay). On the main island of Eleuthera, equipment and information are available at the *Sofitel Cotton Bay Club* (see *Checking In*). Dive sites include a maze of coral reefs around the Six Shilling Channel Islands, a string of small isles between Eleuthera and New Providence; a shallow steamship wreck off the northern coast; and a grounded freighter south of Egg Island Reef. On Harbour Island, the *Romora Bay Club* (see *Checking In*) is fully equipped for instruction and trips. On the Berry Islands, the *Chub Cay Club* (see *Checking In*) has diving equipment and boats; sites include Mamma Rhoda Rock, Whale Cay Reefs, Hoffman Cay, and a mystery wreck with cannon between Little Stirrup and Great Stirrup Cays. All-inclusive, week-long dive cruises from George Town, Great Exuma, to Rum Cay, San Salvador, and Concepcion Island are offered by *Coral Bay Cruises* (phone: 800-433-7262); make arrangements well in advance.

SPORT FISHING Bahamian waters are great grounds for tuna (Allison, bluefin), barracuda, amberjack, bonefish, marlin (blue and white), dolphin, grouper, kingfish, sailfish, tarpon, and wahoo. More than 50 world-record catches have been made off the Bahamas, and over 30 tournaments open to residents and visitors are scheduled every year, including the annual six-tournament *Bahamas Billfish Championship,* held from March through June.

On Grand Bahama, *Reef Tours Ltd.* (see *Sea Excursions,* above) runs half-day fishing trips. Hotels and marinas also can make arrangements.

Best deep-sea sites include Walker's Cay (world-record skipjack tuna) and Cat Island (world-record wahoo); take a boat from the *Current Club* dock in the town of Current, North Eleuthera, to fish that island's western coast (world-record dorado) or some special area that only the captain knows. Known as the bonefishing capital of the Western world, the Bahamas are where the elusive "ghost of the sea" can be stalked on the flats off Bimini, Eleuthera, and the Exumas. See also "Sport Fishing on Bimini" in *Quintessential Bahamas and Turks & Caicos,* DIVERSIONS.

SWIMMING AND SUNNING These 700 islands offer hundreds of miles of sandy beaches of varied shapes, sizes, and colors—all washed by a sea that is truly, incredibly clear. In addition to whatever facilities your hotel offers, there's lots more shore out there.

DREAM BEACHES

Fernandez Bay, Cat Island Though it's not the easiest beach to get to, the good news is that once there, you can count on white sand, turquoise blue sea—and solitude. This lovely strand, lined with lacy casuarina trees, is near the *Fernandez Bay Village* (see *Checking In*), a charming inn run by the Armbrister family, where visitors can rent small sailboats or snorkeling equipment.

Harbour Island, off Eleuthera This 3-mile pink sand beach along Harbour Island's windward shore, serving such hotels as the *Dunmore Beach Club* and *Pink Sands* (see *Checking In* for both), is a perfect place for picnicking, snorkeling (although the surf tends to get a little rough here), and swimming.

Rolleville, Great Exuma Here you'll find miles of secluded beach—interrupted only by clusters of coconut palms and a wooden house here and there—and waters that vary in color from pale aqua to deep turquoise. Except for an occasional yacht or fishing boat passing by, this as-yet-undiscovered strand is all yours.

Other stunning strands include Love Beach and sections of Cable Beach on the north shore of New Providence; Paradise Beach on Paradise Island; Taino Beach at the *Club Fortuna Beach* resort in Freeport, Grand Bahama; and Fortune Beach, also on Grand Bahama.

The outlying islands also boast some excellent beaches. In the Berry Islands, Great Harbour Cay—one of the most handsome beaches in the Bahamas—offers good shelling. There are 2 miles of fine white sand lining the shore at Staniard Creek on Andros. Also oustanding are Stocking Island off George Town on Great Exuma, an ideal destination for day sailing trips and private picnics; the miles-long coral sand shore east of Governor's Harbour, Eleuthera; and the whole sandy rim of unspoiled Mayaguana, a virtually undiscovered island east of Acklins Island, with no accommodations, but the best shelling in the Bahamas.

TENNIS The largest court complex is at the *Club Med* on Paradise Island, with 20 clay-composition courts (eight lighted) plus a full staff of instructors, instant-replay TV, and ball machines. Also on Paradise Island, there are nine courts for day or night play at the *Atlantis* resort and courts at the *Holiday Inn Sunspree* and *Radisson Grand.* In the Cable Beach section of New Providence, the *Forte Nassau Beach* hotel has six lighted courts, the *Meridien Royal Bahamian* has two, and the *Radisson Cable Beach* has 13 Har-Tru and five clay courts (plus three racquetball and three squash courts); the *South Ocean* resort, at the southwestern corner of New Providence, has four courts. Hotels with tennis facilities in the Freeport/Lucaya area of Grand Bahama include the *Bahamas Princess* (12 courts), *Radisson Resort on Lucaya Beach* (four courts), *Club Fortuna Beach* (two courts), and *Xanadu Beach* (three courts). On the outlying islands, the *Sofitel Cotton Bay Club* on Eleuthera has a top layout with four courts, *Treasure Cay* on Great Abaco has six courts, and *Club Med* on San Salvador features 10 courts. See *Checking In* for phone numbers of all hotels listed above. Court time usually is free to guests and available to non-guests at a moderate fee.

WATER SKIING The best sites are off New Providence's Cable Beach, around Paradise Island, and on the protected waters around Freeport/Lucaya, Grand Bahama; some of the larger outlying island resorts (Eleuthera's *Club Med,* for example) also have boats and equipment, though most prefer to concentrate on diving. Many resorts in Nassau/Paradise Island and Freeport/Lucaya also offer parasailing and jet ski rentals.

WINDSURFING Good windsurfing is found on New Providence's Cable Beach; on Paradise Island; at Grand Bahama's Xanadu and Port Lucaya Beaches; in the Abacos at Hope Town, Walker's Cay, and Green Turtle Cay; on Harbour Island, just off Eleuthera; on Andros; at Stella Maris on Long Island; and at Pittstown Point on Crooked Island, south of Long Island.

NIGHTLIFE

Though the Out Islands tend to be quiet after dinner—with maybe a little bar talk or terrace lounging—there is plenty happening on the Nassau/ Paradise Island scene and in Freeport/Lucaya. See *Checking In* for phone numbers of the hotels listed below.

The area around Nassau and Paradise Island offers the greatest variety, starting with two casinos—the enormous *Paradise Island Casino* at the *Atlantis* resort and the equally huge *Crystal Palace Casino,* a rainbow-hued extravaganza on Cable Beach, near Nassau on New Providence. Las Vegas–style shows take place nightly at the *Crystal Palace*'s 800-seat *Palace*

Theater (phone: 327-6200); similar shows are performed Monday through Saturday nights at the *Atlantis* resort's 550-seat *Le Cabaret Theatre*. Also at *Atlantis* is the *Joker's Wild Comedy Club,* featuring comedians from the US (closed Sundays and Mondays). Other hopping nightspots on Paradise Island are the *Paradise Island Casino*'s *Club Pastiche* disco; the *Holiday Inn Sunspree*'s *Mary Reed,* which features live music nightly; and the *Radisson*'s *Le Paon*. Out Cable Beach way, one of the liveliest scenes is apt to be the *Forte Nassau Beach* hotel's *Rock & Roll Café* (see *Eating Out*), which features live bands on Wednesdays and weekends and *karaoke* on Sundays. *Karaoke* also is offered three nights a week at *Forte Nassau Beach*'s *Starlight Terrace*. *King Eric's* nightclub (phone: 327-5321), next to the *Forte Nassau Beach* hotel, features two native shows nightly (except Mondays) with fire-eating, limbo dancing, steel-drum revues, and calypso music. Cable Beach also offers the two-story *Fanta-Z Disco* in the *Crystal Palace Casino*. On West Bay Street, at Saunders Beach near downtown Nassau, is the *Coliseum* (phone: 322-7195), which features a band that plays Bahamian music, reggae, and disco; it's closed weekdays. In Nassau, the *BahaMen,* the Bahamas' leading recording group, have opened the *Culture Club* (Nassau St.; phone: 356-6266), where they feature a *junkanoo* music extravaganza. Another late-night venue with live music in town is *Club Waterloo* (East Bay St.; phone: 393-7324 or 393-0478).

In Freeport/Lucaya on Grand Bahama, there's gambling at the *Princess Casino* at the *Bahamas Princess* resort and at the *Lucayan Beach* resort. The *Casino Royale Theatre* (at the *Princess Casino;* phone: 352-7811) is a major showplace. The *Lucayan Beach* resort also has a revue at the *Flamingo Showcase Theatre*. The *John B. Club* at the *Bahamas Princess*'s *Princess Country Club* offers live Bahamian music in a tropical outdoor setting. Lucaya's hot spot, *Club Estee* (at the *Port Lucaya MarketPlace and Marina;* phone: 373-2777), is another big sound scene, as is the *Studio 69* disco (Midshipman Rd.; phone: 373-4824), which is closed Sundays through Wednesdays. Island shows play at the *Radisson Panache Theatre* and the *Yellow Bird* nightclub at the *Castaways* resort (phone: 352-6682). One of the liveliest of Freeport/Lucaya's after-dark destinations is the *Port Lucaya MarketPlace and Marina,* where calypso and *soca* bands give free concerts several nights a week in Count Basie Square. Make sure to be here for the *junkanoo* festival held every Saturday night, with locals and tourists alike joining in the revelry.

Although several companies offer nightclub and native-show tours (see *Sightseeing Tours*), you don't have to travel with a group to ensure safety; you should be careful at night in Nassau, as in any city, but nowhere on these islands has crime against tourists been a significant problem.

Best on the Islands

CHECKING IN

The hotel situation in Nassau/Paradise Island and Freeport/Lucaya has improved significantly, with many resorts spending millions of dollars on much-needed renovations and room refurbishment. Meanwhile, established inns on the outlying islands—with their stunning beaches, relaxed sports, and genuinely personal service—continue to delight repeat guests. This year, look for two ambitious new luxury resorts to open on the Out Islands— the *Hyatt Cape Eleuthera* on Eleuthera (for updated information, call 800-233-1234; 305-444-7991 in Florida) and the *Bahamas Club* on Great Exuma (for updated information, call 336-2872). A number of Out Island hotels can be reached through the *Out Island Promotion Board* reservation service (phone: 800-OUT-ISLAND; 305-359-8099 in Florida).

Most Nassau/Paradise Island and Freeport/Lucaya hotels quote European Plan (EP) rates (without meals); more resorts on the islands beyond—where there aren't that many places to eat out—include breakfasts and dinners (Modified American Plan, MAP), and sometimes all meals (Full American Plan, FAP), in their rates. A 4% government room tax plus a 4% resort levy are added to all hotel bills; many hotels also add a 10% or 15% service charge. Unless otherwise indicated, rooms in all hotels listed below feature air conditioning, private baths, and TV sets. Almost all hotels in the Bahamas have in-room telephones, except a very few small, family-run places in the Out Islands; it's a good idea to check ahead about amenities if you're planning to stay at one of these smaller establishments.

Expect to pay $150 or more per night in winter for a double room without meals in a hotel listed here as expensive; between $110 and $150 in one designated moderate; and less than $110 in inexpensive digs. Some hotels offer MAP add-ons (covering breakfast and dinner) for about $30 to $45 per person per day. All-inclusive resorts have been categorized according to the estimated rate for the room alone. Between late April and mid-December, prices in all categories drop by about 20% to 40%. All telephone numbers are in the 809 area code unless otherwise indicated.

We begin with our favorite havens, followed by recommended hotels listed by price category.

SPECIAL HAVENS AND PRIVATE ISLANDS

Club Med–Columbus Isle, San Salvador Overlooking sparkling Bonefish Bay, this vacation village is ideally situated on 3½ miles of pristine beach. Geared toward honeymooners and couples, the luxurious resort is decorated in shades of blue and green that evoke images of the sea, and the prevailing themes of the overall decor are the sun, the moon, and the stars—the three elements Columbus used to navigate his ships. The artwork that graces the public areas and the 216 guestrooms was brought here from exotic locales such as Bali, Africa, China, and India. Understandably, Club Med markets this resort as one of its three most elegant in the Western Hemisphere. Facilities include a scuba center, as well as every kind of water sport, 10 tennis courts (with instruction), an open-air theater with nightly entertainment, a pool, and three restaurants. All activities and meals (but not drinks) are included in the rate. Bonefish Bay (phone: 331-2000; 800-CLUB-MED; 212-750-1687 in New York City; fax: 331-2458; 212-750-1697 in New York City).

Dunmore Beach Club, Harbour Island, off Eleuthera Probably Harbour Island's most exclusive enclave for the rich and famous (it was a private club for 25 years), this is also a favorite with honeymooners and laid-back nature lovers seeking a luxurious retreat. The place is small, with 12 rooms in six cottages, all done up in tropical pastels—try to book accommodations in the "Pink" or "White" cottages. The restaurant overlooking the beach is renowned for both its fine fare and its elegance—men are required to wear jackets and ties at dinner (jacket only from April through August). There's a 3-mile-long beach, a tennis court, and a variety of water sports nearby. Closed September and October. No credit cards accepted. Near Dunmore Town on Colebrook La. (phone: 333-2200; 800-235-3505; fax: 333-2429).

Graycliff, New Providence If there's one place that epitomizes Bahamian history, grace, and style, it's this Old World–style, 12-suite luxury hotel housed in a Georgian colonial mansion in Nassau. The decor is Empire and Victorian; prints of London and of English royalty hang on the pale pastel walls, and Persian rugs warm the polished wood floors. There's a pool hemmed by a dense thicket of palms and ferns, a sauna, a Jacuzzi, and a small gym. The in-town location, however, means that the beach is a rather long walk away. Suites are individually decorated with a mix of modern and antique furnishings that create a wonderfully eclectic look. *Graycliff* also has one of the few first class restaurants in the Bahamas (and arguably the most expensive as well; see *Eating Out*). West Hill St., opposite *Government House*, Nassau (phone: 322-2796; 800-633-7411; fax: 326-6110).

Ocean Club, Paradise Island Built in the 1930s as a private estate (with two colonnaded stories around a pink patio) and transformed into an exclusive resort by millionaire Huntington Hartford in 1962, this is certainly the most handsome place on Paradise Island—or New Providence, for that matter. Sun International purchased the resort in 1994 and gave it a $7.5-million face-lift. Secluded, set amid formal Versailles-style gardens, it has 71 rooms, including four suites, with ceiling fans (in addition to air conditioning), satellite TV, mini-bars, and all of the little amenities that denote a luxury resort; five private villas also have Jacuzzis and enclosed patios. Rounding out the amenities are a beautiful big pool, a postcard-perfect beach (with waitress service for drinks and lunch), water sports, and the *Courtyard Terrace* (see *Eating Out*), a lovely, galleried dining patio. Golf and tennis are available nearby. Ocean Club Dr. (phone: 363-3000; 800-321-3000; 305-891-3888 in Florida; fax: 363-2424; 305-893-2866 in Florida).

The Villas on Silver Cay Here, on the private island of Silver Cay, are 22 elegant (and pricey) villas tailor-made for honeymooners and other lovebirds. While the villas are part of the *Coral World Marine Park* complex (entrance to the park is complimentary), they are separate from the hubbub and crowds, with a private beach. Snorkeling gear (handy for exploring the marine park's Pleasure Reef snorkeling trail) and frequent shuttles to Cable Beach and downtown Nassau are also complimentary. The villas are beautifully appointed with king-size beds, unobstructed sea views, modern kitchenettes, living room/dining areas, a sun deck, and spacious marble bathrooms; each also has a fenced-in courtyard featuring a private swimming pool with Jacuzzi. Breakfast (which is included in the rate) is delivered each morning. Silver Cay, off New Providence (phone: 328-1036; 800-328-8814; fax: 323-3202).

NASSAU AND CABLE BEACH, NEW PROVIDENCE

EXPENSIVE

Marriott Resort and Crystal Palace Casino This mammoth casino and resort hotel has nearly 900 rooms dispersed among the Casino Tower, also called the Crystal Tower, and four Palace Towers. When a Marriott franchiser purchased the former Carnival Cruise Lines property in 1994, the company swiftly launched a $30-million renovation program, including the scheduled refurbishment of all the upscale, amenity-laden rooms. The property offers a staggering array of bars, restaurants, and recreation areas, a casino that vies with the one on Paradise Island as the largest in the Bahamas, a glitzy cabaret, a two-story disco, a landscaped pool deck with a bilevel water slide, two lagoons, and a complete water sports facility. Tennis courts and an 18-hole golf course are nearby. Beach lovers will be disappointed, however, as there's only a manmade sandy area. Cable Beach (phone: 327-6000 or 327-7070; 800-222-7466; fax: 327-6801).

Le Meridien Royal Bahamian Upscale yet unpretentious, this wonderful resort retains its quiet elegance and the feel of a private club, which it once was. There are 146 good-size rooms in its six-story Manor House tower, and 27 one-bedroom villas surrounded by gardens (two with private pools, wet bars, and whirlpool baths in master suites). Also here are a health spa, an enormous free-form pool, a wide beach with extensive water sports, a beachside café, a romantically elegant dining room, and two tennis courts. Cocktail parties are held weekly in the statue-filled courtyard. Cable Beach (phone: 327-6400; 800-543-4300; fax: 327-6961).

MODERATE

Best Western British Colonial Once the queen of Bahamas hotels, this pink palace has lost a bit of its splendor. But even though its patina is somewhat faded, the grande dame still boasts a prime location in the heart of Nassau. It has 325 guestrooms, two restaurants, and four bars, as well as a private beach, a health club, a water sports center (with snorkeling and sailing complimentary to guests), and three lighted tennis courts. 1 Bay St., Nassau (phone: 322-3301; 800-528-1234; fax: 322-2286).

Breezes Formerly the Wyndham company's *Ambassador Beach* resort, it joined Jamaica's all-inclusive SuperClubs chain in 1994. Following a $13.5-million refurbishment, the property, with 400 rooms set on 1,800 feet of sandy white beach, now offers a full slate of amenities, all included in the price of a stay. Guests enjoy complimentary snorkeling and sailing at the beach, and tennis, squash, and racquetball at a fully equipped fitness center. There are several bars and restaurants and a pool. The guestrooms are comfortable, but not luxurious. Cable Beach (phone: 800-859-SUPER; 305-925-0925 in Florida; fax: 305-925-0334).

Forte Nassau Beach A 410-room, colonial-style fixture on Cable Beach, this is the liveliest property in the Nassau area, with lots of land and water sports, planned activities, and happenings day and night. Many of the guestrooms are furnished with antiques, and there are six restaurants, including the popular *Rock & Roll Café* (see *Eating Out*). Tennis, snorkeling, and sailing are complimentary to guests. This is a good choice if you're up for convivial, but not overpowering, action. The Palm Club, located in the west wing of the hotel, offers guests an all-inclusive option—with three meals a day plus unlimited cocktails and beverages, tennis, and water sports. Cable Beach (phone: 327-7711; 800-225-5843; fax: 327-7615).

Radisson Cable Beach All 700 rooms and suites in this property are arranged in a U shape around a landscaped garden area with a free-form pool, a lagoon, and waterfalls. The rooms, decorated in blue and white, are comfortably furnished and feature small balconies, many overlooking a wide stretch of beach and the ocean. It's a lively, family-oriented property; the Camp Junkanoo program entertains children with day-long activities and a video room. There's also a shopping arcade that is connected to the casino next door. The hotel's fitness center offers 18 tennis courts, three squash and three racquetball courts, and a fully equipped exercise room; in addition, golfers get a discount on greens fees at the *Cable Beach Golf Club.* There are lots of dining options, with four restaurants and several bars. While not luxurious, this resort offers good value. Cable Beach (phone: 327-6000; 800-333-3333; fax: 327-6987).

Casuarinas of Cable Beach This attractive, homey, 91-room member of the Days Inn chain offers a recreation room, a pool, and tennis courts on the premises; other sports and activities can be arranged. The beach is just across the street, and there is a complimentary shuttle to the casino and downtown. The *Round House* restaurant is one of the island's best seafood places (see *Eating Out*). Owned and operated by Nettie Symonette, a well-known local businesswoman, the property emphasizes personalized, attentive service. West Bay St., Cable Beach (phone: 327-8153; 800-325-2525; fax: 327-8152).

PARADISE ISLAND

EXPENSIVE

Atlantis Acquired by Sun International in 1994, the former *Paradise Island Resort & Casino*—already a luxurious resort—is now a spectacular celebration of sea life. The new centerpiece of the property's lavishly landscaped grounds is the world's largest outdoor aquarium, where visitors can observe over 100 species of marine life. The impressive "waterscape" also includes three freshwater swimming pools, two saltwater swimming lagoons, a quarter-mile-long "river ride," and Turtle Beach, where guests can observe and even help care for Bahamian sea turtles rescued through a licensed program. The revamped resort retains its luxury feel, with 1,150 rooms, including 94 rooms in the posh Reef Club and 64 one-bedroom villas. There are 12 restaurants, and all-inclusive meal plans are offered. Other amenities include the 30,000-square-foot *Paradise Island Casino,* nine tennis courts, Camp Atlantis, a supervised activities program for children ages five to 12, and golf nearby at the *Paradise Island Golf Club.* Those who visited this venerable resort in the past have ample reason to return: It's now something entirely unique. Casino Dr. (phone: 363-3000; 800-321-3000; 305-891-3888 in Florida; fax: 363-3524; 305-893-2866 in Florida).

Club Land'Or Set in a quiet cove on a lagoon opposite the *Atlantis* resort, this charming resort has 72 rather small one-bedroom suites with full kitchenettes and patios or balconies. Facilities include a pool, a lovely courtyard, the *Blue Lagoon* restaurant (serving fine seafood), and the *Oasis Bar* with piano entertainment. The service is attentive and efficient, and there are extensive daily activities. Paradise Beach Dr. (phone: 363-2400; 800-321-3000; fax: 363-3403).

Radisson Grand This modern hotel, formerly rather run-down and tired looking, has become an elegant (but fun) resort. A beachfront high-rise, it has 360 rooms, each with cable TV, a mini-bar, a balcony, direct-dial telephones, and modern furnishings. Guests can choose from a wide array of beach and water activities, bicycle tours, beach aerobics, and more. Restaurant choices include the elegant *Rotisserie*, the *Sundeck Bar and Grill* (see *Eating Out* for both), and a terrace restaurant serving buffet breakfasts and theme dinners twice a week. Other features include tennis courts, a dive shop, a pool with a waterfall, an activities and games center, a small straw market, and a shopping arcade. Located next to the *Atlantis* resort on Casino Dr. (phone: 363-3500; 800-333-3333 or 800-777-7800; fax: 363-3900).

MODERATE

Club Med This resort offers the chain's familiar camaraderie, geared toward couples and singles, but with an emphasis on tennis (20 courts, a teaching staff, and TV playback are at guests' disposal). All the usual *Club Med* pursuits can be found, too—from morning yoga to late-night disco to water sports galore, plus a wide, dreamy beach. Rooms on the top floor have king-size beds, while the rest of the 389 rooms have double beds. The absence of TV sets, radios, and clocks enhances the escape from civilization. Weekly rates cover all activities (including tennis instruction) and all meals, including house wines. Casuarina Dr. (phone: 363-2640; 800-CLUB-MED; 212-750-1687 in New York City; fax: 363-3496).

Comfort Suites One of the island's newer hotels, its 150 junior suites feature satellite TV, mini-bars, and coffee makers. Continental breakfast is complimentary. There's an indoor/outdoor restaurant and bar and a laundromat, and guests have full access to the facilities at the *Atlantis* resort across the street. At the intersection of Casino Dr. and Paradise Island Dr. (phone: 363-3680; 800-228-5150; fax: 363-2588).

Holiday Inn Sunspree More upscale than most other members of the chain, this high-rise property on Pirate's Cove features 564 comfortably and elegantly appointed rooms, a beautiful lagoon with a fine beach, a huge free-form pool, theme buffets, tennis courts, a shopping arcade, four bars, three restaurants (including the pleasant *Junkanoo Café;* see *Eating Out*), and a host of water sports. The resort is a boon for families—there's no charge for children under 12—and it's popular with both children and adults for its free daily activities programs. At the end of Casuarina Dr. (phone: 363-2100; 800-23-HOTEL; fax: 363-2206).

Paradise Paradise This informal, low-rise hotel is on the beach for which the island was named. Purchased by Sun International in 1994, the hotel was set to be renovated at press time as part of its new owners' $250 million–plus investment in the island (much of it poured into its sister *Atlantis* resort). It has 100 simply furnished, balconied rooms, a pavilion restaurant, and a cocktail lounge. The all-inclusive rates cover such sports activities as sailing, snorkeling, windsurfing, water skiing, hydroslides, day and night tennis, aerobics, volleyball, and bicycling. Eschewing luxury, this resort is geared toward a young, sports-minded crowd. Casuarina Dr. (phone: 363-3000; 800-321-3000; fax: 363-2540).

Villas in Paradise Popular with Europeans, this place offers comfortable accommodations in 25 low-rise stucco villas, 15 of which feature private swimming pools in enclosed patios. Villas have fully equipped kitchens, three bedrooms, and two full baths. There are also 16 one- and two-bedroom apartments, which fall into the inexpensive category. Complimentary one-day car rental is included with a seven-night stay. Note that some of the villas could use a refurbishing, and a number of the apartments are in dire need of renovations. Casino Dr. (phone: 363-2998; 800-321-3000; fax: 363-2703).

WESTERN NEW PROVIDENCE ISLAND

EXPENSIVE

South Ocean Golf and Beach Resort In southwestern New Providence, this former Ramada property, now run by the Winfare Management Group, has a $1-million scuba and water sports center and a fabulous 18-hole Joe Lee–designed golf course (see *Top Tee-Off Spots*). The 130 beachfront rooms are housed in plantation-style greathouses painted in pastels and luxuriously appointed with two-poster beds, wet bars, mini-fridges, whirlpools, and patios or balconies. Another 120 rooms are in the main building, but these are older, darker, and smaller. Tennis courts, two pools, a jogging trail, water sports, and two dining rooms, including the elegant *Papagayo* restaurant, round out the offerings. At the southwestern tip of the island (phone: 362-4391; fax: 362-4728).

GRAND BAHAMA

EXPENSIVE

Bahamas Princess Freeport's largest resort (with a total of 965 rooms and suites) is divided into two distinct properties located across the street from each other: the *Princess Tower* and *Princess Country Club.* The dramatic Moorish-style *Princess Tower* adjoins the 20,000-square-foot *Princess Casino* and is within strolling distance of the *International Bazaar;* quieter than its sister property (most of the guests are busy gambling or meeting in the extensive business facilities), its 400 rooms are also larger and more comfortable. The *Country Club*'s nine low-rise buildings (with 565 units) encircle a huge South Seas–style pool with rock gardens and tiered waterfalls. In addition there are two championship 18-hole golf courses, 12 tennis courts, another pool, 10 restaurants (including *Guanahani's* and the *Crown Room;* see *Eating Out*), six bars, a nightclub, a fitness center, a jogging trail, a shopping arcade, and Camp Seashells, a supervised activities program for children ages five and up. There's no beach here, but a complimentary shuttle whisks guests to the *Xanadu Beach* resort, where they have full use of all facilities. Freeport (phone: 352-6721 or 352-9661; 800-223-1818; fax: 352-6842).

Club Fortuna Beach One of Freeport's newer hotels and the only all-inclusive resort on Grand Bahama, this is a successful copycat of *Club Med* geared toward sports-minded couples in search of a moderately priced holiday. The room rate includes all meals, most sports, a daily activities program, entertainment, and all taxes and gratuities. Huge Italian buffets, an international crowd, and topless sunbathing on the gorgeous, private beach add to the European ambience. Scuba diving is offered at an extra charge. The 204 rooms are rather basic but do provide two queen-size beds. There's even a playground for the children. Fortuna Beach, Freeport (phone: 373-4000; 800-847-4502; fax: 373-5555).

Deep Water Cay Small and exclusive, this lodge attracts celebrities and keen sport fishers. It offers a luxury two-bedroom cottage and seven smaller cottages, a private airstrip, a restaurant, a bar overlooking the pool, and superb bonefishing. A barrier reef that's a short swim from the sandy beach is perfect for snorkeling (equipment is provided). There's a minimum stay of three nights, and rates include all meals, tips, and taxes, as well as a boat and a bonefishing guide. Closed July through September. East End (phone: 359-4831; 407-684-3958; fax: 359-4831; 407-684-0959 in Florida).

Lucayan Beach Although ideally located on a 1,500-foot strip of white sand, this 243-room dowager queen has lost some luster over the years. However its newest owners, a *Carnival Cruise Lines* subsidiary, have completed a much-needed, $1.4-million renovation (be sure to request a refurbished room), and there are still plenty of reasons to stay here: several top-notch dining choices, including *Les Oursins* (see *Eating Out*); a huge casino (recently upgraded and expanded); a nightclub; tennis courts; and a water sports center. The dedicated staff is another plus. Lucaya, just across from the *Port Lucaya MarketPlace and Marina* (phone: 373-7777; 800-772-1227; fax: 373-2826).

Port Lucaya Resort and Yacht Club Opened in 1994 with its own full-service, 50-slip marina, this resort appeals not only to the yachting crowd, but to anyone who enjoys a spectacular—and virtually guaranteed—ocean view. The 160 rooms are housed in 10 two-story units set on a peninsula; the property also features an oversize swimming pool and Jacuzzi, a playground, and a Caribbean-style restaurant, the *Tradewinds Café*. Nearby is the *Port Lucaya Marketplace,* a lively square with more than 80 shops and restaurants; the casino at the *Lucayan Beach* resort (above) is only a short walk away. Lucaya (phone: 373-6618; 800-LUCAYA; fax: 373-6652).

MODERATE

Clarion Atlantik Beach and Golf Resort Popular among Swiss and German visitors, this Swiss-owned beachfront resort now boasts the most attractive accommodations in the Lucayan Beach area. There are 175 guestrooms, a third of which are one-, two- and three-bedroom suites with kitchens, ideal for families traveling with children. A large pool and water sports facility are on site, along with three restaurants and a small shopping arcade. A free shuttle takes golfers to the 18-hole *Lucaya Golf and Country Club,* where guests enjoy special rates. Guests also have tennis privileges at the *Radisson* next door, and diving is just across the street at *UNEXSO.* A semi-inclusive package provides soft drinks, two meals a day, bike tours, snorkeling and sunset tours, taxes, tips, airport transportation, and a supervised activities program for children ages five to 12. Lucaya Beach (phone: 373-1444; 800-622-6770 in the US; 800-848-3315 in Canada; fax: 373-7481).

Radisson Resort on Lucaya Beach This 500-room hotel, which recently underwent a complete (and much-needed) renovation, offers four restaurants and bars, a cabaret, a gallery of shops, and afternoon calypso bands at poolside. A popular family resort, it runs a free supervised activities program for children ages four to 12, plus a full complement of land, beach, and water sports activities. Ask for a renovated room. Lucayan Beach (phone: 373-1333; 800-835-3597; fax: 373-8662).

Xanadu Beach Once home to billionaire Howard Hughes, this resort features 179 elegantly decorated rooms in hues of peach, pink, and green. Facilities include a pool, three lighted tennis courts, a 77-slip marina for large yachts, two restaurants, a beach club with a comprehensive water sports facility, a dive shop, and several boutiques. Additional pluses include a free nightly shuttle to the *Princess Casino,* good service, and live calypso on the beach. Freeport (phone: 352-6782; 800-772-1227; fax: 352-5799).

INEXPENSIVE

Running Mon A pastel-pink motel and marina, it caters mainly to boaters and those in search of a quiet place outside town. The 32 comfortable rooms are tastefully decorated and feature kitchenettes. The glass-sided hexagonal restaurant serves fresh seafood and Bahamian dishes and overlooks the 66-slip marina and marine supply shop. Free bus service is offered to the *Princess Casino,* the *International Bazaar,* and Xanadu Beach. Kelly Court and Knotts Blvd., Freeport (phone: 352-6834; fax: 352-6835).

THE ABACOS

EXPENSIVE

Great Abaco Beach One of Great Abaco's most charming spots, it has 80 deluxe rooms, including a new 60-room wing, and six luxury villas, all overlooking the ocean. The hotel adjoins *Boat Harbour Marina,* which offers 160 slips and complete marina services. There is also a good restaurant, two tennis courts, two free-form pools (one with a swim-up bar), and lots of camaraderie—the pleasant staff has won many enthusiastic returnees. Marsh Harbour, Great Abaco (phone: 367-2158; 800-468-4799 or 800-521-0643; fax: 367-2819).

Green Turtle Club One of the Abacos' most charming "in" spots, it has a 32-slip marina and fishing and diving facilities. The resort comprises 30 guestrooms and five balconied bayside and poolside villas spread over extensive grounds, plus a tennis court and a freshwater pool. Two small beaches are within walking distance. Rooms are decorated in colonial style and come complete with hardwood floors, mahogany headboards and dressers, and minifridges; villas have kitchens. Restaurant options include a dockside alfresco eatery for breakfast and lunch and an air conditioned, candlelit dining room for dinner. Green Turtle Cay (phone: 365-4271; 800-825-5099; fax: 365-4272).

Inn at Spanish Cay This upscale, European-owned resort is set on 185 acres, with 7 miles of private shoreline, an idyllic setting for swimming and beachcombing; to add to the sybaritic delight, the resort has its own airstrip and 70-slip marina. Accommodations are in seven beautifully appointed one-, two-, and three-bedroom apartments or in five suites. Other amenities include two restaurants, four lighted tennis courts, nature trails, and boats available for fishing excursions. Spanish Cay, 12 miles northwest of Green Turtle Cay (phone: 365-0083 or 359-6622; 800-688-4752; fax: 365-0466).

MODERATE

Abaco Inn This small gem, ensconced between the Atlantic on one side and the calm blue water of White Sound on the other, has 12 rooms, a unique swimming pool that mimics the shape of the shoreline, and a fleet of bicycles for guests' use. The inn can arrange snorkeling, diving, fishing, and sightseeing trips. The fine restaurant serves lobster, snapper, and grouper, and offers both alfresco oceanside dining and an indoor area. The atmosphere is homey, but geared to adults; children under age 10 are not allowed. Hope Town, Elbow Cay (phone: 366-0133; 800-468-8799; fax: 366-0113).

Guana Beach On a small island completely ringed by gorgeous, deserted beaches, this suitably unpretentious island inn has 18 rooms for those who *really* want to get away from it all. The property has a small marina in front and a superb beach at the back. There's also a pool, a friendly bar, and an extremely informal restaurant. Great Guana Cay (phone/fax: 367-3590; 800-BARE-FOOT).

Walker's Cay Club Sport fishing was originally this private island's biggest attraction—and is still quite a lure. The resort caters to sport fishing and diving enthusiasts (March through early September is high season), and a major billfish tournament is held here each April. The 100-acre cay offers 62 double rooms, four villas, four private suites, a 75-slip marina, a dive facility providing dives to great underwater scenery (plus certified instruction), two all-weather tennis courts, and two pools, one freshwater and one salt-water. Lunch may be a buffet at the marina; dinner is in the hotel restaurant, where the freshest seafood is served. Once a refuge for rumrunners, today the island is more accessible—only a 20-minute flight from Freeport, Grand Bahama. There is also a flight from Ft. Lauderdale daily except Tuesdays. Walker's Cay (phone: 352-5252; 800-WALKERS; 305-359-1400 in Florida; fax: 305-359-1414 in Florida).

INEXPENSIVE

Coco Bay Cottages This unique hideaway is situated on the north end of Green Turtle Cay along a 550-foot point that separates the Atlantic Ocean from the Sea of Abaco. The beach here is protected by an outlying reef that's ideal for snorkeling. Shaded by flowering fruit trees, the five-acre property features four two-bedroom cottages decorated with island fabrics and light rattan furniture. Ceiling fans and trade winds take the place of air conditioning, while large, wraparound sundecks provide space for sunning or daydreaming over an evening cocktail. The cottages all have kitchens, but there's no restaurant. There's also no phone on the premises, but a VHF radio is available for making dinner, diving, and fishing charter reservations. No credit cards accepted. Green Turtle Cay (phone: 365-4464; 800-752-0166).

Conch Inn A favorite with scuba divers and yachting enthusiasts, this inn has its own 60-slip marina and 10 rooms featuring satellite TV and balconies with harbor views. The dockside restaurant specializes in seafood; there's also the *Conch Out Bar,* a popular horseshoe-shape outdoor patio serving light seafood lunches, and, on the nearby artificial beach, a cabaña-style restaurant offering grilled burgers and sandwiches. Other pluses are a small pool and a dive shop. Marsh Harbour, Great Abaco (phone: 367-4000; fax: 367-4004).

Hope Town Harbour Lodge A former island commissioner's home is the nucleus of this relaxed resort with its own dock on one side and beach on the other. Right in the heart of Hope Town, it offers 21 air conditioned rooms and one cottage (with a kitchen). Sailing, scuba, snorkeling, water skiing, and deep-sea fishing are all close by and management is happy to make the arrangements. Next to the pool is a friendly bar that serves informal lunches, a traditional meeting spot for locals in this cozy little town. Hope Town, Elbow Cay (phone: 366-0095; 800-316-7844; fax: 366-0286).

Linton's Beach and Harbour Cottages Situated on Green Turtle Cay, this very private hideaway features just two cottages set on 22 acres and 3 miles of beach in a lush, subtropical landscape. Built following World War II by Captain Stephen Cliff, Winston Churchill's personal wartime pilot, and owned since

THE ISLANDS BAHAMAS

1960 by the Linton family, each cottage has two bedrooms, a screened-in porch, and loads of local charm. The cottages feature fully equipped kitchens (there's no restaurant, but cooks can be arranged), ceiling fans in every room (instead of air conditioning), and daily maid service. TV sets with VCRs are available for an additional fee; the only telephone is in the care-taker's cottage a short walk away. There are plenty of recreational facili-ties nearby in the village of New Plymouth, accessible on foot or by the Lintons' motor launch, and the Lintons will be happy to arrange fishing or diving excursions. Green Turtle Cay (phone: 365-4003; 615-269-5682 in Tennessee; fax: 365-4003).

New Plymouth Inn This charming in-town choice with friendly American manage-ment is in New Plymouth's most elegant old residence. The place is beau-tifully maintained, with nine high-ceilinged, cozy rooms out of another cen-tury. Rates include both breakfast and dinner. New Plymouth, Green Turtle Cay (phone: 365-4161; 800-688-4752; fax: 365-4138).

Treasure Cay Probably the Abacos' most complete resort complex, appealing to golfers, tennis buffs, and water sports enthusiasts. Clustered around a wide cresent-shape expanse of exquisite white sand dotted with coconut palms, this property boasts a 150-slip marina. It offers snorkeling, scuba, fishing, sailing, windsurfing, water skiing, and other beach and water sports, as well as a championship 18-hole golf course, two pools, and six tennis courts. Accommodations are in 45 rooms and suites or eight luxury beachfront vil-las. There is a restaurant. Treasure Cay (phone: 367-2570; 800-327-1584; fax: 367-3362).

ANDROS

EXPENSIVE

Cargill Creek Lodge Popular with fishermen, these 17 Mediterranean-style cot-tages are comfortable but basic—they're not air conditioned, but they do have satellite TV. There's also a gameroom, a bar, and a seafood restau-rant. Rates include three meals a day and unlimited fishing. Cargill Creek (phone: 368-5129; 800-533-4353; 312-263-0328 in Chicago; fax: 329-5046).

Small Hope Bay Lodge This is a resort for dedicated divers and discriminating trav-elers alike, with 20 rooms and a palm-lined beach. There are daily diving trips to the magnificent reef a mile offshore, underwater photography sem-inars, specialty dives to blue holes and coral caverns, bonefishing trips to the Andros Flats, and, at the end of the day, a beach-based hot tub. The atmosphere is very informal; if you're rash enough to wear a necktie, one of the staff may well snip it off with a pair of scissors. All-inclusive fishing and diving packages are available. Nearby (and accessible by water taxi) is the resort's *Coakley House,* a three-bedroom, three-bath villa once owned by the British royal family; sitting on two acres of land with a private dock, it is ideal for families or couples vacationing together. A small grocery store is nearby, and guests can opt to hire a maid and a cook. Closed September and October. Small Hope Bay (phone: 368-2014; 800-223-6961; fax: 368-2015).

MODERATE

Emerald Palms by the Sea An elegant seaside spot replete with lush landscaping, all of its 20 rooms feature four-poster beds and spacious tiled patios, and half overlook the sea. There also are two beachfront lanai suites. Guests can use the tennis court, bicycles, snorkeling equipment, and windsurfers, while divers can arrange trips to the famed Tongue of the Ocean just minutes offshore. A first-rate restaurant and bar round out the amenities. Congo Town (phone: 369-2661; 800-688-4752; fax: 369-2667).

Lighthouse Yacht Club and Marina A splendid property, it offers 20 rooms (some with king-size beds), a 15-slip marina, and diving facilities available through *Small Hope Bay Lodge.* Also on the premises are a pool, a tennis court, and a restaurant. Andros Town (phone: 368-2305; 800-825-5099; fax: 368-2300).

INEXPENSIVE

Nottages Cottages Overlooking Behring Point, this hotel has 10 rooms, a bar, a dining room serving native seafood dishes, and a two-bedroom cottage. Behring Point (phone: 368-4293).

BERRY ISLANDS

EXPENSIVE

Chub Cay Club Offering eight rooms, eight villas, and two townhouses, the condominium buildings that comprise this resort are clustered around a complete marina. The focus is on deep-sea fishing, bonefishing, and boating. Facilities include a restaurant, a small market, and a tennis court. Chub Cay (phone: 325-1490 or 324-7800; 800-662-8555; fax: 322-5199).

Great Harbour Yacht Club & Marina Situated on Great Harbour Cay and boasting an 80-slip marina, this resort caters to yachtsmen. It's set among lush gardens along 8 miles of unspoiled white sand beach with the festive *Beach Club,* an open-air bar and restaurant, as the daytime center of activity. The *Wharf* bar and restaurant and the *Tamboo Dinner Club,* both located in the marina, offer more formal venues for evening dining. A variety of accommodations is available: There's a four-bedroom beach villa, a four-bedroom duplex on the island's nine-hole golf course, four two-bedroom waterfront townhouses, and 15 beachfront efficiencies, which can accommodate from two to four people. All units feature full kitchens and daily maid service. There's also a pool. The management arranges yacht charters as well as private air-charter service to the island from Ft. Lauderdale. Great Harbour Cay (phone: 367-8838; 800-343-7256; 305-921-9084 in Florida; fax: 305-921-1044 in Florida).

BIMINI

EXPENSIVE

Bimini Big Game Fishing Club Simple and friendly, it has a 100-slip marina that can arrange deep-sea and bonefishing charters as well as accommodate visiting yachts. There's a dive shop, a pool, a tennis court, and a trio of bars that tend to liven up when the boats come in. Many of the 49 rooms feature patio grills for guests who want to cook their own catch. But you won't go hungry even if you come back empty-handed: There are also two good restaurants. Alice Town, North Bimini (phone: 347-3391 or 347-3393; 800-327-4149; fax: 347-3392).

INEXPENSIVE

Bimini Blue Water A simple 12-room inn overlooking the sea, up the hill from its own marina, it's home to several fishing tournaments each season, but open to non-anglers, too. There's a good restaurant, a friendly bar, and a pool. Anchorage, North Bimini (phone: 347-3166; fax: 347-3293).

Compleat Angler Ossie Brown's decades-old hotel is one of the funkiest places in all of the Bahamas. Hemingway used to hang out here, and it still attracts an extraordinary cast of characters. There's great people watching in the lobby and at the bar. The bar walls are lined with hundreds of photos chronicling Bimini's fishing tournament history. Though not for everyone—there are only 12 plain, noisy rooms—this place is worth seeing. Alice Town, North Bimini (phone: 347-3122 or 347-3128).

CAT ISLAND

EXPENSIVE

Fernandez Bay Village A lovely, lazy group of 10 villas, sized to sleep two to six people, each individually and appealingly decorated and equipped with a full kitchen. Maid service is included, and there's a grocery on the property. First-rate dinner buffets are offered nightly on the beach beneath a thatch-roofed dining area with an honor bar, and there's also a casual restaurant. Situated on 50 acres of land fronting one of the most beautiful and serene beaches in the Bahamas, it's ideal for swimming, sunning, beachcombing, snorkeling, fishing, small-boat sailing, and scuba diving. A private six-seater plane picks up arriving guests in Nassau or Long Island. Fernandez Bay (phone: 342-3043; 800-940-1905; 305-474-4821 in Florida; fax: 305-474-4864 in Florida).

ELEUTHERA

EXPENSIVE

Club Med Eleuthera Located 8 miles from *Governor's Harbour Airport*, this all-inclusive (except drinks) resort has 288 rooms fronting the beach or garden.

While the accommodations are far from luxurious, this family-oriented place offers supervised activities for children ages two and up (there's even a circus workshop complete with a trapeze), as well as three restaurants, two pools (one just for children), eight tennis courts, and a marina. Near Governor's Harbour (phone: 332-2270; 800-CLUB-MED; 212-750-1687 in New York City).

Sofitel Cotton Bay Club Closed indefinitely at press time, this posh retreat is expected to resurrect itself under another company's aegis. A lovely, quiet oasis, it was formerly a private playground for dignitaries and tycoons. Once it opened as a hotel with 77 guestrooms and a six-bedroom luxury villa, it attracted the likes of former Presidents Bush and Nixon and occasional movie stars, while still maintaining that priceless, get-away-from-it-all ambience. The property features an indoor-outdoor dining room overlooking the ocean, a beach, a golf course (see *Top Tee-Off Spots,* above), tennis courts, and water sports. Rock Sound (phone: 334-6101; fax: 334-6082).

INEXPENSIVE

Rainbow Inn Small and family-run, this pavilion-style stucco inn overlooking the sea is known for its fine restaurant and family atmosphere. The spacious accommodations (five rooms, a two-bedroom house, and a three-bedroom house) have wet bars, mini-fridges, gas grills, and double or twin beds. There's a tennis court, a pool, and complimentary snorkeling equipment and bicycles. The hotel is not on the beach, but offers shuttle transportation to a good strand nearby. Closed mid-September to mid-November. Hatchet Bay (phone: 335-0294; 800-688-4752; fax: 335-0294).

HARBOUR ISLAND, OFF ELEUTHERA

EXPENSIVE

Coral Sands Loaded with charm and hospitality, this beachfront hotel with 33 rooms and suites shares its stunning, pastel-hued beach with the *Pink Sands* (see below). Its owner, onetime actor Brett King, worked with John Wayne and Bette Davis and dated Elizabeth Taylor (he'll show you pictures to prove it!). The property is an active one, offering an array of complimentary water sports—including rowboats, sailboats, kayaks, jet skis, and snorkeling equipment. There's also tennis, a gameroom, a nightclub, and a restaurant with a surprisingly good wine cellar. A recently expanded beach bar is a gorgeous—and popular—spot for lunch and sunset cocktails. The hotel also rents bicycles, motor bikes, cars, even golf carts for tooling around the grounds. Closed September through mid-November. Chapel St. (phone: 333-2350; 800-468-2799; fax: 333-2368).

Pink Sands Having added 20 new villas, this newly renovated upscale resort now has a total of 30 one- and two-bedroom units, some with ocean views. With its own glorious 3-mile, reef-protected stretch of sand that actually is pink, this tranquil spot attracts a very loyal following of repeat visitors. Facilities include a pool, tennis courts, and two restaurants. Chapel St. (phone: 333-2030; 800-OUTPOST; fax: 333-2060).

Romora Bay Club This 37-room inn exudes a tropical ambience, with lush grounds and terraced flower gardens. Though it's in need of a face-lift, it's popular with divers and bonefishing enthusiasts. Main-house dinners are an occasion (book a table early, even if you're a hotel guest). A dive shop on the premises offers scuba (including instruction) plus daily snorkel trips. There's a tennis court, a hot tub, a pink sand beach a short stroll away, and a cove-side pavilion for lunch buffets, sunset gatherings, and informal nighttime entertainment. Closed mid-September through October. Colebrook La. (phone: 333-2325; 800-327-8286; 305-427-4830 in Florida; fax: 333-2500; 305-427-2726 in Florida).

Runaway Hill Club An intimate Bahamian-style inn overlooking a hillside pool and lovely wide beach, it has only 10 rooms (the two in the duplex bungalow across from the main building are best), tastefully but simply decorated with terra cotta floors, white wicker, and *Casablanca*-style ceiling fans. There's a good restaurant, and a calypso group performs Tuesdays in winter. Closed September through mid-November; no children under age 16 are allowed. A half mile from Dunmore Town (phone: 333-2150; 800-728-9803; fax: 333-2420).

MODERATE

Valentine's Yacht Club & Inn Right on the sound, this 21-room inn with a 37-slip marina is popular with fishing, diving, and yachting folk. There's a pool, and the management can arrange sailing, snorkeling, and diving trips, as well as bone-, bottom-, and reef fishing. It's informal, but a thoughtful management and staff are always ready to help. The nautically decorated restaurant serves good seafood dishes. Closed September and October. Dunmore Town (phone: 333-2142 or 333-2080; 800-323-5655; fax: 333-2135).

EXUMAS

MODERATE

Club Peace and Plenty Here's a classic island hostelry with 35 rooms, an informal guesthouse atmosphere, and agreeable staff. It's virtually in town, with a small swimming pool overlooking the harbor. There's ferry service to the beach club (with bar and snack service) on beautiful Stocking Island, just across the water. Sailing, snorkeling, and world class bonefishing can be arranged. Occasional evening entertainment is also offered. The bar is the local meeting and greeting place. Queen's Hwy., George Town (phone: 336-2551; 800-525-2210; fax: 336-2093).

Coconut Cove Next door to the *Peace and Plenty Beach Inn* (see below), this 10-room place features a beachside patio and a pool with a swim-up bar, plus rock gardens and a pond stocked with subtropical fish. The dining room has a fireplace and paintings by local artists, and rooms are decorated in pastels and wicker. The luxurious honeymoon suite, the Paradise Room, has its own terrace with a hot tub, and a Jacuzzi. Queen's Hwy., George Town (phone: 336-2659; 800-688-4752; fax: 336-2658).

The Palms at Three Sisters The name tells the story: Enormous palm trees punctuate the lush landscape of this beautiful beach resort, while the Three Sisters, a famous trio of rocks, jut out of the placid waters just offshore. A charming 12-room inn built of stucco and native stone, it has a terrace overlooking the property's splendid white sand beach. Snorkeling out to the rocks is a favorite pastime, and guests often return with a lobster or grouper for the chef to prepare to their liking. In addition, the inn can arrange a wide variety of water activities. The rooms are spacious, with satellite TV and either air conditioning or ceiling fans; three private cottages are also available for rent. Meals are served in the dining room, which features a lounge and bar. The inn is located 3 miles west of the airport and 3 miles from some excellent bonefishing flats just west of George Town. Queen's Hwy., just northwest of George Town (phone: 358-4040/3; 800-688-4752; fax: 358-4043).

Peace and Plenty Beach Inn This property's greatest asset is the 100 yards of beach right outside the door. Its 16 rooms are decorated plantation-style, with floral fabrics, tile floors, ceiling fans (plus air conditioning), and terraces with views of the pool and beach. There's a restaurant, and cocktail parties are given on Monday and Friday nights (one guest who can be counted on to show up for the free chicken wings is a barracuda named Clyde). Quiet reigns here, but guests seeking more action can hop aboard the free shuttle to the affiliated *Club Peace and Plenty* (see above), where they enjoy free use of all the facilities. Queen's Hwy. outside of George Town (phone: 336-2250; 800-525-2210; fax: 336-2253).

Staniel Cay A good value, this small, private yacht club has six rustic cabins with balconies overlooking the marina, a cozy bar, and a restaurant serving native and American seafood dishes. Guests come for the bonefishing in the flats and good offshore snorkeling. Each cabin comes with the use of a 13-foot skiff, and the room rates include three meals a day. Staniel Cay (phone: 355-2024; 800-825-5099; fax: 355-2044).

INEXPENSIVE

Two Turtles Inn A colony of two-story tropical hardwood cabins set around a stone courtyard overlooking Elizabeth Harbour, it has 14 rooms, a good seafood restaurant, and a popular outdoor bar. Friday night is barbecue night for most local residents. Cycling, boating, diving tours, and tours of the island can be arranged. George Town (phone: 336-2545; 800-688-4752; fax: 336-2528).

LONG ISLAND

EXPENSIVE

Cape Santa Maria Beach Resort This resort, highly acclaimed for its great fishing, still manages to maintain the air of a well-kept secret. The property stretches along 4 miles of pristine white sand beach, with accommodations in 12 white-roofed beachfront cottages (10 doubles and two that can sleep four), all with screened verandahs facing the ocean and connected to public areas by a bleached-wood boardwalk; the cottages don't have telephones or TV sets. Amenities include a pool and a restaurant that serves local island delicacies either indoors or under the stars. Bicycling, sailing, windsurfing, and snorkeling are complimentary, but the most favored pastime here is fishing: The outlying waters are rich with record-breaking marlin, snapper, dorado, barracuda, kingfish, grouper, and bonefish. Guided charters are offered several times daily, and interested non-anglers can attend special fishing clinics. Cape Santa Maria (phone: 357-1006; 800-663-7090; fax: 604-598-1361 in Vancouver).

MODERATE

Stella Maris Resort Club A beautiful little cottage resort set in a sizable oceanside palm garden, it features 50 rooms, apartments, and one-, two-, and four-bedroom villas. Three swimming pools, five separate beach areas, a tennis club, and a marina are all on the premises, and there is excellent fishing nearby. Also available are diving facilities, an array of other water sports, bicycle and car rentals, two weekly boat excursions, and an in-house air service offering connections with nearby islands as well as aircraft rentals. There are even daily educational programs covering local history and ecology. The casual, friendly resort is known for its excellent food, service, and island-style evening entertainment. Stella Maris (phone: 338-2051 or 336-2106; 800-426-0466; fax: 359-8238).

SAN SALVADOR

MODERATE

Riding Rock Inn An easy walk to town, this longtime favorite haunt of scuba buffs has 24 standard and rather small rooms, 18 deluxe oceanfront rooms (the best value), and six time-share villas. Guests enjoy a pool, tennis, a restaurant, a bar, and an excellent dive facility, complete with photo lab and instruction. Good vacation packages are available. Located about a half mile down the road from the *Club Med–Columbus Isle* resort (phone: 331-2631; 800-272-1492; 305-359-8353 in Florida; fax: 331-2803; 305-359-8254 in Florida).

EATING OUT

Meals in the larger Nassau/Paradise Island and Freeport/Lucaya hotels tend to be expensive and unimaginative, with too many "surf and turf" specials that do justice to neither the filet mignon nor the lobster tail involved. When it comes to good restaurants, the Freeport/Lucaya choice is limited, and the Out Islands are, with some notable exceptions, lacking in restaurants that offer much beyond local fare. Nassau does somewhat better, with several places where first-rate chefs use their continental skills to make the most of fresh local fish and seafood (except for chicken, most meat is imported frozen). There are also some tasty Bahamian places that serve good, home-cooked food at moderate to inexpensive prices.

Favorite island dishes include conch (pronounced *conk*), which is served as "salad" (that is, ceviche—raw and marinated in lime), fritters, chowder, and "cracked" (pounded thin and deep-fried); spiny lobster; baked Bahamian crab; broiled or boiled grouper; and peas (really beans) and rice. On the outlying islands especially, most bread is locally baked—fresh, crusty, and delicious. Sweet, fresh Eleutheran pineapple turns up frequently as a breakfast starter or a dessert. And rum, in just about any form, is the favorite local drink.

Expect to pay $80 or more for a meal for two at the restaurants we have listed in the very expensive category; $50 to $80 at expensive places; $30 to $50 at moderate ones; and under $30 at those restaurants described as inexpensive. Prices do not include drinks, wine, or tip. Restaurants are open for lunch and dinner unless otherwise noted; to avoid disappointment, call ahead. All telephone numbers are in the 809 area code unless otherwise indicated.

NASSAU

VERY EXPENSIVE

Graycliff Leisurely continental and Bahamian meals are served with true English elegance in what once was the home of Lord Dudley, the Earl of Staffordshire. The menu includes perfectly steamed fresh lobster, elegant grilled grouper with white truffles, tender *nodino di vitello* (a special cut of veal rarely found outside Italy), luscious chocolate mousse, and lots more, but be prepared: Dinner for two can easily cost upward of $200—without wine. Cocktails are served in the antiques-filled drawing room; service is perfect; the wine list, with 175,000 bottles, is unparalleled; and the ambience is simply unforgettable. Jacket required at dinner. Closed for lunch weekends. Reservations necessary. Major credit cards accepted. West Hill St. opposite *Government House* (phone: 322-2796).

EXPENSIVE

Buena Vista In a rambling house built in the early 1800s is one of the most pleasant all-around eating experiences in Nassau, with a soothing atmosphere, deft service by tuxedoed waiters, and excellent food. The menu features a number of great grouper recipes (*en coquille,* au gratin, baked in white-wine sauce, or Bahamian-style), delicate veal Buena Vista (veal in a cream sauce with sherry and mushrooms), and incredible dessert crêpes (a house specialty). There's also a five-course prix-fixe menu that's a good value. The place is prettiest in warm weather, when tables are set on the verandah. Jackets suggested. Open for dinner only; closed Sundays. Reservations necessary. Major credit cards accepted. Delancey St. (phone: 322-2811).

Sun and ... Dining here is outdoors in a fountain-centered garden or inside in a wood-paneled main dining room, depending on the weather. The romantic atmosphere—glinting crystal, silver, candlelight—is a big draw; book well in advance. The conch chowder is memorable, and you might follow it with a poached grouper soufflé, veal piccata, or roast rack of lamb. Leave room for Chef Ronny's outstanding dessert soufflés. Jackets required. Open for dinner only; closed Mondays, August, and September. Reservations necessary. Major credit cards accepted. Lakeview Dr. off East Shirley St.—take a taxi so you won't miss the turn (phone: 393-1205).

MODERATE

The Cellar Choose this spot for a casual lunch or dinner in a Bahamian-style pub or on an outdoor garden patio. The local seafood dishes include grouper fingers, cracked conch, grouper in white-wine sauce, and seafood *en coquille.* There's also regular evening entertainment. Reservations advised. Major credit cards accepted. 11 Charlotte St. (phone: 322-8877).

Green Shutters Inn For years a favorite haunt of English expatriates and visitors, it offers such specialties as a ploughman's platter, steak-and-kidney pie, shepherd's pie, bangers and mash, and other English pub favorites. Owner Francis Davis also delights in serving Bahamian dishes such as grouper with johnnycake and fried chicken with peas and rice. There's a different special for lunch every day, while dinners feature fish and seafood, from baked grouper Provençal to cracked conch. Closed Sundays. Reservations advised. Major credit cards accepted. 48 Parliament St. (phone: 325-5702).

Mai Tai This restaurant features Chinese fare in pleasant surroundings overlooking gardens that border a lake. Specials include orange beef and Caribbean lobster Cantonese. Reservations advised. Major credit cards accepted. Waterloo Lodge, East Bay St. (phone: 393-5106).

Pick-A-Dilly Creative Bahamian and international dishes such as vegetarian plates, conch fritters, shrimp, and seafood/pasta combinations are served in two settings at this popular eatery: There's a broad, covered terrace/garden (wear a sweater during the winter) alive with tropical birds, and an intimate, air conditioned dining room. The bar—famous for serving the best daiquiris on the islands—is popular with local businesspeople. A singer performs calypso music some evenings. Closed Sundays. Reservations advised. Major credit cards accepted. 18 Parliament St. (phone: 322-2836).

Poop Deck Long a popular hangout for boating people, this nautically decorated landmark offers marina and harbor views and an always-informal atmosphere. Bahamian favorites like cracked conch and grouper share the menu with stuffed crab and fisherman's platter combinations. Sandwiches are served at lunch. Reservations unnecessary. Major credit cards accepted. *Nassau Yacht Haven,* East Bay St. (phone: 393-8175).

Rock & Roll Café Cable Beach's top choice for enjoying good food, hanging out with friends (or making new ones), and dancing. This Bahamian version of the *Hard Rock Café* is located next to the *Forte Nassau Beach* hotel in *Frilsham House,* the former colonial home of a British newspaper baron. Music memorabilia, like platinum records from John Lennon, the *Eagles,* and *Foreigner,* line the walls. Appetizers, soups, salads, and burgers are served on the boardwalk at lunch. The dinner menu (served indoors) features steaks, charbroiled lobster tail, and cracked conch. Sporting events are shown on a large-screen TV set in the front bar; rock and roll bands entertain Wednesdays and weekends; and Sunday is *karaoke* night. Reservations advised. Major credit cards accepted. Cable Beach (phone: 327-7639).

Round House Part of the *Casuarinas of Cable Beach* complex, this eatery does delicious things with old Bahamian recipes and local ingredients—especially conch, fresh fish, and other seafood. Closed Tuesdays. Reservations unnecessary. Major credit cards accepted. West Bay St., Cable Beach (phone: 327-7921/2).

Tamarind Hill A converted Bahamian cottage with tables set in a courtyard around a huge tamarind tree, this eatery is a delightful inland retreat. The menu emphasizes American appetizers, such as chicken wings and peel-and-eat shrimp, and local food prepared in innovative ways. The English beer on tap and the live music on Wednesdays and weekends are big attractions. Reservations advised on weekends. Major credit cards accepted. Village Rd. (phone: 393-1306).

Traveller's Rest If you must lay over at *Nassau International Airport,* there's no better place to do it than here. Just a stone's throw from the terminal, this breezy waterfront café with a tropical atmosphere offers up abundant local specialties and seafood, all accompanied by fruity frozen drinks. And the adjacent *Sea Grape* gift shop is a good place to pick up some last-minute souvenirs. Open daily. Major credit cards accepted. West Bay St., Gambier (phone: 327-7633).

Café Johnny Canoe Vivid *junkanoo* colors are splashed over the walls and ceiling of this festive café boasting a menu of American favorites and Bahamian specialties. The service is the fastest on the island, the Caesar salad the best on Cable Beach, and the portions generous. Try tender cracked conch, blackened grouper, or grilled chicken breast, but be sure to leave room for the New York–style cheesecake or guava duff (a kind of jelly-roll cake). The party atmosphere is great for kids, especially on Friday nights, when a *junkanoo* parade winds right through the dining room. There's dancing to live music on the outdoor terrace Thursdays through Sundays. No reservations. Major credit cards accepted. West Bay St., Cable Beach (phone: 327-3373).

Roselawn Café Homemade pizza, pasta, and calzone plus island dishes such as grouper or steamed conch are served indoors or in the garden. This place is renowned for its late-night supper menu and live calypso band Thursdays through Sundays; it stays open until 6 AM. Closed for lunch on weekends. Reservations unnecessary. Major credit cards accepted. Bank La. off Bay St. (phone: 325-1018).

PARADISE ISLAND

VERY EXPENSIVE

Café Martinique For sophisticated dining, reserve a table at this former home surrounded by greenery and water views—an intimate setting rare on Paradise Island. The menu of French dishes includes appetizers such as *crevettes dejonge* (shrimp baked in a creamy garlic-and-herb sauce) or escargots *bourguignons,* followed by Dover sole *véronique* or duckling in Grand Marnier sauce. For dessert, the incomparable soufflés will linger in your memory long after the meal is over. Service is gracious but at times exasperatingly slow; be prepared for a leisurely dining experience. There's an excellent Sunday brunch as well. Jackets are required. Open daily. Reservations necessary. Major credit cards accepted. At the *Atlantis* resort (phone: 363-2222).

Courtyard Terrace One of the prettiest dining spots in the Nassau area, it features alfresco dining in a galleried courtyard framed by swaying palms and embellished with a fountain. Chefs are Swiss and Irish; service is sometimes slow, but the setting is worth the often only average cuisine. Open daily. Reservations necessary. Major credit cards accepted. At the *Ocean Club* (phone: 363-2501 or 363-3000).

EXPENSIVE

Boathouse Grill Overlooking Paradise Lagoon, it features steaks sizzled to your taste on tableside grills plus seafood. Open daily. Reservations advised. Major credit cards accepted. At the *Atlantis* resort (phone: 363-2222).

Rotisserie Nothing exotic, but everything is done with flair, from appointments and service to food preparation and wine selection. Notable starters include marinated seafood in a *sauce caribe* and cauliflower soup with shrimp. Surf and turf here becomes a superb *filet de boeuf grillé* and *langouste fraîche*. Open daily. Reservations necessary in season and on weekends. Major credit cards accepted. At the *Radisson Grand,* Casino Dr. (phone: 363-3500).

Villa d'Este Another of the deluxe dining places appended to the *Atlantis* resort. The decor is Mediterranean, and the Italian menu features some tasty pasta dishes and plenty of veal—it's a good place to get away from grouper if you've been here awhile. Open daily. Reservations necessary. Major credit cards accepted. At the *Atlantis* resort (phone: 363-2222).

MODERATE

Blue Marlin Nestled among the shops in *Hurricane Hole Plaza,* this cozy place specializes in local seafood. There's live music, beginning early in the evening, on Thursdays, Fridays, and Saturdays (reservations advised on those nights). Open daily. Major credit cards accepted. Harbour Rd. (phone: 363-2660).

Junkanoo Café Tucked away in the *Holiday Inn Sunspree,* it offers an attractive selection of sandwiches, salads, and lighter entrées. The grilled chicken breast teriyaki sandwich is filling and reasonably priced. Open daily. No reservations. Major credit cards accepted. Casuarina Dr., Pirate's Cove (phone: 363-2100).

INEXPENSIVE

Island This is the only thing still operating at the old *Chalk's* seaplane terminal, and the only genuinely Bahamian restaurant on the island. The menu features such dishes as boiled fish and grits; conch fritters; stewed conch, chicken, or fish; steamed pork chops; and spareribs, all served with hearty homemade bread. Open daily. No reservations. No credit cards accepted. Just off Paradise Beach Dr. (phone: 363-3153).

Sundeck Bar and Grill Salads, sandwiches, conch burgers, and hamburgers are served quickly and efficiently at this alfresco poolside eatery. The decor is bright and colorful, with life-size murals of Nassau scenes. Open daily for lunch and early dinner. No reservations. Major credit cards accepted. At the *Radisson Grand,* Casino Dr. (phone: 363-3500).

FREEPORT/LUCAYA

EXPENSIVE

Arawak Away from the hotel bustle, this elegant dining room at the *Lucaya Country Club* specializes in seafood and continental fare such as filet of lamb Provençal, pheasant, and duckling *à l'orange.* There's a daily lunch buffet, and free transportation is provided from all Lucaya area hotels. Closed

Sunday dinner. Reservations advised. Major credit cards accepted. Albacore St. off Sgt. Major Dr., Lucaya (phone: 373-1066, ext. 55).

Crown Room Best bet for pre-show or pre-casino dining at the *Princess,* although the standard fare, while well prepared and efficiently served, offers no surprises or spices. Closed Mondays. Reservations advised. Major credit cards accepted. *Bahamas Princess,* Freeport (phone: 352-6721, ext. 54).

Guanahani's A garden and waterfall view plus soothing music afford diners a welcome change from the usual Freeport hustle and bustle, although the fare is not very exciting. Start with deep-fried grouper fingers, then try Bahamian lobster and fish pot or ribs and chicken. Follow it all up with chocolate fruit fondue. Closed Fridays and Saturdays. Reservations advised. Major credit cards accepted. In the *Princess Country Club, Bahamas Princess,* Freeport (phone: 352-6721).

Les Oursins Tucked within the *Lucayan Beach* resort is this dining spot offering excellent food in an intimate, romantic setting. The decor is muted and elegant, with low lighting, hand-painted silk artwork on the walls, and plush carpeting. The menu combines such French and continental dishes as stuffed lobster thermidor, black Angus sirloin steak *au poivre,* and snails. Be sure to leave room for the flambéed bananas Foster for dessert. Jackets suggested but not required. Open for dinner only; closed Mondays. Reservations advised. Major credit cards accepted. Across from the *Port Lucaya MarketPlace and Marina,* Lucaya (phone: 373-7777, ext. 4245).

MODERATE

Buccaneer Club This Swiss-run spot serves European versions of Bahamian dishes—lobster bisque, conch fritters, and broiled lobster—as well as such traditional European favorites as Wiener schnitzel. Its lovely beachside setting is well worth the trip to Deadman's Reef, about half an hour from Freeport; there's a complimentary shuttle service from area hotels. Try to get here early enough to catch the spectacular sunset. Open for dinner only; closed Monday and early September to mid-November. Reservations advised. Major credit cards accepted. Deadman's Reef (phone: 352-5748 or 348-3794).

Pier One A restaurant on stilts, it's a longtime favorite for Bahamian specialties, seafood, and sunsets on the waterfront. Every evening the eatery puts on a unique floor show: At 8 and again at 9 PM, about a dozen hungry reef and lemon sharks show up to dine on fresh fish courtesy of the management. Open daily. Reservations necessary. Major credit cards accepted. Freeport Harbour (phone: 352-6674).

Stoned Crab A breezy beachside eatery, this place serves the freshest seafood and steaks broiled over hickory charcoal. Try the guava lobster soup as an appetizer, followed by yellowfin tuna steak. Open daily for dinner only.

Reservations advised. Major credit cards accepted. Taino Beach (phone: 373-1442).

INEXPENSIVE

Fat Man's Nephew The fat man is no more, nor is his eatery at Pinder's Point, but his nephew carries on in this spot, where tourists and locals dine out on conch specialties, chicken and pork dishes, and local lobster. Open daily. Reservations unnecessary. Major credit cards accepted. *Port Lucaya MarketPlace and Marina,* Lucaya (phone: 373-8520).

Freddy's Place This place gets high marks from savvy Bahamians. The menu includes all kinds of conch (salad, chowder, cracked, or steamed), grouper, and local lobster (the seafood platter samples all three), plus steaks and such daily island specials as pea soup and dumplings, short ribs, and souse (a mélange of pig parts pickled with onion, cucumber, and pepper). Open for dinner only; closed Sundays. Reservations unnecessary. No credit cards accepted. At Hunters Village, Pinder's Point (phone: 352-3250).

Outriggers This beachfront restaurant is better known as *Mama Flo's,* after the matriarch of the family who runs it. Mama Flo was born in Smith's Point, where the restaurant is located, and she enjoys reminiscing about the early days before Freeport was built. This is the place to be on Wednesday nights, when the restaurant throws a beach party that features an outdoor fish fry, served up with peas and rice, salad, and macaroni and cheese. Starting around 6 PM, Kalik beers are poured, the stereo is turned up, and the jovial atmosphere spills outside onto the beach. Closed Sundays. Reservations unnecessary. No credit cards accepted. Smith's Point (phone: 373-4811).

Pusser's Country Store and Pub A fun place to meet, with terrace dining, seafood specials, and exotic rum cocktails. Closed Sundays. Reservations advised. Major credit cards accepted. *Port Lucaya MarketPlace and Marina,* Lucaya (phone: 373-8450).

Scorpio's Authentic Bahamian food—cracked conch, spicy conch salad, steamed chicken, plus daily specials—is the draw here. Open daily for breakfast, lunch, and dinner. Reservations unnecessary. Major credit cards accepted. Downtown at West Mall Dr. and Explorer's Way (phone: 352-6969).

Turks & Caicos

"Turks and *what?*" ask friends when you tell them where you're headed. It doesn't take long to find out that much of the world has never heard of the Turks and Caicos Islands, in spite of the fact that they're closer to the US than Puerto Rico or the Virgin Islands. You'll probably need a magnifying glass to find the minute archipelago called the Caicos and the neighboring cluster of tiny islands known as the Turks on a map. Roughly 40 miles southeast of Mayaguana in the Bahamas and about 90 miles due north of Haiti, the islands' location and landscape (similar to that of the Bahamas' Out Islands, they are almost totally flat, with shining edges of sand and some low green hills) should make them a logical extension of the Bahamas archipelago. In fact, they were part of the Bahamas until 1874, when they came under Jamaican jurisdiction. When Jamaica declared its independence in 1962, the Turks and Caicos remained a British Crown Colony with a governor appointed by the queen; a 1976 constitutional amendment provided for an elected ministerial government as well.

Seven of the eight major islands—Grand Turk and Salt Cay in the Turks group and the Caicos islands of Providenciales (called Provo), Pine Cay, and South, Middle (Grand), and North Caicos—are inhabited, as are a few of the 40-odd mite-size cays. About 14,000 people (including seasonal residents) inhabit the islands; well over half live on Provo and Grand Turk. Altogether the islands encompass only 193 square miles of land, plus an almost equal expanse of tidal banks teeming with sea life. This relatively small amount of earth owes its outsize tourist potential (until recently almost totally unexploited) to 230 miles of beautiful white-sand beaches—many undisturbed by humans for days at a time—and to vast surrounding rings of live coral reefs and spectacular drop-offs that lure a small, steady stream of divers from all around the world. Then there's the fishing—so fine that the bonefishers who've found it are reluctant to share their discovery with other anglers.

What has deterred other tourists? For years accommodations have been extremely limited, with styles ranging from attractively simple to downright rustic, and the government tourist board's small budget has meant limited advertising to attract travelers. In the last decade, however, there have been significant changes in the islands' tourist picture. In 1984, *Club Med Turkoise* opened on a 70-acre section of Provo's 12-mile Grace Bay Beach, bringing the first major resort to the Turks and Caicos. The *Ramada Turquoise Reef* followed in 1990 with a sizable 228-room resort along a neighboring stretch of Grace Bay Beach, and in 1993 the *Grace Bay Club* brought upscale sophistication to the area. In addition, the previously spotty air service to the islands has stabilized in recent years, with *American Airlines* providing daily flights to Provo from Miami.

But if the islands are just now being discovered by tourists, they were discovered by others long ago. Sometime before the 10th century, Lucaya Indians arrived from islands to the south to settle on Middle Caicos. It is possible that their name, "Lucaya," may have been the origin of the name "Caicos," or the name may simply be another version of *cayos,* the Spanish word for "keys." On the other hand, everyone agrees that the Turks isles, to the east of the Caicos, were named for the native Turk's head cactus, whose scarlet top looks like a Turkish fez.

For years it was believed that Juan Ponce de León was the first European to discover the islands, having stopped by in 1512 on his quest for the fountain of youth. More recent evidence suggests that Columbus may have landed here in 1492. In fact, Grand Turk may have been the site of Columbus's first landfall in the New World, rather than the Bahamian island of San Salvador. During the 16th and 17th centuries, some of the region's most notorious pirates found the Caicos convenient for hiding out and provisioning. It was not until 1678 that more law-abiding settlers from Bermuda made their appearance. The Lightbournes, Astwoods, and Butterfields came to harvest the wealth of sea salt on the Turks and South Caicos. Despite the continued depredations of pirates, a short-lived Spanish invasion in 1706, and three French attacks in the course of the next 70 years, the Bermudians kept returning, rebuilding their salt pans, and sustaining a trade that became a staple of Bermuda's economy. Loyalist families fleeing the American Revolution, among them the Gardiners, Williamses, and Stubbses, arrived circa 1787 to establish sisal plantations on the Caicos Islands, bringing slavery with them. By the time slavery was abolished in 1838, most of these plantations were no longer in operation; by 1950 the introduction of synthetic fibers had made the sisal industry obsolete. When the British nationalized salt production in 1951, many whites left the Turks and Caicos for good. But after three centuries of intermingling and intermarrying, the old names persist among island residents today.

Despite their pristine beaches and colorful sea life, the Turks and Caicos are not for every traveler. Don't rush to pack your bags and take flight for these islands if you're happy only in five-star hotels (not all the islands' rooms are air conditioned); if the absence of a social director sends you into a deep depression (except for those at *Club Med,* there are none); or if bus touring, Las Vegas–style entertainment, or acres of shops are essential features of your ideal island holiday (you won't find them here). And epicures take note—meals here can be good, even delicious, when the fish or lobster is fresh and subtly sauced, but because so much food is imported frozen, haute cuisine is the exception, not the rule. Finally, if totally reliable, split-second timing is essential to your peace of mind, the Turks and Caicos aren't the places to seek it. Waiters and waitresses, maids, guides, taxis, and airplanes all come and go according to "island time"—always later than advertised, sometimes not at all.

But if your natural vacation pace is a saunter; if quiet doesn't scare you; if you genuinely enjoy miles of undeveloped beach, uninhabited cays, and shelling, fishing, snorkeling, windsurfing, and (especially) scuba diving; if you'd rather shoot the breeze in a waterfront bar than tromp through a museum (the *Turks and Caicos National Museum* on Grand Turk is the only one on the islands)—in short, if you really mean it when you say you want to get away from it all—then by all means book your passage, and do it soon. Progress is on the way, so discover the Turks and Caicos while they are still widely unknown and genuinely unspoiled.

Turks & Caicos At-a-Glance

FROM THE AIR

The more than forty islands and cays that make up the Turks and Caicos archipelago lie 575 miles southeast of Florida, halfway between Miami and Puerto Rico and 90 miles north of Haiti. The islands continue the southeasterly line of the Bahamas, with the Caicos grouped in a rough semicircle and the Turks clustered a bit farther southeast across the Turks Island Passage. From above, the two island groups form a sort of rough question mark. The flight from Miami to Grand Turk or Provo takes about an hour and a half; the flight from Nassau to South Caicos or Provo takes about the same amount of time.

SPECIAL PLACES

Though the islands can't accurately be described as lovely—they're generally flat, dry, and covered with stunted pines or scrub—the Turks and Caicos do have some extraordinary beaches, and the turquoise waters that surround them are a diver's paradise. Each island has its own attractions—some modest, some quite spectacular. For additional details on touring each of the main islands, see the *Turks and Caicos* routes in DIRECTIONS.

GRAND TURK This is the most historic of the islands; weatherbeaten colonial homes line the narrow streets of Cockburn Town, the island's main settlement and the colony's capital. Some maintain that Columbus landed on nearby Pillory Beach in 1492. The dramatic relationship between the sea and these islands can be examined at the *Turks and Caicos National Museum* on Cockburn Town's main street, which is known as Front Street (although its official name is Duke Street). Housed in the former *Guinep Lodge,* a historic stone building on the waterfront, its main displays are artifacts from the oldest shipwreck discovered in the Americas, the Molasses Reef wreck, which dates from about 1512. The museum is closed Saturday afternoons and Sundays; there's an admission charge (phone: 62160).

Only a quarter mile off the west coast of Grand Turk in the Turks Island Passage is one of the most extraordinary diving spots in the world, where the coastal shelf drops to a 7,000-foot abyss (see *Quintessential Bahamas and Turks & Caicos* in DIVERSIONS).

SALT CAY Just 9 miles south of Grand Turk and also part of the Turks archipelago, Salt Cay is another historic spot. Windmills dot the dazzling white salt pans on the island, and tidy Balfour Town has many relics of the island's whaling and salt-raking days, including a badly decayed warehouse with walls of salt still standing where the sides of the building have fallen away.

PROVIDENCIALES (PROVO) If the Turks are the place for history, Provo in the Caicos is the place for fun. Provo boasts a handful of world class resorts, including the *Grace Bay Club,* the *Ramada Turquoise Reef,* and the *Club Med Turkoise* (see *Checking In*). These hotels occupy one of the most spectacular beaches in the colony, a 12-mile beauty that stretches from Turtle Bay on the north coast to Grace Bay near the eastern tip of the island. At Sapodilla Bay, another good beach on the south coast, the bonefishing is excellent. (If the locals tell you it's not, pay no heed; they say this just to keep the hordes at bay.) Well-heeled travelers who find the crowds on Provo too harrying can escape to the *Meridian Club* (see *Checking In*) on Pine Cay, a nearby private island.

OTHER CAICOS ISLANDS The other links in the Caicos chain have their own attractions: bonefishing and bird sanctuaries (North Caicos); limestone caves and Lucaya Indian ruins (Middle Caicos); sailing and diving off deep Cockburn Harbour (South Caicos). Those who really want to get away from it all can hop on a charter and spend the day on one of the uninhabited isles such as West Caicos, where the honey-hued beaches and great dives make you forget that there's nary a bar nor grill in sight.

EXTRA SPECIAL

Protected by international treaty, the wetlands of the *Ramsar Site,* located on the south side of Middle (Grand), North, and East Caicos, are home to thousands of water birds and intertidal and shallow-water plant life, and are an important nursery area for conch, lobster, and myriad marine species. The Silver, Navidad, and Mouchoir Banks, also protected areas, lie between the Turks and Caicos and the Dominican Republic and are the only known breeding grounds for western Atlantic humpback whales. These nature reserves are fairly inaccessible, and a permit is required to enter some of them, but it's well worth the effort. Contact the *Turks and Caicos Department of Environment and Coastal Resources* on Grand Turk (phone: 62855) to arrange a memorable marine-life adventure.

Sources and Resources

TOURIST INFORMATION

The *Turks and Caicos Tourist Board* has offices in the back courtyard of the *Government Building* in Cockburn Town, Grand Turk (Front St.; phone: 62321; 800-241-0824; fax: 62733) and in the *Turtle Cove Landing* shopping center on Provo (phone: 64970).

LOCAL COVERAGE The *Free Press* comes out biweekly. *Times of the Islands* magazine is published quarterly and includes articles about things to do and where to shop, as well as restaurant reviews. The *Turks and Caicos Pocket Guide,* published biennially, offers comprehensive information for visitors.

TELEPHONE The area code for the Turks and Caicos is 809. When calling from outside the islands, dial the area code + 94 + the five-digit local phone number. When calling on the islands or between islands, dial the five-digit local number only.

GETTING AROUND

CAR RENTAL In addition to large international agencies (see GETTING READY TO GO), there are several local companies. In Provo, *Provo Rent-A-Car* (phone: 64404) is located at the airport, and *Highway Rent-a-Car* (phone: 15262) and *Island Rent-a-Car* (phone: 64475) are located on Leeward Highway. On Grand Turk, *Dutchies* (phone: 62244) rents cars, while *Tropical Auto Leasing* (phone: 63000) specializes in jeeps. On North Caicos, try *Sierra Rent-A-Car* (phone: 67317).

FERRY *Caicos Express* (phone: 67111) offers regularly scheduled ferry service from *Leeward Marina* on Provo to Sandy Point on North Caicos, with stops at Pine Cay, Parrot Cay, and sometimes Middle Caicos.

INTER-ISLAND FLIGHTS *Turks and Caicos Airways* (*TCA;* phone: 64255), a privately owned airline, flies regularly from Provo to North, Middle, and South Caicos and Grand Turk. Flights usually are fully booked, with standbys waiting, so reserve ahead. *TCA* also provides service to Nassau and Freeport in the Bahamas; Puerto Plata and Santo Domingo, Dominican Republic; Kingston, Jamaica; and Cap Haïtien, Haiti. Several air charter services also fly between the islands. Based in Provo are *Blue Hills Aviation* (phone: 64388); *Cactus Air Airport* (phone: 64152); *Charles Air Service* (phone: 64352); and *Provo Air Charter* (phone: 64296). On Grand Turk there's *Flamingo Air Service* (phone: 62109). *Inter-Island Airways* (phone: 15481) serves both Grand Turk and Provo.

MOTOR BIKES AND DUNE BUGGIES On Provo, dune buggies are available from *Rent-A-Buggy* (phone: 64158), while motor bikes can be hired at *Scooter Bob's Rental* (phone: 64684). On Grand Turk, the *Kittina* hotel (see *Checking*

In) rents scooters. Bicycles are available both at the *Kittina* and at *CJ Rentals* (phone: 62744).

SEA EXCURSIONS For more than a dozen years, Chloe Zimmerman of Provo-based *Turtle Tours* (phone: 64393; fax: 64048) has been putting together half- and full-day Turks and Caicos excursions on land, by air, and both under and over the water. Choices include a flight to North Caicos with a guided tour of the island and its crab farm, and a five-hour sail-swim-picnic trip to uninhabited cays.

Among the other tour operators on Provo are *Provo Turtle Divers,* with two locations—at the *Turtle Cove Inn* (phone: 64232; 800-328-5285) and at the *Ocean Club* (see *Checking In*)—and *Dive Provo* (phone: 65040; 800-234-7768) at the *Ramada Turquoise Reef.* Both outfits run glass-bottom boat trips. There's also *Undersea Tours* (phone: 15926), which operates a two-person submarine and the *Grand Adventure* party boat. Visitors can arrange day cruises aboard the *Beluga* (phone: 64544), *Caicos Sol* (phone: 67111), *Christina* (phone: 65047), *Ocean Outbacks' Kon-Tiki* (phone: 15810), and the *Tao* and *Two Fingers* (phone: 64393).

TAXI Renting a taxi for an island tour is one of the best ways to get the lay of the land. Most cabbies have tours already designed. Ask your hotel to make arrangements, and be sure to agree on a price before you set out. The initial asking price will be high, particularly on Provo, but since most drivers own their cars, there's room for negotiation. Drivers will usually charge by the passenger, with each additional passenger receiving a discounted fare.

SPECIAL EVENTS

The *Commonwealth Regatta,* also called the *South Caicos Regatta,* is the biggest event on the islands, taking place on South Caicos the last weekend in May. The *Queen's Official Birthday* is celebrated June 10 with police parades on both Grand Turk and Provo. The *Turks and Caicos Islands International Billfish Tournament* is held on Provo in June and July (see *Sport Fishing,* below). The *Provo Summer Festival,* the islands' major fete, is a week-long annual celebration in late July or early August with races, parades, regattas, and a Miss Turks and Caicos beauty pageant. On Grand Turk, islanders celebrate a *Carnival* that begins the last few days in August and continues into the first week in September.

SHOPPING

The browsing and buying opportunities are certainly not spectacular here, although there are some excellent boutiques featuring swimwear, shell jewelry, and other souvenirs. Liquor is a relative bargain, especially rum from Haiti or the Dominican Republic.

On Provo there are several small shopping centers along Leeward Highway and in the crossroads area known as "town," or "downtown." The *Town Centre Mall* is where you'll find the *Bank of Nova Scotia* (phone: 64750); the *Island Pride Supermarket* (phone: 64211); and *Rosie's Pioneer*

Boutique (phone: 64214), which sells beachwear. Nearby, on the same side of the road, is *Island Photo* (phone: 64686), the only film processor in the islands. Across the way is *Butterfield Square,* with *Barclay's Bank* (phone: 64245) and *Tasty Temptation,* a café and take-out shop (see *Eating Out*). A little east of these two centers is the *Market Place,* where you'll find *Bamboo Gallery* (phone: 64748), featuring fine Caribbean art. Just down the road is *Central Square,* which is home to *Greensleeves* (phone: 64147), an arts and crafts supply store; a couple of souvenir shops; a small supermarket; *Scooters Rentals;* and a great watering hole called *Hey José* (see *Eating Out*). Elsewhere on Provo, *Turtle Cove Landing* has a number of shops, including *Tropical Fashion* (no phone), which sells hand-painted T-shirts and beachwear; there are also a few shops at the *Ramada Turquoise Reef* resort at Grace Bay (see *Checking In*).

Shopping opportunities are more limited on Grand Turk. On Front Street in Cockburn Town is the *Seaview Gift Shop* (no phone), featuring lots of T-shirts, aprons, and totes, many hand-painted in Haiti. Also on Front Street, near the center of town, is *Blue Water Divers* (phone: 62432), with the best collection of T-shirts on the island. *Dot's Gifts* (on Moxey's Folly, east of the Red Salina; phone: 62324) has some unique souvenirs as well as some books and records dealing with the Turks and Caicos' history and folk traditions.

SPORTS

BIRD WATCHING There are bird and butterfly sanctuaries everywhere, with particularly interesting species at French Cay in the Caicos and at Penniston, Gibb, and Round Cay, a patch of small islands near Grand Turk.

GOLF The only course on the islands is the 18-hole, 3,202-yard Carl Litten–designed *Provo Golf Club* in Provo (Grace Bay Rd.; phone: 65991).

PARASAILING Suspended beneath a parachute, participants float high above the sea, taking off from and landing on the deck of a towboat; thrill seekers can request a dip in the water as well. Book through your hotel or contact the *Turtle Cove Inn* (see *Checking In*).

SAILING AND WINDSURFING *Dive Provo* (see *Sea Excursions,* above) offers windsurfing and sailing lessons and equipment rentals; it also rents easy-to-maneuver ocean kayaks. On Grand Turk, the *Kittina* hotel (see *Checking In*) has a complete water sports shop.

SNORKELING AND SCUBA Both are spectacular—underwater buffs flock from all over the world to the stunning 7,000-foot Turks Island Passage drop-off and the reefs that circle Grand Turk and the Caicos. Local divers are extremely protective of their undersea fauna and flora; they take the motto of the Provo-based organization *PRIDE (Prevention of Reefs and Islands from Degradation and Exploitation)* very seriously: "Take only pictures; leave only bubbles."

Island dive outfits are excellent; most offer certified instruction and full equipment rental as well as dive and snorkeling trips. You'll find all this at *Tradewind Divers* (phone: 67377) on North Caicos; *Porpoise Divers* (phone: 66927) on Salt Cay; *Blue Water Divers* (phone: 62432) and *Off the Wall Divers* (phone: 62159) on Grand Turk; and *Flamingo Divers* (phone: 64193), *Turtle Inn Divers* (phone: 15389; 800-359-3483), *Provo Turtle Divers,* and *Dive Provo* (see *Sea Excursions,* above, for information on the last two) on Provo. Scuba enthusiasts can also set out for longer excursions on live-aboard dive boats: *Sea Dancer* (phone: 800-932-6237), based at *Caicos Marina* on Provo; *Turks and Caicos Aggressor* (phone: 800-348-2628) and *Island Diver* (phone: 15810) on Provo; and *Aquanaut* (phone: 62160) on Grand Turk. There is a decompression chamber on Provo at *Dr. Jon Menzies Cottage Hospital* (Leeward Hwy.; phone: 64242). For more details, see *Quintessential Bahamas and Turks & Caicos* in DIVERSIONS.

SPORT FISHING It's marvelous off Grand Turk, Salt Cay, South Caicos, and Provo, and generally very good on all the islands. Boats can be rented for the day through most hotels. Provo has a trim marina with dockage for visiting sport boats. Deep-sea fishing catches include marlin, sailfish, sawfish, wahoo, dolphin, tuna, mackerel, and barracuda. Be aware that it can take up to an hour to get to deep-water fishing areas.

Aficionados who've already tried it hope you won't believe the stories you hear about the incredible bonefishing in the shallows off the Caicos. Privately, they say it's some of the best in the world—especially in the waters that wash the west-lying Caicos Bank. For more information, contact the *Turks and Caicos Tourist Board* (see *Tourist Information*).

Among the charter operators on Provo are *Sakitumi,* with Captain Bob Collins in charge (phone: 64203 or 64393), and the *Fair Tide* (phone: 64684); on Grand Turk try *Off the Wall Divers* (phone: 62159). If bonefishing is your passion, Captain Barr Gardiner operates *Bonefish Unlimited* (phone: 64874) on Provo. On Parrot Cay, call *Parrot Cay Charters* (phone: 64551), where Albert Musgrove directs the operation. Other guides include Earl Forbes and Lem "Bonefish" Johnson on Provo; Julius Jennings on South Caicos; Dolphus Arthurs at Conch Bar, Middle Caicos; and the Talbots on Salt Cay. They communicate mostly by radio, so ask your hotel for help in contacting them.

The Turks and Caicos seem to be following the lead of the Bahamas and the Cayman Islands, which have had success drawing top sport fishers to summer tournaments. The *Turks and Caicos Islands International Billfish Tournament,* held on Provo each June and July, is a release-format tournament offering cash prizes. For details, contact the tournament organizers (PO Box 145, Providenciales, Turks and Caicos Islands, BWI; phone: 64307; fax: 64771).

SWIMMING AND SUNNING It's hard to go wrong on any of the islands' cays. With some 230 miles of beaches, the real joy of a Turks and Caicos vacation is to find a stretch of sand you like and relax with a book, a beverage, and nothing else but time.

DREAM BEACH

Grace Bay, Providenciales Busy, but still beautiful, this reef-protected beach stretches along Provo's north shore for almost 12 miles. Thirty years ago Grace Bay was a deserted place, but time and progress have brought hotels—the *Grace Bay Club, Club Med Turkoise,* and the *Ramada Turquoise Reef,* the largest resort in the colony—to its shores. No matter. The sand here is still so fine that it's almost like powder, and when the beach gets too crowded, snorkelers and divers can take to the water and frolic with the fish.

Other splendid strands include Governor's Beach, Grand Turk; the northern coast of Salt Cay; Conch Bar, Middle Caicos; almost any of the coasts on North Caicos; and Sapodilla Bay on Provo.

TENNIS Courts are available at the *Prospect of Whitby* resort on North Caicos and the *Windmills* on Salt Cay. On Provo you'll find courts at *Grace Bay Club, Treasure Beach Villas, Ramada Turquoise Reef, Club Med Turkoise, Turtle Cove Inn, Erebus Inn, Le Deck,* and the *Ocean Club.* (See *Checking In* for hotel phone numbers and addresses.)

NIGHTLIFE

A nightcap (or several) and some talk around the hotel bar or other watering hole is about as exciting as most evenings on the Turks and Caicos get, though the entertainment scene is beginning to heat up on Provo. The *Banana Boat, Alfred's Place,* and *Jimmy's* are late-night favorites with expatriates in the Turtle Cove area (see *Eating Out* for information on all three), while locals head for *Erebus Inn* (see *Checking In*), *Smokey's* (near the *Island Princess* hotel; phone: 13466), or *Fast Eddie's* (see *Eating Out*) for dancing to live music. Grand Turk boasts *The Lady* (on the north end of the island; no phone) for dancing on Friday and Saturday nights. Hotels usually take turns hosting music nights, with Tuesdays and Sundays belonging to the *Salt Raker Inn* on Grand Turk (see *Checking In*). But when there's a dance anywhere in the islands, everybody's invited—and almost everybody comes. Check the *Free Press* for listings. The first—and only—gambling casino in the Turks and Caicos is located at the *Ramada Turquoise Reef* hotel (see *Checking In*); it features blackjack, roulette, video poker, and slot machines and is open from 4 PM to 2 AM. It's closed Sundays (although it's sometimes open daily in winter). Several other establishments around the islands feature slot machines.

Best on the Islands

CHECKING IN

There are only about 1,200 tourist rooms scattered throughout the islands—half of them distributed between *Club Med Turkoise* and the *Ramada Turquoise Reef*. Most hotels have fewer than 50 rooms and take pride in the personal service their small size allows them to offer. All of the properties listed below have rooms with private baths unless otherwise indicated; most hotel rooms listed below also are equipped with air conditioning, TV sets, and telephones.

In winter, expect to pay $300 or more per night for a room for two, without meals, in a hotel listed as very expensive; $150 to $300 in an expensive place; $90 to $150 in a place we list as moderate; and under $90 in an inexpensive hotel. Some hotels offer a meal plan that includes breakfast and dinner for an extra $25 to $35 per person per day. There is a 7% room occupancy tax and a 10% or 18% service charge on room rates and anything charged to the room. Hotels also are free to charge whatever they want for telephone calls, local or long distance. Packages—particularly those run in conjunction with one of the dive operations—can offer considerable savings on posted room rates.

There are a number of bed and breakfast establishments on the islands, but not all operate year-round. Information on bed and breakfast accommodations can be obtained from the tourist board (see *Tourist Information,* above). Hostelries with fewer than four rooms do not collect government taxes or mandatory gratuities. All telephone numbers listed below are in the 809 area code unless otherwise indicated; for information on dialing from outside the Turks and Caicos, see *Telephone,* above.

We begin with our favorite haven, followed by recommended hotels listed by price category.

A PRIVATE ISLAND

Meridian Club, Pine Cay Barefoot-casual (but still pricey), this resort on private Pine Cay has 12 suites fronting its gorgeous 2-mile-long beach and 11 additional cottages, all pleasingly rustic. (Don't expect to find air conditioning, TV sets, or telephones *anywhere* on this island.) The central clubhouse has a big, homey lounge, family-style dining, and a pool; also offered are an array of water sports, fishing, nature walks, a tennis court, and boat trips to neighboring islands. Pine Cay, three quarters of which is set aside as a nature preserve, is noted for the unspoiled beauty of its land and sea life—no spearfishing is allowed. Several houses near the resort may be rented by the week. For international travelers, Pine Cay is most accessible from Provo. No credit cards accepted. Closed

July through October. Pine Cay (phone: 800-331-9154; 212-696-4566 in New York City; fax: 65128; 212-689-1598 in New York City).

TURKS ISLANDS

GRAND TURK

EXPENSIVE

Kittina Fifteen years ago the Fenimore family built this hotel themselves, even quarrying the stone locally, and it has been popular ever since. There are eight standard rooms as well as 20 big and airy deluxe beachfront rooms complete with kitchens and with balconies overlooking the courtyard or the sea. Also on the premises are a good dining room (the *Sandpiper;* see *Eating Out*), a popular bar, and a dive shop. Front St., Cockburn Town (phone: 62232; 800-KITTINA; fax: 62877).

MODERATE

Gordon's Guest House There's just one guestroom at this establishment, which is also the home of Douglas and Angie Gordon, who owned the *Salt Raker Inn* (below) for years. Located upstairs and with its own private entrance, the room is spacious, with twin beds, a ceiling fan, cable TV, a small refrigerator, and a roomy porch with a table and two comfortable chairs. Continental breakfast is included in the room rate. Front St., Cockburn Town (phone: 62470).

Guanahani Beach On the beach north of Cockburn Town, this 16-room hotel also has a saltwater pool. It's a simple, isolated place, but the staff is attentive, and the location is a bonus for beach lovers. The good restaurant is another plus (see *Eating Out*). Dive packages are available. Pillory Beach (phone: 62135; 800-821-6670; fax: 61152).

Salt Raker Inn A 150-year-old Bermuda-style inn set in a former private home with a flowering garden, this place offers three large suites and 10 rooms, all with refrigerators and most with TV sets and telephones. There's an outdoor pub, a bar/lounge, a guest library and reading room, and a very good alfresco restaurant (see *Eating Out*). Guests can scuba, snorkel, or swim at the beach across the road, and rental bikes are available nearby. The inn is only a stroll from the center of town. Front St., Cockburn Town (phone: 62260; fax: 62432).

INEXPENSIVE

Ocean View This spartanly furnished establishment has 10 large rooms, some with TV sets and mini-refrigerators, and a deck. There's also a small restaurant. Pond St., Cockburn Town (phone: 62517).

Turks Head Inn Renovated by local artist Xavier Tonneau in the style of a Bahamian country inn, this is one of Cockburn Town's designated historic buildings. Each of the six rooms has a ceiling fan (as well as air conditioning), cable TV, a large balcony, and some antique or period furniture. Breakfast is included in the room rate. There's also a restaurant and bar on the premises (see *Eating Out*). Front St., Cockburn Town, (phone: 62466; fax: 62825).

SALT CAY

VERY EXPENSIVE

Windmills A re-creation of a colonial plantation by architect S. Guy Lovelace, it has four suites and four rooms (none air conditioned). The rates are Full American Plan (three meals a day and all drinks included) and remain the same year-round. The minimum stay is three nights. North Bay Beach (phone: 66962; 410-819-0562 in Maryland; 800-822-7715 elsewhere in the US; fax: 66930; 410-820-9179 in Maryland).

MODERATE

Mount Pleasant Guest House This refurbished historic building with seven guest-rooms (only one has a private bath) caters mostly to divers. The rates are Modified American Plan (breakfast and one other meal included). North Bay Beach (phone: 66927).

CAICOS ISLANDS

MIDDLE (GRAND) CAICOS

INEXPENSIVE

Eagle's Rest Villas These eight villas—six of which are brand new—offer a peaceful, comfortable place to get away from it all on this most remote and undeveloped of the Caicos. The units—some in red-tile-roofed, one-story duplexes, others in elevated, modern-style, octagonal bungalows—have verandahs facing a gorgeous 5-mile stretch of unspoiled beach, and one of them is only 75 feet from the gentle surf. Each villa can accommodate up to six guests, with two bedrooms, two baths, a sleeper sofa, a full kitchen, TV with VCR (not that there's anyplace to rent movies nearby), and a washer/dryer; some villas are air conditioned, while others have ceiling fans only. For those who want to scuba dive, snorkel, or sportfish, equipment and two boats with guides are available; car rental and cook and maid service can also be arranged. But be warned—this is really getting away from it all: You can either catch your dinner yourself, get it from a local fisherman, or—if you're not in the mood for seafood—bring it along with you when you come to the island (phone: 66122; 800-484-1882, ext. 7177; 813-793-7157 in Florida).

NORTH CAICOS

EXPENSIVE

Ocean Beach Located on the gorgeous beach are 10 condominiums (studios and one- or two-bedroom units) with full kitchens; there's a commissary and a small restaurant on the premises as well. Guests can enjoy the pool, scuba diving, snorkeling, and tennis; deep-sea and bonefishing facilities are nearby. Weekly rates are available. Whitby (phone: 67113; 800-710-5204; 905-336-2876 in Ontario; fax: 67386; 905-336-9851 in Ontario).

Prospect of Whitby A venerable and elegant resort on lovely North Beach, it boasts 24 rooms and four suites with a choice of views, a freshwater pool, tennis, scuba diving, a bar, a restaurant, and plenty of seclusion and privacy. North Beach (phone: 67119; fax: 67114).

MODERATE

Pelican Beach With 6 miles of powder-white beach at its doorstep, this 14-room shoreside retreat offers snorkeling, fishing, boat trips to nearby islands, and flying excursions as far as the Dominican Republic (the owner is a first-rate pilot). There's also an informal bar and a dining room. Whitby (phone: 67112; fax: 67139).

PROVIDENCIALES (PROVO)

VERY EXPENSIVE

Grace Bay Club This full-service resort, which resembles a Mediterranean village, features 22 elegantly appointed deluxe suites. Each is individually decorated in contemporary-style earth tones with Asian and Central and South American touches such as rattan furniture, handmade Guatemalan pottery, and plaited rugs. Suites have full kitchens and either terraces or patios, and all are equipped with cable TV, refrigerators, and washer/dryers. There are two restaurants (the *Anacaona* and *Grill Room;* see *Eating Out* for both), a freshwater pool, a Jacuzzi, a cabaña bar, and an excellent beach. A wide variety of activities is offered, including half- or full-day trips on the hotel's 21-foot motorboat or catamaran, scuba diving, a full range of water sports, deep-sea and bonefishing, and tennis on two lighted courts. The island's only golf course is nearby. Grace Bay (phone: 65757 or 65050; 800-946-5757; fax: 65758; 800-946-5758).

EXPENSIVE

Le Deck Beach Club On Grace Bay, it boasts 26 rooms and a honeymoon suite, all in Bermuda-pink buildings. The rooms have ceiling fans (in addition to air conditioning) and cable TV. There's also a restaurant and a swimming pool; most water sports are available. Grace Bay (phone: 65547; 800-223-9815; fax: 65770).

Erebus Inn Overlooking *Turtle Cove Marina,* this hilltop resort, with 22 rooms and eight chalet and bungalow units, boasts one of the loveliest views on Provo. Rooms have ceiling fans (along with air conditioning) and cable TV. There are also two swimming pools, lighted tennis courts, a first class fitness center, a bar, and *La Crêperie* restaurant (see *Eating Out*). Turtle Cove (phone: 64240; fax: 64704).

Ocean Club A condominium development on the beach near *Club Med,* it has 41 units (studios and two- and three-bedroom suites); all feature full kitchens, cable TV, and patios or terraces. Some units include a washer/dryer. Also on the premises are a freshwater pool, a Jacuzzi, a cabaña bar, a full-service dive shop, and lighted tennis courts. Grace Bay (phone: 65880; fax: 65845).

Ramada Turquoise Reef There's not a single bad room at this 228-room, modern property on Grace Bay—almost all have ocean and/or pool views. On-site facilities include a large pool with a poolside bar and grill; two restaurants, including the elegant *Portofino* (see *Eating Out*); a full dive shop and water sports operation; and, last but not least, the only casino in the Turks and Caicos. A tour operator, rental car service, and shops are in the lobby. Grace Bay (phone: 65555; 800-854-7854; fax: 65522).

Turtle Cove Inn Yachters and divers take full advantage of the full-service marina just yards from this waterfront inn with two suites and 28 standard rooms. The beach is a few minutes' walk away, with shuttle service twice daily in season. Two lighted clay tennis courts, a pool, and two restaurants, including *Jimmy's* (see *Eating Out*), round out the amenities. Turtle Cove (phone: 64203; 800-887-0477; fax: 64141).

MODERATE

Club Med Turkoise This rambling 70-acre retreat on gorgeous Grace Bay Beach offers every imaginable activity: sailing, snorkeling, scuba diving, water skiing, deep-sea and bonefishing, tennis on eight courts (four lighted), picnic cruises, aerobics classes, a 12-station fitness center, and beach games. If you're not too tired in the evening, there are also shows and dancing in the resort's disco. The 298 rooms are comfortable but basic, without TV sets or telephones. Meals (all are included in the rate) are served in two specialty restaurants, a grill, and a pizzeria. Rates include everything—right down to beer and wine with lunch and dinner. Grace Bay (phone: 65500; 800-CLUB-MED; 212-750-1687 in New York City; fax: 65501).

Sun Worshipers Pelican Beach Club With one of the islands' most beautiful views, this charming place has 25 good-size rooms, an attractive dining room, and an on-site bakery. It's all surrounded by gardens and suffused with a pleasantly private atmosphere; the beach is a short walk away. Sapodilla Bay (phone/fax: 64488).

Treasure Beach Villas An attractive apartment alternative on Grace Bay Beach, this place offers 18 beachfront one- and two-bedroom combinations, each with a living/dining room, terrace, and fully equipped kitchen. There's also a pool and a laundromat on the premises, but no restaurant. The Bight (phone: 64211; fax: 64108).

INEXPENSIVE

Columbus Slept Here Louise Fletcher, one of Provo's most knowledgeable sources for local history, archaeology, and sightseeing tips, has three guestrooms in her home. Breakfast is included in the rate, but there's no restaurant. The Bight, near Grace Bay Beach (phone: 65878; 800-241-0824; fax: 65758).

SOUTH CAICOS

MODERATE

Club Caribe With 24 units, this beach resort caters to scuba and snorkeling enthusiasts. There is a bar and restaurant, and Modified American Plan rates (breakfast and one other meal included) are available. Cockburn Harbour (phone/fax: 63444).

EATING OUT

In general, there are very few restaurants on these undeveloped islands, and dining is almost exclusively in hotels. Only Provo, in the Caicos chain, and Grand Turk, in the Turks, offer a number of eating establishments and again, except on Provo, these are almost all hotel dining rooms. A typical menu might feature many different kinds of fresh fish and such island specialties as whelk soup, conch chowder, turtle steaks, and lobster. Expect to pay $55 or more for dinner for two, not including drinks, wine, or tip, at a restaurant we list as expensive; $40 to $55 at a restaurant described as moderate; and less than $40 in a place in the inexpensive category. There is an 8% meal tax, and many restaurants add a 10% or 15% service charge to your bill. Unless otherwise noted, restaurants are open daily for lunch and dinner, but to avoid disappointment, it's a good idea to call ahead. All telephone numbers are in the 809 area code unless otherwise indicated.

GRAND TURK

EXPENSIVE

Sandpiper The dining room of the *Kittina* hotel specializes in fresh seafood, including lobster, herbed turtle steaks, and conch. Landlubbers can sample the veal chops. Reservations unnecessary. Major credit cards accepted. Front St., Cockburn Town (phone: 62232).

Turks Head Inn The bar here stays busy, especially on Thursday and Friday nights, when complimentary hors d'oeuvres include spicy conch fritters. The dining room serves up generous portions, with nightly specials ranging from beef Stroganoff to curries. Reservations advised for dinner. Major credit cards accepted. Front St., Cockburn Town (phone: 62466).

Guanahani Beach This hotel restaurant strives to offer items not found on other island menus—stone crab claws and two-claw lobsters, for example—but there are also plenty of delicious standards, including cracked conch, grouper, chicken, and the best conch chowder you will find anywhere. Reservations unnecessary. Major credit cards accepted. Pillory Beach (phone: 62135).

Salt Raker Inn Here you'll find seafood and steaks served alfresco in a tropical garden. Reservations necessary. Major credit cards accepted. Front St., Cockburn Town (phone: 62260).

INEXPENSIVE

Water's Edge As its name suggests, this casual eatery is perched atop a small sand dune near the sea. Many diners arrive by boat, tying up at the nearby dock. The menu features fish soup, leg of lamb, and curried lobster, as well as excellent island specialties. Closed Mondays. No reservations. American Express accepted. Front St., Cockburn Town (phone: 61680).

PROVIDENCIALES (PROVO)

EXPENSIVE

Anacaona Well-prepared seafood and lamb specialties and innovative appetizers such as smoked conch and tuna carpaccio are served in this open-air dining room at the *Grace Bay Club*. The swaying palm trees surrounding the tables and the sound of the waves lapping at the beach add to the tropical atmosphere. Reservations advised. Major credit cards accepted. Grace Bay (phone: 65060).

Grill Room Adjacent to *Anacaona* and also in an attractive open-air setting, the *Grace Bay Club*'s other restaurant serves steaks and an appealing variety of seafood prepared on a charcoal grill. Reservations necessary. Major credit cards accepted. Grace Bay (phone: 65880).

Portofino The elegant upstairs dining room of the *Ramada Turquoise Reef* resort offers Italian seafood and pasta dishes in a relaxed atmosphere. There's an extensive wine list. Closed Sundays. Reservations advised. Major credit cards accepted. Grace Bay (phone: 65555).

MODERATE

Alfred's Place This terrace dining room and bar affords guests a wonderful view of Turtle Cove, and it's a favorite spot with locals for snacking on potato skins and Buffalo chicken wings at happy hour. For serious diners, there are lobster and veal entrées, and the gastronomically intrepid may even be tempted by the conch sashimi (served raw). For those who prefer their food cooked, the hot roast beef sandwich—a slab of first-rate beef on home-made bread with lettuce, tomato, onion, and grated horseradish—is a bargain. Reservations advised on weekends or when there's entertainment, usually on Tuesdays and Fridays. Major credit cards accepted. Off Leeward Hwy. at Suzie Turn (phone: 64679).

Banana Boat Grouper, marlin, snapper, and other local fish, served either grilled or with Jamaican jerk spices, are the specialties at this waterfront restaurant. Continental dishes are also served. Reservations advised for dinner. Major credit cards accepted. Turtle Cove (phone: 15706).

Bonnie's Arthur Bonnie presents a tropical soul food buffet every Saturday night, featuring fish, conch, lobster, turtle, pork chops, and chicken, and accompanied by live music. The rest of the week offers a tamer menu selection of some of the same delicious island and soul food specialties. Open daily. Reservations advised, especially for the Saturday buffet. No credit cards accepted. In *Provo Plaza,* Leeward Hwy. (phone: 64072).

La Crêperie The restaurant at the *Erebus Inn* presents French dishes with an island accent. The menu specializes in crêpes filled with seafood, including lobster and conch. Try to be here at dusk; the view of the sun setting over the waters of Turtle Cove is splendid. Reservations advised. Major credit cards accepted. Turtle Cove (phone: 64240)

Fast Eddie's Owner Eddie LaPorte runs the kitchen himself at this popular hangout, a favorite of the younger local crowd for its fresh island dishes and homemade bread. There is live music on Wednesdays and Saturdays, when reservations are necessary; reservations unnecessary at other times. No credit cards accepted. Airport Rd. (phone: 64075).

Gilley's at Leeward The airport snack bar owned by Gilmore "Gilley" Williams was so popular that he opened this second eatery, which has expanded his clientele to include boat owners, day-trippers, and residents of Leeward Going Through. The location is wonderful and the menu has lots of local flavor—selections include ribs, steamed conch, and fried chicken served with peas and rice or macaroni salad. Dinner specials include steaks, shrimp scampi, and stone crab. Reservations unnecessary. Major credit cards accepted. *Leeward Marina* (phone: 65094).

Hey José Transplanted Californians Jeff and Diane Rollings run a friendly, popular spot with a full bar and a menu featuring *chimichangas,* burritos, tacos, and the best salsa this side of Mexico. There's also a selection of pizza, and they don't skimp on the cheese or toppings; Wednesday is barbecue night. This is the place to head when you're "conched" out. Closed Sundays. No reservations. Major credit cards accepted. In the *Central Square* shopping center, Leeward Hwy. (phone: 64812).

Hong Kong Owner Bosco Chan serves up Chinese dishes that are somewhat sweeter than those found in the Chinatowns of New York and San Francisco. Also look for island-influenced specials such as sweet-and-sour lobster and conch with black-bean sauce. Closed Sunday lunch. Reservations unnecessary. Major credit cards accepted. Grace Bay Rd. near *Club Med* (phone: 65678).

Jimmy's The eclectic menu here features steaks, ribs, fried chicken, assorted pasta, and pizza topped with everything from Canadian bacon to jalapeño peppers. Open daily for dinner only. Reservations unnecessary. Major credit cards accepted. Upstairs at the *Turtle Cove Inn* (phone: 15575; 15676 for takeout or delivery).

INEXPENSIVE

Dora's Large and friendly, this eatery offers sandwiches for under $5. Lunch and dinner specials include cracked or creole conch, barbecued pork chops, steamed or fried fish or chicken, and steamed turtle. (Note that "steamed" here is analogous to "smothered" in Dixie culinary parlance.) There's a seafood dinner buffet on Mondays; on Friday and Saturday nights the restaurant stays open into the wee hours (4 or 5 AM). Reservations advised for large parties. No credit cards accepted. Leeward Hwy. (phone: 64558).

Pub on the Bay The first pub on the islands features both international dishes and local fare ranging from barbecued chicken and ribs to seafood. There's live music on Saturday evenings. Reservations advised. Major credit cards accepted. In Blue Hills, across from Northside Beach (phone: 15309).

Sweet T's A wide selection of takeout snacks, sandwiches, light breakfast food, and ice cream are dished up at this roadside trailer. No reservations. No credit cards accepted. Leeward Hwy. (no phone).

Tasty Temptation This French Canadian sandwich shop also sells pâtés, meat, and cheeses by the pound. It's got the best breakfast downtown—you can select your own coffee beans, then savor the fresh-brewed java with pastries or croissants baked on the premises. Open for breakfast and lunch; closed weekends, except Saturdays during the winter. No reservations. No credit cards accepted. In *Butterfield Square* shopping center (phone: 64049).

Top O' the Cove The islands' only New York–style deli, serving great hoagies, lox and bagels, and more. Eat in or order a picnic lunch to go. Reservations unnecessary. Major credit cards accepted. Leeward Hwy. (phone: 64694).

Where It's At Here you'll find island specialties with a Jamaican accent, including salt fish, curried goat, oxtail, and jerk pork and chicken. Fresh fruit and vegetable juices are also available. The size of your appetite is the only limit here; portions are huge and prices are low—meals start at $6. Reservations unnecessary. No credit cards accepted. Airport Rd. (phone: 64185).

Diversions

Exceptional Pleasures and Treasures

Quintessential Bahamas and Turks & Caicos

To Americans, the Bahamas (and the neighboring Turks and Caicos) are both foreign and familiar. The countries have the same language—though the Bahamian "conch accent" is a good deal more lilting than anything you'll hear stateside—and some of the same history as the United States. But just because the islanders speak English, and even though some of the Bahamian and Turks and Caicos cays bear a strong resemblance to the Florida Keys, visitors shouldn't be misled into thinking that they've never left home. The islands have their own distinct identities, with a rich folklore, lively music, and centuries-old traditions. Some of the sights and sounds here can't be experienced anywhere else. Here are a few that shouldn't be missed.

JUNKANOO No matter how tired you are, nor how early you customarily hit the hay, there are two nights a year when visitors to the islands simply have to stay awake until the break of dawn: *Christmas*—the night before *Boxing Day,* that ever-so-British holiday—and *New Year's Eve.* Both witness the all-night celebration of *junkanoo*—a costumed dance-and-music happening. If there's one cultural tradition that's synonymous with the Bahamas, this is it.

Ask a group of Bahamians about the origins of the name *junkanoo,* and you'll get a dozen answers. The most popular version is that the name is a corruption of John Canoe, a legendary figure among African slaves in the New World. The name doesn't really matter—it's the music that counts. Even tourists who would rather die than be dragged to a dance floor will find their feet tapping when they hear the *junkanoo* beat.

The music starts early—usually at 3 or 4 AM—on *Boxing Day* (and again six days later on *New Year's Day*). It begins with a blast from a conch-shell horn or a brass trombone or a big plastic foghorn—whatever is at hand. Then the drums join in. They're African drums made of wood and tanned goatskin, and their rhythm is infectiously wild. Once the drums start, the dancers follow: hundreds of them, all dressed in fantastic multicolored costumes fluttering with crêpe-paper fringe. They may be dressed like Christopher Columbus, like the Puritan colonists who sailed here in the 17th century, or like Lucaya Indians, astronauts, giant spiders, or the Greek muses. Each dancer belongs to a clan—they used to be called gangs—and each clan represents a neighborhood. As they jive their way down the street, the dancers "scrap" and "rush" at each other, as if they were fighting a stylized street battle. The sparring is all in good fun. Though the dance was once linked, rightly or wrongly, to hooliganism or social protest, today it's perfectly proper and respectable; even government ministers join in. But that's not to say that it's staid—it's one of the craziest and most colorful extravaganzas in the Bahamas.

Each dancer makes his own costume, and glueing on the crêpe-paper fringe takes patience and a practiced hand. Months of planning go into the spectacle, which lasts only a few hours. But as one dancer—Jackson Burnside, a Nassau architect and member of the *Saxon Superstars,* a redoubtable *junkanoo* clan—says, "It's not the dance itself that matters, it's the process." *Junkanoo* symbolizes freedom—freedom from everyday drudgery, slavery, colonial masters, and colonial governments—and freedom can be an evanescent thing. When the final drumbeats die away after the *New Year's Day junkanoo* parade, the costumes are discarded, and the ritual awaits another *Boxing Day.*

SPORT FISHING ON BIMINI Let's face it: If Bimini didn't have fish, few people would bother to come here. It's a one-track-minded place: monomaniacal fishermen talking monotonously about marlin—or wahoo or tuna or barracuda. In fact, it borders on being boring, unless you happen to love to fish.

If Ernest Hemingway hadn't fallen in love with the place, even anglers might have passed it by. But Hemingway immortalized Bimini in *Islands in the Stream* and—indirectly—in *The Old Man and the Sea,* whose hero (or antihero) is a big blue marlin. Today, the whole island is suffused with the Hemingway mystique, with the *Compleat Angler* bar the most authentic repository of the colorful writer's spirit.

And there aren't just marlin here. Some game fish are temporary visitors, like the tuna, which glide past Bimini on their tours along the Gulf Stream. Sailfish can be found here year-round; white marlin abound in the late winter and spring; and larger blue marlin are most plentiful from mid-June to mid-August. But anglers never know exactly where and when a school of game fish will show up—that's part of the fun. The big fish change their feeding grounds from year to year. As Hemingway wrote in August 1934: "This year, there were many small marlin taken off Miami, and the big ones appeared off Bimini just across the Gulf Stream several months before they run into Cuba."

East of the Gulf Stream, in the waters of the Great Bahamas Bank, swim the mackerel, amberjack, wahoo, dolphin fish, and barracuda, as well as tasty eating fish like grouper and snapper. Bonefish teem in the flats just offshore. (Tourists who manage to catch a bonefish shouldn't attempt to make a meal of it on the beach, unless they know a native who will cook it.

The bones must be expertly cracked before the fish can be filleted—not an easy task for a neophyte.) Eating your catch is secondary, though. It's the struggle that counts—and the stories you collect. Spend a week or two off Bimini and you'll have plenty, even if you can't recount them as well as Papa did.

THE ISLAND(S) OF DISCOVERY While no one is sure exactly where in the New World Christopher Columbus first stepped ashore, natives of several Bahamian isles have laid claim to the honor. Historians have disqualified one candidate—Cat Island—leaving two contenders: San Salvador and Grand Turk (although the small, virtually uninhabited Samana Cay has its supporters, too). San Salvador and Grand Turk are remarkably similar, and it's easy to see how either one could be "Guanahani," as the Lucaya Indians called the isle where Columbus landed.

Guana means "water" in Arawak, and both San Salvador and Grand Turk have plenty. The interiors of both islands are flecked with sea-fed ponds and lakes, although early settlers dammed the pools on Grand Turk to create the salt pans that sustained the local economy for many years. Both isles are roughly bean-shaped, which corresponds to the description recorded by the bishop who accompanied Columbus. Treacherous coral reefs lie off the east coast of both islands, while their sheltered western shores could have made a perfect spot for a landing. Both isles have a protected harbor large enough to hold "all the fleets of Christendom," as Columbus described it. Archaeologists have unearthed evidence that the two islands were populated by Indian tribes who could have been the natives that Columbus said greeted the ship by "calling us and giving thanks to God."

If in doubt about which island to visit, go to both. Standing on the eastern shore of either, imagine what it must have been like for the lookout on the *Pinta* who sighted land on the night of October 12, 1492. From the shore you can spot the ponds in the islands' interiors and know what Columbus did not: that the water in them is brackish, not fresh and sweet as the explorer thought. Walk along the beaches on the western side of each of the islands and imagine where the admiral might have rowed ashore to plant the standard of Ferdinand and Isabella. And imagine the excitement—probably tinged with fear—that the Lucaya must have felt when they beheld the bearded creatures wearing scarlet-and-blue doublets and metal helmets disembarking from a boat larger than any they had ever seen. Cynics can amuse themselves by scouting out the numerous monuments erected on San Salvador that mark the "exact" spot where Columbus landed.

VISIT A LOYALIST TOWN Perhaps no place better embodies the colonial spirit on the islands than Harbour Island. "Briland" (the natives elide the first syllable) is a quaint little town on a small isle of the same name located just off the northern tip of Eleuthera. The main settlement is officially known as Dunmore Town, after John Murray, the fourth Earl of Dunmore, a

Governor of the Bahamas who built a summer home here in the 1780s. The earl came to the islands after serving as royal governor of the Virginia colony, where his astounding arrogance made him a target of Patrick Henry's vituperative spleen. He behaved no better in the Bahamas, where he so besmirched his reputation with rumors of nepotism, womanizing, and greed that the self-respecting residents of straitlaced Harbour Island refused to call their town by his name.

The Brilanders still have reason to be proud. Their town is one of the oldest in the Bahamas, and its residents earned a reputation early on for perseverance and patriotism. Many of the island's early settlers arrived during the late-17th and early-18th centuries from New Providence, where life was frequently disrupted by attacks by pirates and Spanish galleons. The colonists of Harbour Island carved out a hardscrabble life for themselves, surviving storms and epidemics, until a large contingent of Tories landed here soon after the American Revolution and injected new life into the town. The Loyalists launched a building boom, refurbishing churches such as Anglican *St. John's,* and erecting many of the tidy clapboard houses that still line the streets in the old parts of town.

If you stroll down the quiet, tree-lined lanes of Harbour Island, you can see evidence of the island's past at almost every turn. The narrow lanes were plotted by the Earl of Dunmore in 1791. (The earl wasn't motivated by civic duty; he planned to charge rent on the 190 lots carved from portions of his estate.) The bluff called Barracks Hill, near the town's cricket grounds, is named for the barracks that the earl built for the troops who patrolled his estate. Some of the cannon that guarded the earl's property now stand in the yards of various private homes—ramble around and see how many you can find. There are many historic churches, including *St. John's,* which has a bell tower added in the 1860s, and the magnificent *Wesley Methodist Church* at the corner of Dunmore Street and Chapel Road, which was erected in the 1840s. Virtually all the early colonial buildings in town were damaged in the Great Bahama Hurricane of 1866, but many were later rebuilt. Tourism boomed after World War II, and many old buildings were refurbished and new ones added—tastefully and unobtrusively, for the most part. The town is more prosperous now than it was in the days when the locals relied on shipbuilding and sugar refining. But the place isn't grand enough to put on airs, and the locals aren't so besieged by tourists as to be unfriendly. Go now, before everybody else discovers the place. (Also see *Eleuthera* in DIRECTIONS.)

STROLL ALONG A PINK BEACH If you go to Harbour Island off Eleuthera, don't spend too long dallying in town. There's another attraction that shouldn't be missed: the perfect rose-tinted beach on the eastern strand. The beach stretches the length of the island, roughly 3 miles in all, and although it's lined with guesthouses and hotels, it still manages to preserve a sense of peace and quiet. This is a morning beach; the sun soon chases the slight chill that lingers from the night, and tiny sand creatures scurry to escape the tide. The waves are slight, for the coral reef just offshore bears the brunt of the ocean's force, and there are good places to snorkel nearby. Islanders have pretty much scoured the beach of shells, but it's a wonderful place for a stroll or a leisurely morning of soaking up the sun.

PICNIC ON STOCKING ISLAND This skinny 5-mile-long island is misnamed: It's much better explored in bare feet. Located near the mouth of Elizabeth Harbour off Great Exuma, it's the perfect place for a lazy afternoon. To get here, jump on a ferry from the dock near *Club Peace and Plenty* in George Town. The owners of the hotel bought up most of Stocking Island a few years ago and have turned it into a semiprivate reserve for their guests. The ferry is free for those staying at the hotel; for the rest, it's $8 round trip. The sand on the island's two beaches is as fine and white as sugar—not the coarse tan sugar that the British love, but the powder-fine, driven-snow American kind. Bring a picnic lunch and a thermos of rum cooler, or stop by the *Beach Club* on the island for a hamburger. On weekends, the *Beach Club* cooks up a seaside barbecue. Take a walk down the beach and explore the many secluded coves and inlets, or hunt for starfish and sand dollars if the tide is low. Divers can explore the 400-foot-deep blue hole known as Mystery Cave.

DIVE THE WALL OFF GRAND TURK Imagine leaping from the rim of the Grand Canyon, and you'll have a sense of what diving off the underwater wall west of Grand Turk Island is like. Barely 300 yards offshore, just a stone's throw from Cockburn Town, is one of the most precipitous drop-offs in the western Atlantic. Divers scoot along the shallow coastal shelf, where the depth is only 50 or 60 feet, and then *whoosh!* The floor drops away, and they're gazing into an abyss more than 7,000 feet deep. Humpback whales skim along this channel—called Turks Passage, and now also known as Columbus Passage in honor of the recent quincentennial—on their way to their breeding grounds in the Silver and Mouchoir Banks.

The wall itself is a craggy, coral-encrusted cliff riddled with odd formations. There's the Black Forest, a shallow indentation in the rock covered with three species of black coral. At the same depth, about 40 feet, is the Amphitheater, a broad gallery where divers can rest and watch for whales. Near a particularly large coral arch (waggishly called *McDonald's*), schools of grouper and yellowtail mill about waiting for a handout. By following a series of passageways called the Tunnels, divers emerge from the reef at a depth of 80 or 90 feet. There they find themselves amid a forest of purple sponges and odd gorgonia, with spadefish and schooling jacks darting through the crystal-clear water. Night divers head for the Library, where black coral and a rare nocturnal orange anemone grow, and where octopuses and eels undulate through the currents. The seas off Grand Turk are at their best from April through October—provided a hurricane doesn't swoop by.

A Few of Our Favorite Things

Though the Bahamas and the Turks and Caicos boast plenty of fine hotels, spectacular beaches, great golf courses, and snorkeling and scuba diving sites, we've singled out a few select spots that are guaranteed to delight pursuers of a variety of pleasures. Follow our lead; we promise you won't be disappointed.

Each place listed below is described in detail in the specific island chapter.

SPECIAL HAVENS AND PRIVATE ISLANDS

The following are our particular favorites for a stay on the islands. Some are large, self-contained resorts, others are small and intimate, but each in its own way offers the highest caliber of service, food, and tropical ambience. Complete information about our choices can be found on pages 57 to 59 of the *Bahamas* chapter and on pages 92 to 93 of the Turks and Caicos chapter in THE ISLANDS.

Bahamas
Club Med–Columbus Isle, San Salvador
Dunmore Beach Club, Harbour Island, off Eleuthera
Graycliff, Nassau
Ocean Club, Paradise Island
The Villas on Silver Cay, Silver Cay

Turks & Caicos
Meridian Club, Pine Cay

DREAM BEACHES

Of the seemingly endless miles of sandy shores these islands have to offer, the following strips are guaranteed to deliver the best combination of sun, sand, and turquoise sea. And as some of these places haven't yet been discovered by the masses, you may even be able to enjoy the much sought-after but often elusive gift of solitude. Complete information about our choices can be found on page 54 of the *Bahamas* chapter and page 91 of the *Turks & Caicos* chapter in THE ISLANDS.

Bahamas
Fernandez Bay, Cat Island
Harbour Island, off Eleuthera
Rolleville, Great Exuma

Turks & Caicos
Grace Bay, Providenciales

TOP TEE-OFF SPOTS

Despite their level terrain, the Bahamas offer some prime challenges for golfers. The courses listed below—our favorites—are the creations of some of golf's most illustrious architects, including Robert Trent Jones Sr., Joe Lee, and Dick Wilson. And the views surrounding them are so striking that you may have trouble keeping your eye on the ball. Complete information about our choices can be found on page 49 of the *Bahamas* chapter in THE ISLANDS.

Bahamas

Paradise Island Golf Club, Paradise Island
Sofitel Cotton Bay Club, Eleuthera
South Ocean Golf and Beach Resort, New Providence

BEST DEPTHS

In order to see all there is to see in and around the Bahamas, you have to look below the surface (of the ocean, that is). There are a multitude of dive sites throughout the 700 Bahamian islands; the following afford the ultimate underwater experience. Complete information about our choices can be found on pages 51 to 53 of the *Bahamas* chapter and pages 89 to 90 of the *Turks & Caicos* chapter in THE ISLANDS.

Bahamas

Andros (particularly the Andros Barrier Reef)
Bimini (particularly the Bimini Wall)
Eleuthera (especially the Current Cut and Devil's Backbone)
Grand Bahama (particularly Treasure Reef)
Long Island
New Providence and **Paradise Island** (especially Goulding Cay Reefs, Gambier Deep Reef, and Booby Rock Channel)
San Salvador

Turks and Caicos

Grand Turk (especially the Turks Island Passage drop-off)
Caicos Islands

WHERE THEY BITE

One of the prime sportfishing grounds in the world, the Bahamas and Turks and Caicos attract enthusiastic anglers from all over. Almost every variety of deep-sea game fish—and some world-record catches—have been taken in these waters. The best bite sites are listed below. Complete information about our choices can be found on pages 53 to 54 of the *Bahamas* chapter page 90 of the *Turks & Caicos* chapter in THE ISLANDS.

Bahamas
  Bimini (also see "Quintessential Bahamas and Turks & Caicos," above)
  Cat Island
  Eleuthera
  The Exumas
  Walker's Cay

Turks and Caicos
  Grand Turk
  Providenciales (Provo)
  Salt Cay
  South Caicos

Sunken and Buried Treasure

It's certainly childish, and rather a poor way to try to repay your gambling debts, but who can resist the urge to hunt for buried treasure? The odds of striking it rich are not in your favor—but neither are they at the casinos in Nassau and Freeport. There are plenty of wrecks off the Bahamas to explore. In fact, many of the ships that met their end here may have been sunk deliberately. During the lean years in colonial times, many Bahamian communities made a living by "wrecking"—scavenging goods from ships that foundered on the reefs and shoals offshore. Legend has it that the residents of some towns, like Port Howe on Cat Island, deliberately lured ships aground—and then rowed out to claim their treasure.

There are many kinds of wrecks in the Bahamas: Spanish galleons, sloops that patrolled the waters during the American Civil War, freighters, and pleasure boats. For all we know, there might be a sunken submarine in the 6,000-foot-deep trough east of Andros called the Tongue of the Ocean, where the British and American navies conduct secret maneuvers. But there are few shipwrecks that are a bit easier to find.

For starters, go to Man-O-War Cay in the Abacos, where the steam-powered sloop USS *Adirondack* lies in the shallows 27 feet below the surface. The ship hit a reef soon after dawn on August 23, 1862, on its way to Nassau, where it was being sent to monitor the activities of the Confederate blockade runner *Alabama*. The crew of the *Adirondack* fortunately was saved, and the ship's cargo was divided between the captain and the "wreckers" that rowed over from the Abacos to assist the crew. Divers can investigate 14 of the ship's cannon, some of which lie only 10 feet below the surface of the water.

Nearby, off Green Turtle Cay, lies the wreck of the *San Jacinto,* a Union gunboat that sank on *New Year's Day* in 1865. The ship was chasing a blockade runner when it mistook a light on the cay for the renegade craft and ran aground a reef offshore. Divers can also explore the hulk of the *Potomac,* which lies in 20 feet of water off Andros; the cement-hulled *Sapona* (built by Henry Ford in World War I), which lies near South Bimini; the remains of the *Frascate,* a steel-hulled freighter that sank off San Salvador Island in 1902; and the *Hydrolab,* an underwater research station abandoned off Grand Bahama about 20 years ago.

Some of the recent wreckage was sunk deliberately. *Theo's Wreck,* off Grand Bahama, is a 228-foot steel freighter intentionally sunk in a hundred feet of water in 1982. Freeport's dive operations use it for exploratory dives and underwater photography sessions. The waters off New Providence are littered with wrecks that were deliberately scuttled to provide backdrops for James Bond movies.

Landlubbing treasure seekers on the Out Islands can explore Morgan's Cave, at the northern tip of Andros, near the village of Morgan's Bluff. Henry Morgan was one of the most successful pirates in the Caribbean, and the treasure caches he is said to have buried in the cave have never been found.

None of these sites can compare with Treasure Reef off Grand Bahama, where four divers discovered the wreck of a Spanish galleon in 1965. The wreck lies in shallow water about 3 miles due east of the beach at Port Lucaya. The ruins yielded a fabulous treasure trove: 10,000 silver coins minted by Hernán Cortés in Mexico. Initially valued at $9 million, their worth plunged rapidly once collectors were faced with the prospect of a flooded market. Their value was later pegged at $2 million and then halved. Subsequently the Bahamian government enacted a law giving itself a 25% stake in all wrecks—and said that the law applied retroactively. If that wasn't enough, the four divers soon found themselves embroiled in expensive legal disputes with other claimants to the find. One of the divers, a lad named Jack Slack, summed up the whole frustrating experience in a book entitled *Finders, Losers.* Don't get discouraged, though. There may still be plenty of treasure worth finding.

Casino Countdown

The Bahamas are home to some of the flashiest casinos around, and the islands have become an attractive destination for gambling junkets—trips organized to deliver high rollers to the tables by the planeload. There are now four casinos in operation in the Bahamas: the huge, rainbow-hued *Crystal Palace* at Cable Beach on New Providence; the equally gargantuan but more tastefully decorated *Paradise Island Casino* at the *Atlantis* resort; and the *Princess* and *Lucayan Beach* casinos on Grand Bahama. The *Crystal Palace* and *Paradise Island* casinos are similar in ambience and style. Both have cavernous gaming rooms, huge theaters featuring extravagant stage shows, shops hoping to entice lucky gamblers to spend their winnings, and loud, crowded discos. The casino on Paradise Island is—at 30,000 square feet—one of the world's largest, but there are no windows, and thus nothing to remind you that you are in the Bahamas except the soothing lilt of the dealers' accents. The *Princess,* whose Moorish decor matches Donald Trump's Atlantic City *Taj Mahal* in style and (questionable) taste, and the less crowded *Lucayan Beach* are favored destinations of Florida junkets.

The first casino in the Out Islands is expected to open this year on Great Exuma at the *Bahamas Club.* There is only one casino in the Turks and Caicos, at the *Ramada Turquoise Reef* resort on Provo.

Most of the big casinos offer all the usual diversions: slot machines, blackjack, roulette, craps, and wheels of fortune, plus baccarat for big spenders. The minimum bet at the casinos is $5 (except at baccarat tables, where the stakes are usually *high*), but in the evening this figure tends to rise depending on the day of the week, the crowd, and who's in charge. The Bahamas prohibit their own nationals from gambling, but tourists aren't stopped at the door (the islands are so small that the management knows local residents by sight) or charged admission. Complimentary lessons on the major games are offered daily. Drinks are available free to players at casinos in the Bahamas and for a small charge at the casino in the Turks and Caicos. The minimum age for gambling is 18. Bahamian casinos are open from 10 AM until 4 AM; several keep slot machines operating 24 hours a day. The *Ramada Turquoise Reef* casino on Provo operates from 6 PM to about 1 AM, Mondays through Saturdays (and sometimes Sundays in season).

A Shutterbug's View

The Bahamas and the Turks and Caicos offer more photo opportunities than you could exhaust in a lifetime of visits. There's the hustle and bustle of Bay Street shoppers in Nassau; festive Floridians arriving at the dock in Freeport; the clusters of fishing boats off Bimini and at the yacht haven at Walker's Cay; the surf-kissed beaches throughout the islands; and the simple images provided by islanders going about their daily business.

Sunsets and sailboats, flowers and flamingos, farmers and fisherfolk, pomp and circumstance, *junkanoo* and jump-ups—all the color and excitement the islands have to offer is waiting to be captured on film. Whatever your pleasure—nature photography, portraiture, architecture, or fast-action sports shooting—the diversity of the Bahamas affords a cornucopia of images. Even a beginner can achieve remarkable results with a surprisingly basic set of lenses and filters or a camcorder. Equipment is, in fact, only as valuable as the imagination that puts it to use.

LANDSCAPES AND SEASCAPES Nassau's busy downtown, its historic buildings, and its waterfront area are the favored subjects of most visiting photographers. But the island's green spaces, bustling Potter's Cay, and the rest of New Providence provide numerous photo possibilities. East of Nassau, for instance, lies a residential area with many unusual homes, including one built in the shape of a lighthouse. West of town, at Cable Beach and in the heights above, are even more luxurious residences, including former Prime Minister Pindling's home and the former residence of Mrs. Harry Oakes, the widow of the near-legendary financier. On the south shore of New Providence is the tiny community of Adelaide, where photographers can capture images of a placid lifestyle that has all but disappeared from the rest of the island.

The more pristine—and much less photographed—Turks and Caicos Islands offer a range of unusual landscapes: Salt Cay's eerie, chalk-white salinas (salt ponds), dotted with abandoned windmills, provide an almost postapocalyptic image. And if you're on the island in the late winter or early spring, you may be lucky enough to photograph a giant humpback whale swimming up Turks Island Passage to its spawning grounds.

Color and form are the obvious ingredients in these types of photos, and how you frame your pictures can be as important as getting the proper exposure. Study the shapes, angles, and colors that make up the scene, and create a composition that uses them to best advantage.

Lighting is another vital component of landscapes and seascapes. Take advantage of the richer colors of early morning and late afternoon whenever possible. The overhead light of midday is often harsh and without the shadows that can add to the drama of a scene. This is when a polarizer is used to best effect. Most polarizers come with a mark on the rotating ring. If you can aim at your subject and point that marker at the sun, the sun's rays are likely to be right for the polarizer to be effective. If not, stick to your skylight filter, underexposing slightly if the scene is particularly bright. Most light meters respond to an overall light balance, with the result that bright areas may appear burned out.

Although a standard 50mm to 55mm lens may work well in some landscape situations, most photographers will benefit from a 20mm to 28mm wide-angle lens. A beach shot from a hotel balcony, for example, is the kind of panorama that fits beautifully into a wide-angle format, allowing not only the overview but also the inclusion in the foreground of people or other points of interest to provide a sense of perspective. For instance, try including people in the foreground of a shot of the Paradise Island Bridge.

To isolate specific elements of any scene, use your telephoto lens. A particular carving on a historic church or the interplay of light and shadow on a pier lined with boats can make lovely shots. The successful use of a telephoto means developing your eye for detail.

PEOPLE As with taking pictures of people anywhere, there are going to be times in the Bahamas when a camera is an intrusion. People are often sensitive to having a camera suddenly pointed at them, and a polite request, while getting you a share of refusals, will also provide a chance to shoot some wonderful portraits that capture the spirit of the islands as surely as the scenery does. For candids, an excellent lens is a zoom telephoto in the 70mm to 210mm range; it allows you to remain unobtrusive while the telephoto lens draws the subject closer. And for portraits, a telephoto can be used effectively as close as five or seven feet.

For authenticity and variety, select a place likely to produce interesting subjects. The *Straw Market* in New Providence is an obvious place for visitors, but if it's local color you're after, visit Potter's Cay, where fishermen and produce growers unload their boats every day and the islanders do their shopping. Or go to the village of Gambier, west of Cable Beach, which is more like an Out Islands community than a suburb of Nassau. Take a walk to "Over the Hill," where the less wealthy residents of Nassau live. Aim for shots that tell what's different about the islands. In portraiture, there are several factors to keep in mind. Morning or afternoon light will add richness to skin tones. To avoid harsh facial shadows cast by direct sunlight, shoot where the light is diffused.

SUNSETS When shooting sunsets, keep in mind that the brightness will distort meter readings. When composing a shot directly into the sun, frame the picture in the viewfinder so that only half of the sun is included. Read the meter, set, and shoot. Whenever there is this kind of unusual lighting, shoot a few frames in half-step increments, both over and under the meter reading. Bracketing, as this is called, can provide a range of images, the best of which may well be other than the one shot at the meter's recommended setting.

Use any lens for sunsets. A wide-angle is good when the sky is filled with color-streaked clouds, when the sun is partially hidden, or when you're close to an object that silhouettes dramatically against the sky.

Telephotos also produce wonderful silhouettes, either with the sun as a backdrop or against the palette of a brilliant sunset sky. Bracket again here. For the best silhouettes, wait 10 to 15 minutes after sunset. Unless using a very fast film, a tripod is recommended.

Orange, magenta, and split-filters are often used to accentuate a sunset's picture potential. Orange will help turn even a gray sky into something approaching a photogenic finale to the day and can provide particularly beautiful shots linking the sky with the sun reflected in the ocean. If the sunset is already bold in hue, the orange will overwhelm the natural colors, as will a red filter, though both can still produce dramatic, if highly unrealistic, results.

NIGHT If you think that picture possibilities end at sunset, you're presuming that night photography is the exclusive domain of the professional. If you've got a tripod, all you'll need is a cable release to attach to your camera to assure a steady exposure (which is often timed in minutes rather than fractions of a second).

For situations such as evening shows outdoors at a hotel or nighttime harbor cruises, a strobe does the trick, but beware: Flash units are often used improperly. You can't take a view of the skyline with a flash. It may reach out as far as 30 feet, but that's it. On the other hand, a flash used too close to a subject may result in overexposure, resulting in a "blown-out" effect. With most cameras, strobes will work with a maximum shutter speed of 1/125 or 1/250 of a second. If you set the exposure properly and shoot within range, you should come up with pretty sharp results.

CLOSE-UPS Whether of people or of such objects as flower blossoms, close-ups can add another dimension to your photography. There are a number of shooting options, one of which is to use a 70mm or a 210mm lens at its closest focusable distance. Unless you're working in bright sunlight, a tripod will be worthwhile. If you are very near your subject and there is a good deal of reflective light, it may pay to underexpose a bit in relation to the meter reading.

If you do not have a telephoto lens, you can still shoot close-ups using a set of magnification filters. Filter packs of one-, two-, and three-time magnification are available, converting your lens into a close-up lens. Even better is a special macro lens designed for close-up photography.

A SHORT PHOTOGRAPHIC TOUR

Here are some of the islands' truly great pictorial perspectives.

POTTER'S CAY, New Providence Early in the morning, the photo possibilities here are endless, with the rows of vendors' stalls fronted by heaps of produce: vivid green limes, bright red tomatoes, brown-skinned onions, multicolored peppers, bright orange carrots, yellow and green bananas, and green-crowned pineapples. The conch sellers are partially hidden from view by the piles of pink-tinged shells that are stacked in front of them; island women fry their conch fritters to a golden brown in vats of bubbling-hot oil; and the jostling crowds of shoppers pick up their daily groceries. At the outer piers, the mail boats—even in this modern age—are still the lifeline to the Out Islands, carrying mail, bulky cargo, and occasional passengers. An unusual perspective can be gained by shooting from the Paradise Island Bridge. There are sidewalks on each side of the bridge's roadway, so no matter what time of day you're shooting, one view or the other will be shadow-free. (Higher up on the Paradise Island Bridge, you can get some spectacular views of downtown Nassau, the cruise-ship dock, the *Coral World* observation tower to the west, and Nassau's East End to the east.)

DIXON HILL LIGHTHOUSE, San Salvador The temptation on San Salvador will be to shoot anything and everything having to do with Christopher Columbus and the Bahamian claim that this was the island on which the Great Navigator first set foot in the New World. But most of the Columbus memorabilia is of recent origin, while the lighthouse is nearly 140 years old. One of the few remaining hand-operated, kerosene-powered lights in the world, it sits 163 feet above high water, has 40,000 candlepower, and its beam is visible up to 19 miles out to sea; its light emits a double flash every 25 seconds. Its internal workings—with weights that must be pulled by hand, much like those on an antique grandfather clock—can be photographed, but a strobe or flash is necessary. The lighthouse's observation deck provides views of the island's network of saltwater, sea-fed lakes, connected by channels hacked by hand out of solid limestone.

PREACHER'S CAVE, Eleuthera This wide-mouthed cavern has a vaulted roof that soars as high as 100 feet in some places, providing plenty of light (and a bat-free experience for those on the ground). There is a caretaker who keeps the cave clean, so no trash or litter mars your picture. This is the cave where William Sayles led his band of shipwrecked survivors, the remnants of the Eleutherian Adventurers who settled the islands in the middle of the 17th century. The cave offered these devout Puritans shelter and a natural site for religious services. Holes in the cave's roof allow shafts of light to penetrate the interior, enhancing its otherworldly ambience.

THE SALINAS OF GRAND TURK Grand Turk was settled for one reason: the production of salt. In the 1640s, Bermudian salt rakers established the industry by damming the naturally occurring salt ponds and clearing trees to reduce rainfall and increase evaporation. Salt production ended only about 30 years ago and the vast ponds remain, now crisscrossed by causeways and attractive to waterfowl of all sorts. Shoot early in the morning, with the sun peeping over the hills in the east; in the morning hours there's also a better chance of luring one or more of the island's roving donkeys, or perhaps a lone stroller or solitary car, into the picture.

JUNKANOO Whether you are in the islands for the real thing on *Boxing Day* (December 26) or *New Year's Day* or find yourself at one of the mock *junkanoos* staged for visitors at other times of the year, this is an opportunity to capture a quintessentially Bahamian experience. It's one time that islanders don't mind at all if you point your camera at them and snap away. In fact, many of the dancers and revelers will stop and pose for you. The costumes are unbelievably colorful and elaborate, but the action is often so fast that you have to be prepared to shoot at a moment's notice. You will need a strobe or flash for a nighttime *junkanoo* (the *Boxing Day* and *New Year's Day* festivities begin around 3 or 4 AM). Another problem you may have to cope with are the surging crowds joining the action; they may be more preoccupied with having fun than with helping you take the perfect picture.

Directions

Introduction

What best describes the Bahamas and Turks and Caicos Islands? Glitzy casinos, championship golf courses, and great scuba diving and game fishing come readily to mind. But most folks don't know about the 18th-century saltbox houses in the Abacos and on Eleuthera, each painted a different pastel shade; the grand Georgian homes on Queen Street in Nassau; the ruined Loyalist plantations on Eleuthera; or the old saltworks on the Turks Islands. Nor do many visitors think of spending a Sunday morning in a whitewashed church listening to a rousing revival meeting, or dancing to 1950s-style *goombay* music or a rake-and-scrape band on a Saturday night, or watching a *junkanoo* parade.

There is more to the Bahamas than most people realize, and each island has something special to offer. Anglers go to Bimini; sailors to Abaco and the Exumas; and divers to Andros, the exquisite coral gardens off the Abacos, and the pristine reefs off Grand Turk and Providenciales. But don't expect to find everything on each of the islands. There's no casino on San Salvador, but there is great surfing nearby; and while Grand Turk has little in the way of wildlife aside from a few herds of wild donkeys, it has some of the finest reefs this side of Australia.

Here, then, are a dozen island tours. They first take you to the best-known isles: New Providence (including its capital, Nassau, and Paradise Island just offshore) and Grand Bahama. Then they follow a zigzag course through the outlying isles, tacking southwest from Grand Bahama to Bimini; east to the Abacos; south to Andros; east and south to the slender isles of Eleuthera, Cat Island, and the Exumas; and even farther east to tiny San Salvador, where Christopher Columbus *may* have landed in 1492. The tours end in the Turks and Caicos, the British Crown Colony more than 500 miles east of Florida. Several of our tours describe walks through historic towns like Nassau, Harbour Island just off Eleuthera, George Town in the Exumas, and Cockburn Town on Grand Turk. For those with a good map and time to spare, there are also several driving routes. The hardy may want to follow some of the driving routes by bike, though the Bahamas aren't as bike-and moped-friendly as, say, Bermuda. Along the way, our tours point out old plantations and historic churches, great restaurants (or, on the remote isles, the only eateries open after 2 PM), pineapple farms, rum factories, and the perfect spots for a variety of activities, from swimming to spelunking to shelling. Finding the best places in the Bahamas can take some patience and perseverance, but the rewards are well worth the effort.

Note: Unless otherwise specified, all phone numbers are in the 809 area code (for information on dialing the Turks and Caicos, see *Telephone* in GETTING READY TO GO).

Nassau

The capital of the Bahamas, Nassau has attracted a mixed crowd over the years. In the 17th century, Puritans settled in Nassau (known as Charles Town until 1695), and the Anglican church dominated life here until well into the 19th century. Freebooters came to Bay Street to sell their stolen goods, Spanish galleons periodically assaulted Nassau's forts, and American revolutionaries captured the town briefly in 1776. Pirates and money-grabbing clergymen abandoned Nassau long ago, to be replaced by gamblers, tourists, and offshore banks. Despite this hurly-burly, the town has remained pleasantly civilized and old-fashioned. Skyscrapers and sprawling developments are strictly controlled, and many of the town's historic forts and government buildings have been given a face-lift. Rambling mansions overlook the harbor on the east side of town, and the pastel Georgian houses that line some shady side streets are more than 200 years old.

There is so much to do and see in Nassau that it's best to have a plan of attack before starting out. For those visitors planning a lunchtime break, keep in mind that most restaurants open between 11 AM and noon and close around 2:30 PM. When a cruise ship is in port, most restaurants are jammed, so be prepared for a long wait—or pack a picnic basket and head for the *Nassau Botanical Gardens* or *Fort Charlotte* (see *New Providence* in this section). The walking tour described here, which takes in several picturesque and historic spots, can be completed in a leisurely few hours.

The tour starts in Rawson Square in the center of town, just steps from Prince George Wharf, where cruise ships are berthed. Situated along the wharf is the new *Junkanoo Expo,* which offers a real cultural treat to those not lucky enough to be in town during the *junkanoo* parades on *Boxing Day* (December 26) and *New Year's Day.* The interactive museum and entertainment center showcases the colorful costumes and instruments of this Bahamian celebration. The museum is open daily; admission charge (phone: 356-6266). West of Rawson Square, along Parliament Street is the surrey depot, where horse-and-buggy tours of the city begin. Opposite is the *Churchill Building,* where the prime minister and some government ministries conduct their affairs. The statue in the square is of Sir Milo Butler, a former grocer who became the country's first governor after the Bahamas won its independence from Great Britain in 1973.

Fronting the south side of Rawson Square is busy Bay Street. Just across it is Parliament Square, presided over by a statue of a youthful Queen Victoria. The stately building to the queen's right houses more government offices. To her left is the *House of Assembly,* where the oldest governing body in continuous session in the New World convenes. The *Senate*—the less powerful legislative branch—meets in the building behind the queen.

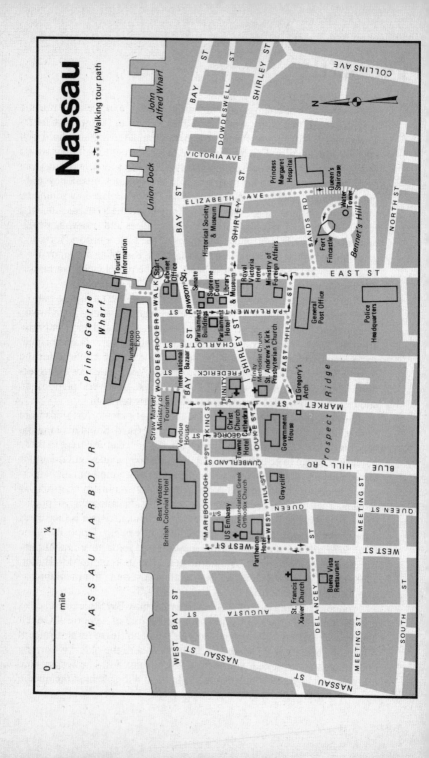

Nassau

····· Walking tour path

NASSAU HARBOUR

Prince George Wharf

Union Dock

John Alfred Wharf

COLLINS AVE

0   ¼   mile

N

WEST BAY ST

WEST BAY ST

Best Western
British Colonial Hotel

Tourist
Information

Junkanoo
Expo

Straw Market/
Ministry of
Tourism

Vendue
House

WOODES ROGERS WALK

Start

Cabinet
Office

Rawson Sq.

Senate

Supreme
Court

Library
& Museum

Parliament
Buildings

Parliament
Hotel

Historical Society
& Museum

Royal
Victoria
Hotel

Ministry of
Foreign Affairs

Princess
Margaret
Hospital

Queen's
Staircase

Water
Tower

Fort
Fincastle

Benner's Hill

NORTH ST

EAST ST

BAY ST

BAY ST

VICTORIA AVE

ELIZABETH AVE

SHIRLEY AVE

DOWDESWELL ST

SHIRLEY ST

BAY ST

SHIRLEY ST

SANDS RD.

International
Bazaar

BAY ST

CHARLOTTE ST

FREDERICK ST

SHIRLEY ST

PARLIAMENT ST

EAST ST

EAST HILL ST

MARKET ST

TRINITY PL

Trinity
Methodist Church

St. Andrew's Kirk
Presbyterian Church

Christ
Church
Cathedral

Towne
Hotel

KING ST

GEORGE ST

Government
House

Gregory's
Arch

Prospect Ridge

General
Post Office

Police
Headquarters

BLUE HILL RD

DUKE ST

CUMBERLAND ST

MARLBOROUGH ST

US Embassy

Annunciation Greek
Orthodox Church

Graycliff

HILL ST

WEST ST

QUEEN ST

WEST ST

Parthenon
Hotel

St. Francis
Xavier Church

AUGUSTA ST

DELANCEY ST

Buena Vista
Restaurant

MEETING ST

MEETING ST

QUEEN ST

WEST ST

SOUTH ST

NASSAU ST

NASSAU ST

These modified-Georgian structures date from the late-18th and early-19th centuries.

Behind the *Senate* building stands the *Supreme Court*. A serene little square separates the courthouse and the *Nassau Public Library and Museum;* in its center stands a cenotaph commemorating the Bahamians who died in both world wars. (A separate plaque honors four members of the Royal Bahamian Defense Forces who were killed in 1980 when their craft was sunk by Cuban MIGs—a traumatic incident that made a deep impression on the national consciousness.) The library, housed in a yellow octagonal building constructed in the 1790s, was once a jail. History buffs should visit the second floor, which is devoted to Bahamian exhibits, including straw plaiting, Bahamian postage stamps, and several artifacts, including a *duho,* a low stone bench made by Lucaya Indians. Climb the stairs to the third floor verandah, which affords a fine view of the city center. The library and museum are open daily; no admission charge (phone: 322-4907).

West of the library, across Parliament Street, is the *Parliament* hotel, built just before World War II. The sandbox trees in front are said to be two centuries old. The nearby *Pick-A-Dilly* restaurant caters to tourists, who come for the daiquiris, and Nassau barristers, who seem to prefer Scotch and sodas and martinis (see "Eating Out" in *Bahamas,* THE ISLANDS).

Continue down Parliament Street to the post office, where collectors can buy colorful Bahamian stamps. A short walk away is Bennet's Hill, which has a magnificent view of Nassau Harbour. To get there, walk east on East Hill Street and turn left onto East Street, right onto Shirley Street, and straight down to Elizabeth Avenue. On the northwest corner is the *Bahamas Historical Society and Museum,* where historic maps and photographs are on display. It's closed Thursdays and Sundays; no admission charge (phone: 322-4231).

Proceed south (away from the harbor) on Elizabeth Avenue to the *Queen's Staircase,* hewn out of limestone blocks sometime in the late 1830s. The stairway leads to Bennet's Hill and an 18th-century fort. Don't give up—the view is worth every one of the 65 steps. Visitors who can muster the energy should climb the 126-foot tower at the top, where the view is even better, particularly at dusk, when the town's lights begin to wink on.

Nearby is *Fort Fincastle,* which was built by Lord Dunmore, a former royal governor of Virginia who came here during the American Revolution. The fort's shape and deck-like ramparts remind some visitors of a Mississippi stern-wheeler. No shot was ever fired in anger from the fort, and it served as a lighthouse until 1816. The fort is open continuously; the tower is closed weekends. There's an admission charge to climb the tower.

Return to the post office by taking the footpath that leads to Sands Road; take a right onto East Street and a left onto East Hill Street. The 19th-century pink-and-white building on the north side of East Hill houses the *Ministry of Foreign Affairs;* it was once the home of Lord Beaverbrook, the newspaper tycoon. Nearby is the modern headquarters of the *Royal*

Bank of Canada, built on the site of an old home called *Glenwood Gardens.* Woodes Rogers, the 18th-century buccaneer-turned-governor, is reputedly buried in the yard. The grave is said to be marked with a skull and cross-bones; don't bother looking for it, though, for the grounds are off limits.

You are now standing on Prospect Ridge, once the dividing line between Nassau's rich and poor. Most of the town's white population lived along the waterfront, while blacks lived "over the hill." Laborers trudged up the steep ridge each night until a tunnel, called *Gregory's Arch,* was put through in 1850. The poor lived in tumbledown villages like Grant's Town, which was settled in the 1820s by freed slaves; the town is now a middle class neighborhood shaded with palms, casuarinas, and royal poincianas.

Ramble down East Hill Street to Market Street; *St. Andrew's Kirk* will be to the right. This fine 19th-century Presbyterian church housed the first non-Anglican congregation in the Bahamas. Straight ahead, on a high hill just west of Market Street, is *Government House,* the official residence of the Governor-General of the Bahamas. (Bahamian governors are mostly figureheads, with the true political power resting in the hands of the prime minister.) The original mansion was destroyed in a hurricane in 1929 and was replaced by this pink-and-white neocolonial building a few years later. A 12-foot statue of Christopher Columbus stands on the steep flight of steps leading to the main doors. The front gates are usually closed at 5 PM, but you can slip in through the side entrances on Market and Cumberland Streets. On alternate Saturdays, the grounds are open for the spit-and-polish changing-of-the-guard ceremony, which takes place at 10 AM sharp.

On the west side of *Government House,* where West Hill Street meets Blue Hill Road, is *Graycliff,* one of the Bahamas' special hostelries. The handsome Georgian house was built in the 1720s by Captain John Howard Graysmith, who made his fortune plundering ships along the Spanish Main. During the American Revolution, it was used as a mess hall for troops of the West Indian Regiment. Polly Leach, a friend of Al Capone's, ran a hotel here in the 1920s. The house was later bought by Lord and Lady Dudley, who restored it with unimpeachable taste. Twelve rooms of the old house have been converted into guestrooms—there are suites and cottages as well—and the restaurant is one of the best in the Bahamas. (Also see "Checking In" and "Eating Out" in *Bahamas,* THE ISLANDS.)

Continue west on West Hill Street. The wall along this street is built with stones from the oldest church on New Providence, which was destroyed by fire in 1703. Across West Street is the *Church of St. Francis Xavier,* erected in 1886. Just south of the church on Delancey Street is the very good *Buena Vista* restaurant (see "Eating Out" in *Bahamas,* THE ISLANDS). Walk north, toward the waterfront, on West Street; on the right side of the street is the beautiful little *Annunciation Greek Orthodox Church.* Pass the church and turn right on Marlborough; walk the short block to Queen Street, and turn right again, which will bring you to the front of the *US Embassy.* Peer through the dense foliage at the stately old homes that line Queen Street; some are more than 200 years old. The pink *Best Western British Colonial* hotel stands near the corner of Queen and Marlborough Streets. Built in 1923, it was run for a time by the near-legendary Nassau entrepreneur Sir Harry Oakes. On the grounds is a replica of *Blackbeard's Well,* named after the infamous pirate, whose real name was Edward Teach.

Continue east on Marlborough and turn right onto George Street, near *Christ Church,* an Island-Gothic Episcopal cathedral. Though the country hasn't been officially Anglican since 1869, many state ceremonies still take place here. The opening ceremony of the Supreme Court, for example, begins with a procession of robed and bewigged judges and barristers to *Christ Church,* accompanied by the *Royal Bahamas Police Band.* Farther up George Street, next to the *Towne* hotel, is a curious old mansion named *Georgeside* that dates from the late 1700s and is said not to have a single right angle, inside or out. (The house is closed to the public.)

A left turn onto Duke Street leads to Market Street, just below *Gregory's Arch.* Proceed north, toward the water; the *Straw Market* is dead ahead. On the right side of the street is the huge *Central Bank Building.* Across from it are two buildings that were once private homes: *Balcony House,* built in the late 18th century, and the somewhat newer *Verandah House.* The Central Bank of the Bahamas, which now owns both houses, plans to open *Balcony House* to the public; *Verandah House* is used for bank functions. Halfway down the block on the right is Trinity Place, a short street that leads to *Trinity Methodist Church,* reconstructed in 1869 after a hurricane.

Backtrack to Market Street and continue north across Bay Street once again. To the left is *Vendue House,* where chattel of all sorts, including slaves, once was auctioned. Today it houses the *Pompey Museum,* where exhibits trace the history and culture of Bahamian slavery. The museum is named after a slave on Exuma who led a revolt in 1830 that resulted in the slaves getting better working hours and the right not to be relocated. Other displays include a slave auction block, colonial-era memorabilia, and a full-sized replica of a chattel house. The artwork of the famous Bahamian painter Amos Ferguson is on permanent exhibit on the museum's second floor. The museum is closed Sundays; admission charge (phone: 326-3566).

At the *Straw Market* on Bay Street, young women will weave you a basket or plait your hair—with beads, if you like—for a dollar or two a strand. The offices of the *Bahamas Ministry of Tourism* occupy the same building. They're closed weekends (phone: 322-7500). North is the waterfront and Woodes Rogers Walk, named for the onetime pirate and former governor.

Stroll east along the walk toward Prince George Wharf, where the cruise ships dock. At the intersection of Charlotte Street is the *Nassau International Bazaar.* Among the shops here is the *Tropical Fine Art Gallery* (phone: 325-7492), where works by watercolorist Darman Stubbs are on display; the gallery is closed Sundays. The wharf, where the water taxis chug back and forth to and from Paradise Island, is just a few paces from Rawson Square, where this tour began.

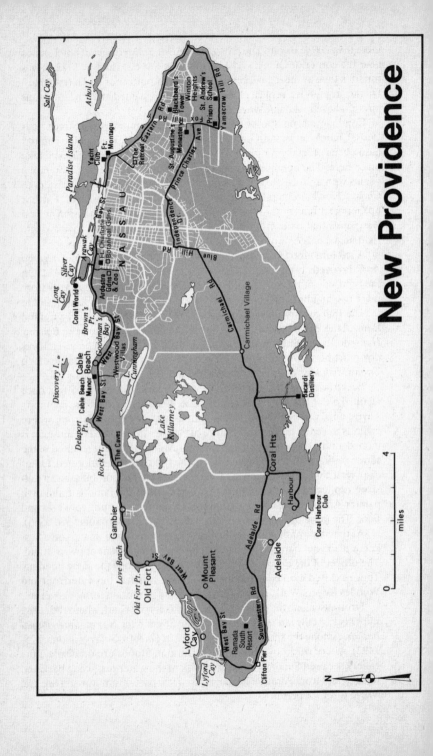

New Providence

New Providence

Two out of every three Bahamians live on New Providence; in fact, the island's population (172,000 at last count) has grown so much in recent years that the government must now import water from Andros. Settled in 1656 by a band of Puritans from Bermuda, New Providence was later chosen as the site of the colony's capital because of its deep natural harbor and abundant fresh water supply. Most of the island's settlements are clustered along the coast; the flatlands in the interior are covered with scrub and groves of palmetto and pine. While the capital city of Nassau is the main attraction here (see *Nassau* in this section), there are plenty of other places worth seeing.

This tour takes a counterclockwise swing around the island, which measures roughly 22 miles long and 7 miles wide. Beginning at Nassau and stopping at some historic forts, grand homes, and quiet beaches along the way, the route merits a leisurely day, whether you go by moped, rental car, or taxi. Celebrity hunters may wish to hire a guide, as no enterprising local soul has yet published a Hollywood-style map to the homes of notables.

Pick up a *Bahamas Trailblazers Map* (offered free at hotels, car rental agencies, and all *Ministry of Tourism* offices) and head west out of Nassau along West Bay Street. About a half mile out of town, turn left at Marcus Bethel Drive and follow the road around to the right to *Fort Charlotte,* atop the hill behind *Clifford Park,* where the annual *Independence Day* (July 10) festivities are held. Built between 1787 and 1789 to protect Nassau's western harbor, the fort was the pet project of Lord Dunmore, then the Governor of the Bahamas. It soon became known as "Dunmore's Folly" because its construction cost about four times the amount budgeted. The largest of New Providence's many fortifications, it is made of solid limestone buttressed with cedar. It was touted as the most impregnable of Nassau's bastions, but the claim was never tested, for it never came under attack. A $1-million restoration was completed several years ago, and it's worth spending an hour or so touring its dungeons, reputed torture chamber, seemingly bottomless well, and drawbridge, which spans the waterless moat. The barricades run about 300 feet along the crest of a hill overlooking the harbor. The fort is closed Sundays. There's no admission charge, but expect to pay a tip if you engage one of the freelance guides who always seem to be loitering around (no phone).

Return to West Bay Street and turn left, heading west again for another half mile to a sign pointing the way to what may well be New Providence's most popular attraction: *Coral World.* Turn right at the sign and drive over the bridge. This is Arawak Cay, an island built by the Bahamian government in the late 1960s as a place to keep the huge storage tanks that hold fresh water shipped in from Andros. Follow the road to Silver Cay, site of the vast *Coral World* complex. Here visitors stand within a large, glass-enclosed underwater observatory. Outside is a live coral reef, with sharks, moray eels, spiny lobsters, and rainbow-hued tropical fish—all moving about in their natural habitat. There is also an underwater snorkeling trail, pools with stingrays and sea turtles, and a shark tank. Young children can visit the shallow "petting pool," where they can touch harmless conch, hermit crabs, starfish, and sea cucumbers. The complex is open daily; admission charge (phone: 328-1036).

From *Coral World* return to West Bay Street, turn right, and after a short block turn left on Chippingham Road. Straight ahead are the peaceful *Nassau Botanical Gardens,* spread over 18 acres of a former limestone quarry. Lush tropical foliage flourishes alongside succulents that thrive in arid regions of the Bahamas. One garden is planted with shrubs used by "bush doctors" on remote cays. There is also a grotto fashioned out of hundreds of conch shells. The gardens are open daily; admission charge (phone: 323-5975). Just down the street are the *Ardastra Gardens and Zoo.* The zoo—the only one in the Bahamas—has a small but excellent collection of monkeys, snakes, margay cats, and tropical birds. There are also a blue-and-green Bahamas parrot (an endangered species), several varieties of iguana, black swans, and peacocks. Children shouldn't miss the trained flamingos, which march briskly in perfect unison to music at 11 AM and 2 and 4 PM. The gardens and zoo are both open daily; admission charge (phone: 323-5806).

Return to West Bay Street and turn left, continuing west. The road twists sharply near Brown's Point, known locally as "Go-Slow Bend." The view is lovely, with Goodman's Bay on the right and the green lawns of the *Cable Beach Golf Club* (phone: 327-6000) on the left. This is the entrance to Cable Beach, named after the first undersea telephone cable; completed in 1892, it runs from this beach to Jupiter, Florida. During the 1930s and 1940s, Cable Beach boasted a number of mansions owned by the rich and famous; over the years, most have been supplanted by resorts and hotels. Two markets selling hats, baskets, and other hand-crafted straw items flourish on the south side of the road directly across from the larger hotels. Farther down the road, condominiums and apartments are springing up across from the beach.

Continue straight on West Bay Street for about five blocks. To see one of the island's most exclusive neighborhoods, turn left onto Malcolm Avenue, across from *Cable Beach Manor.* The area, known as both Westwood Villas and Skyline Drive, was granted by the Crown to Sir Harry Oakes, the Canadian gold mining baron who moved to the Bahamas in the 1930s. His estate stretched about 7 miles from east to west, past the south shore of Lake Cunningham, the second-largest of the island's saltwater ponds. After Oakes's murder in 1943 (the case remains unsolved), his widow lived in this neighborhood until her death. Nearby, on Ridge Road, is the home of former Prime Minister Lynden O. Pindling. Many other government officials live in this area, as do well-heeled Americans, Canadians, and Britons.

Continue along West Bay Street through the roundabout and over Sandy Point Bridge, where pastel townhouses and several expensive yachts line the inlet. Farther west is Delaport Point, where pirates once hid out, according to local legend. Just down the road is *Rock Point,* an estate where scenes from the James Bond film *Thunderball* were shot. On the left, just before Blake Road, are some caves on what used to be the Oakes estate. Arawak Indians purportedly took refuge in them; some locals say Sir Harry found buried treasure here (like many stories about him, it's probably untrue).

At the fork in the road, bear right (you're still on West Bay Street, but there's no sign). Farther down, on the inland side of the road, is the village of Gambier, named for the brothers Gambier. (One was a buccaneer and the other a Governor of the Bahamas—vocations that in the old days weren't all that dissimilar.) A sign proclaims that this village is the oldest permanent settlement in New Providence (it was founded in 1807 by freed slaves). The traditional, close-knit community is much like settlements found in the Out Islands. Near here, the property owned by Oakes ends and the former estate of Harold G. Christie begins. One of the wealthiest of the island's real-estate magnates, Christie was rumored by some to have been involved in Oakes's death. From here, the road parallels Love Beach and skirts several secluded seaside homes, including one owned by singer Julio Iglesias. Offshore is the Sea Garden, a reef favored by snorkelers.

Next comes the district of Old Fort, where the sand is as white and fine as sugar. Stately homes block the view, though, and the only way to see the beach is from the water. Near *St. Paul's Church* the homes begin to thin out until you reach Lyford Cay, which is linked to the main island by a causeway. Harold Christie built a few houses here, but it was Canadian brewing magnate and horse racing enthusiast E. P. Taylor who turned the cay into "the Beverly Hills of the Bahamas" some 30 years ago. The Fords, Vanderbilts, and Rockefellers built homes in this exclusive retreat, as did Sean Connery and Eddie Murphy. The golf course and beaches here are private, and guards keep celebrity seekers at bay.

Turn left at the Lyford Cay roundabout and follow the road to Clifton Point, the western tip of the island; the comfortably bourgeois village of Mt. Pleasant is nearby. There are several industries in this area, including a cement factory; a major power plant; the *Commonwealth Brewery,* which makes Kalik beer; and Clifton Pier, where oil tankers unload and cruise ships once docked. Turn right at the *Atlantis Submarine* sign and follow the road to the beach, which is surprisingly pristine, given its industrial surroundings. Until the *Atlantis Submarine* started running tours from here, the beach was virtually deserted, which may be why a few scenes from *Jaws 4: The Revenge* were shot here in 1983. The crooked pier you see appeared 'n the film. Today, visitors can experience an unusual adventure here: diving 90 feet underwater without getting wet. The air conditioned and pressure-controlled *Atlantis* takes 28 passengers on this voyage beneath the sea. The tour begins with a boat ride to the submarine; on the way, a guide points out Golden Cay, a bird sanctuary where scenes from the movies *Splash* and *Cocoon II: The Return* were filmed. During the 50-minute submarine ride, passengers look through large portholes at a lush coral wall, purple tube sponges, two large wrecks that have been turned into artificial reefs, and several varieties of tropical fish, including groupers and yellowtail snappers. The operation is closed Sundays; the cost of the ride includes round-trip transportation from downtown Nassau (phone: 356-3842/5).

From the beach, continue around Clifton Point, where West Bay Street becomes Southwestern Road. Beyond Clifton Pier, the road passes the pastel plantation-style "greathouses" of the *South Ocean* resort. The sprawling property has a championship golf course (reputed to be the best on the island), condominiums, and a topnotch dive shop. (Also see "Golf" and "Checking In" in *Bahamas,* THE ISLANDS.)

Drive east until you come to a well-marked side road (on your right) that leads to the tiny town of Adelaide on the beach. The village was founded in 1832 by Sir James Carmichael Smyth, then Governor of the Bahamas, who named it for the consort of King William IV. It was intended as a settlement for Africans liberated from the Portuguese slave ship *Rosa.* Not too many years ago, it had its own courthouse, jail, and primary school, but the town has dwindled as people move to Nassau to look for work. The beach here is a narrow spit of sand bordering shallow waters, but it does seem to stretch on forever. On most days two or three men sit by the side of the road selling conch shells, starfish, and coconut-husk gimcracks. One of the men, Allen Albury (he's the one with a ruddy face and white beard), has plenty of stories to tell.

Proceed east on the main road—now called Adelaide Road—and take a right-hand turn at the roundabout to get to Coral Harbour. Begun in the mid-1950s, this development was the darling of Miami banker Lindsey Hopkins Jr. Hopkins hoped to make it the premier resort on the island—and might have done so if he hadn't run out of money. Marines from the Royal Bahamas Defense Forces are billeted in barracks behind the ruins of the never-completed hotel, and the golf course, designed by George Fazio, shows signs of neglect. Many of the homes that line the canals and slips—designed so that yachts could be moored right by each door—are for sale or rent, but several neighborhoods look like they are making a comeback. Other areas have a forlorn quality, like a Miami suburb of 30 years ago. A few businesses have hung on in this residential area: three dive shops; the *Coral Harbour Beach Club Villas* bar and restaurant (phone: 362-1443) on the waterfront; and *Happy Trails Stables* (phone: 362-1820), offering horseback riding.

As you leave Coral Harbour, turn right onto the highway (now called Carmichael Road). A mile or two ahead, past a few tempting fruit stands, take a right for the *Bacardi* rum distillery (phone: 362-1412). No tours are offered, but on weekdays visitors are welcome to stop at their *Hospitality Pavilion* for free rum samples. At the intersection of Carmichael and Gladstone Roads, near the *Carmichael Bible Church,* is the former town of Headquarters, which was renamed Carmichael Village in honor of Governor Sir James Carmichael Smyth. Founded in 1825, it was one of three communities officially established by Governor Smyth for liberated slaves. The area east of here is peppered with housing developments built by the government to ease overcrowding in Nassau.

After another 5 miles or so, Carmichael Road runs into Blue (formerly Baillou) Hill Road. Continue north—the traffic may be heavy—past *A. F. Adderley Senior High School.* At the roundabout, distinctively marked by a huge metal rooster sculpture, go three-quarters of the way around and turn onto Independence Drive. If time allows, stop at the *Caribe Bahamas Perfume Factory* to take a self-guided tour of the facility and perhaps buy some perfume at the gift shop; the factory is open daily (phone: 393-2755). The road veers south and becomes Prince Charles Avenue, which is lined with typical middle class Bahamian homes, most with their own satellite dishes. At Fox Hill Road, a left turn leads to the *St. Augustine Roman Catholic Monastery and College* (phone: 364-1331, monastery; 324-1511, college). Built in 1946, this Benedictine abbey was designed by John Hawkes, an architect and Anglican missionary who came to the Bahamas sometime before World War I. Father Jerome, as he was known after his conversion to Catholicism, designed several churches in the islands before retiring to his retreat on Cat Island. The monks are pleased to offer free tours of the monastery. The gift shop here sells goods made by the monks, including freshly baked bread and guava jelly.

A right turn on Fox Hill Road from Prince Charles Avenue leads to the village of Fox Hill, named for Samuel Fox, a slave who became a prosperous landowner after he won his freedom. Several government buildings line the road, including two reformatories and a forbidding prison. Past the prison grounds, turn left onto Yamacraw Hill Road, which passes by *St. Andrew's,* a 50-year-old Anglican school. As the road sweeps north and west, rounding the tip of the island, the homes that line the north shore become increasingly grand. (Somewhere along here the name of the road changes to Eastern.) There is a mansion on the right side of the road that resembles a lighthouse; it was built by a member of the Solomon clan, a wealthy merchant family. Some of the stateliest homes stand on a hill in an area known as Winton Heights, where an old plantation once stood. Here visitors can catch an occasional glimpse of the harbor; Athol Island lies just offshore. On a hill on the inland side stands *Blackbeard's Tower,* a tottery jumble of stones rumored to be the foundations of a tower where the eponymous pirate once watched for ships sailing into the harbor. A narrow unmarked path wedged between two homes—a pink one on the right and a green-and-white one called *Tower Leigh* on the left—leads to the ruins.

Continue west past Brigadoon Estates, site of an eclectic bunch of mansions built around the 1920s by Nassau's elite. A left turn onto Village Road leads to *The Retreat,* an 11-acre estate formerly owned by Arthur and Margaret Langlois and now the home of the *Bahamas National Trust.* The Langloises collected some 200 species of exotic palms, some of which shade the gardens. Guided tours of the house and gardens are conducted Tuesdays, Wednesdays, and Thursdays at noon; you also can take a self-guided tour of only the gardens. The house and gardens are closed weekends; there's a small admission charge (phone: 393-1317). The main road, now called East Bay Street, leads to *Fort Montagu,* which stands on a bluff overlooking the harbor. Completed in 1742, the fort was protected by 17 massive cannons. The ordnance appears to have done little good, for the fort was captured in 1776 by an American force led by Ezekiel Hopkins; again in 1782 by the Spanish; and once again the following year by American Loyalist Andrew Deveaux. Visitors can roam the grounds as they wish; there is no admission charge, and there are no guided tours. The bridge to Paradise Island looms off to the north of the fort; downtown Nassau is about 2 miles to the west. Nearby, all on East Bay Street, are the *Waterloo* nightclub (phone: 393-7324 or 393-0478); the 1930s-era *Nassau Yacht Club* (phone: 393-5366); and the *Nassau Yacht Haven,* where you'll find the *Poop Deck* (phone: 393-8175), a high-spirited bar that's just the place to revive yourself after an island tour.

Paradise Island

Paradise Island, the tiny cay in Nassau Harbour, is proof of the power of advertising. Hog Cay, as it was known until 1959, has been built up, beautified, and marketed so assiduously that it has become a required stop for many travelers to the Bahamas. Visitors who like Las Vegas and Atlantic City won't be disappointed—or surprised. Though the views *from* the island can be magnificent, many of the sights *on* it have a somewhat familiar look. There are no historical landmarks here, and nothing exotic or ethnic, but for those who like kitsch, or who are looking for a break from Nassau's bustle, this is the place.

Though the island's sights may be lackluster, its history is colorful indeed. In the mid-17th century William Sayle, the leader of the Eleutherian Adventurers, a group of Puritans from Bermuda who also settled the island of Eleuthera, bought the 685-acre island, which lies just 600 feet off the shore of New Providence Island. It was he who named it Hog Cay—possibly because he intended to raise pigs here, though it's not clear if he ever did. Forty-odd years later the island was purchased by Bahamian Governor Nicholas Trott for the price of £50, plus an annual rent of a shilling per acre. Trott maintained his claim to the island even after a London court trial and his subsequent removal from office (his ties with several buccaneers had been uncomfortably close).

By the late 19th century, Nassau entrepreneurs had discovered the island's tourist appeal; ferries shuttled wealthy Nassau residents over to pristine Paradise Beach. During this era, American entrepreneur Joseph Lynch (of the brokerage firm Merrill Lynch) bought the island and built a home here.

In the 1930s, the island was sold to Swedish industrialist Axel Wenner-Gren, who moved into Lynch's old house, which he renamed *Shangri-La,* and launched several beautification projects. He did so partly as a favor to his friend the Duke of Windsor, Governor of the Bahamas from 1940 to 1945, who was looking for ways to employ poor islanders during the war. Wenner-Gren dug a large lake, which was fed by canals leading to the sea, and hired a landscaper to create a replica of the gardens at Versailles.

In 1962, after Wenner-Gren's death, the island was bought by American multimillionaire Huntington Hartford, heir to the A&P supermarket fortune. Hartford gave the island its current name and announced plans to turn it into a resort for a discriminating clientele. "There will be no automobiles, no roulette wheels, no honky-tonks on Hog Island," Hartford told *The New York Times.* (He was wrong on all counts.) Hartford took possession of the former Wenner-Gren estate, finished the formal gardens, and transplanted a 12th-century French cloister, stone by stone, to the grounds. The cloister survives, in a sadly deteriorated state, as do many of the sculp-

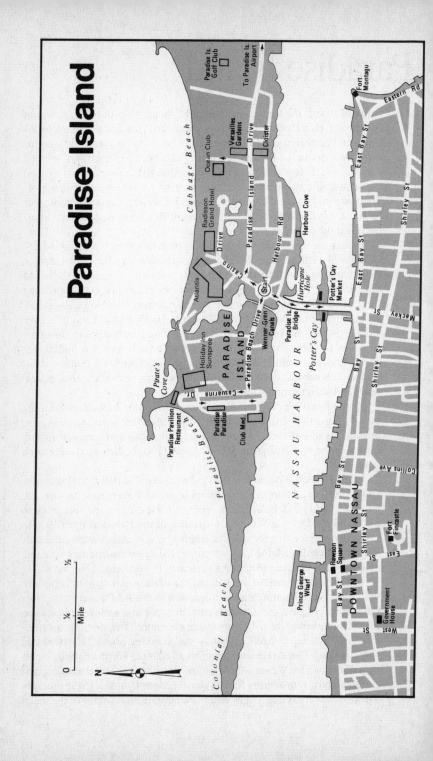

tures Hartford collected, including likenesses—of rather uneven quality—of Franklin D. Roosevelt, African explorer David Livingstone, Hercules, Mephistopheles, Faust, and Napoleon and Josephine.

Hartford also spruced up the island's resorts. Around his estate he built the *Ocean Club,* an 18-hole golf course, the anchorage at Hurricane Hole, and posh riding stables. He also launched a ferry service between the island and downtown Nassau. These ventures, like most of Hartford's projects, generated little profit, and in the late 1960s he sold the island to the Tampa-based Mary Carter Paint Company for about $14 million—considerably less than he reportedly spent refurbishing it.

It didn't take long for the owners of Mary Carter to realize that tourism was more profitable than paint. The company quickly reorganized, and in its new guise, Resorts International, it built the $2-million Paradise Island Bridge in 1967; promoted gambling at the *Paradise Island* casino; and, after American entertainer/entrepreneur Merv Griffin gained control of the company in the 1980s, built the airport on the eastern end of the island. Recently, Resorts International, struggling with financial difficulties, sold its hotels, casino, and airline to Sun International Investments Ltd. Sun International poured $250 million into a total face-lift of its new properties—the *Paradise Island Resort and Casino* (now renamed *Atlantis*), the swanky *Ocean Club,* and *Paradise Paradise.*

What follows are three short walking tours of Paradise Island. To get to the island, take the Paradise Island Bridge. It costs 25¢ per pedestrian or bicycle and $2 per car to cross from Nassau; the return trip is free. The bridge arches high in the center to allow tall ships to glide underneath. Sidewalks run along both sides of the bridge, and the view is equally impressive from both. Look straight down to see the piers at Hurricane Hole on Paradise Island, where deep-sea fishing boats dock in the late afternoon after their daily excursions. To the southwest is the shopping district of downtown Nassau; Prince George Wharf, where cruise liners dock; and, in the distance, Silver Cay. To the southeast is *Fort Montagu* and the fine waterfront homes of east Nassau; tiny Athol Island is to the east, just off Paradise Island. Water taxis also leave for Paradise Island from Dock Five at the Prince George Wharf in downtown Nassau, dropping passengers west of the Paradise Island Bridge, off Casuarina Drive; the fare is $2 one way.

WALK 1

This tour leads to the beaches on the western strand; it's a leisurely 45-minute round trip. At the fountain at the foot of Paradise Island Bridge, turn onto Paradise Beach Drive; the road crosses one of Axel Wenner-Gren's canals and skirts the *Club Land'Or* hotel. Continue down the road past the Shell gas station and turn left at the sign for the *Island* restaurant to see the old seaplane terminal. Planes haven't landed here since the

Paradise Island Airport was built, but the airport restaurant, the *Island,* still serves inexpensive local food; try the conch fritters and stewed fish. (Also see "Eating Out" in *Bahamas,* THE ISLANDS.)

The road dead-ends at Casuarina Drive, and *Club Med* is straight ahead. From here it's a short walk to the left to the Nassau water taxi dock and to the vendors selling pink conch shells, or to the right to the two resort hotels up the road. The drive is lined with stately casuarinas, and a paved footpath runs along the median. Off to the right is the *Holiday Inn Sunspree,* with three restaurants and four bars, including a poolside spot called the *Bonney Anne* that's built like a pirate ship. (Anne Bonney was a pirate—a real swashbuckler, if legend can be believed.) The beach at Pirate's Cove is sheltered and picturesque, but sunbathers take heed: The hotel building casts a shadow on parts of the beach at different times of the day. Bicycles can be rented from a vendor located in the hotel's parking lot. Across the road is the pink, two-story *Paradise Paradise* resort. The waves here are calm, as they are at the *Club Med* beach a stone's throw away, and both beaches are wide, clean, attractive, and accessible to the public.

WALK 2

Our second walk, which will take about three and a half hours, starts from the fountain and heads straight up Casino Drive, a continuation of the road across the Paradise Island Bridge. It's about a five-minute stroll to Paradise Island Drive, past a long block of shops and boutiques at the *Paradise Shopping Plaza.* Turn right at the *Comfort Suites* hotel and walk about a mile to the *Ocean Club.* Follow the signs to the swimming pool, where there is a fine view of the *Versailles Gardens,* the cloister, and, in the background, the east end of Nassau (it's so close you can't even see the water separating the two islands). The gazebo just beyond the cloister is a good breezy spot for a picnic. There's a broad view of the harbor; notice the boats heading for the market at Potter's Cay. A half mile farther east on Paradise Island Drive is the *Paradise Island Golf Club* (phone: 363-3925) on the left, and a block farther on the right, the *Paradise Harbour Club and Marina* (phone: 363-2992). About another half mile farther east, at the end of the road, is the *Paradise Island Airport.*

WALK 3

The last walk is a short stroll of an hour to Potter's Cay, a busy market beneath the Nassau side of the Paradise Island Bridge. (It's no longer a cay, but a finger of land extending into the bay.) Potter's Cay is busy early in the day, when the chefs of the big restaurants in Nassau are rumored to come here to get their produce. Stalls stocked with fish, conch, and fresh produce—most of it from the Out Islands—stretch in parallel rows underneath the bridge, and vendors sell mangoes, pomegranates, passion fruit, sapodillas, and custard apples. Try a conch salad or hot conch fritter or two, or stroll around and look at the baskets and shell gewgaws for sale.

Beyond the stalls are packing houses where seafood is processed for shipment to the US and elsewhere. Several mail boats, the little freighters that are the lifeline of the Out Islands, are moored on the east end of the cay. In addition to delivering mail, the boats also bring manufactured goods from Nassau to remote islands; they return laden with crates of produce, bales of cotton or fragrant tree bark, and other agricultural products destined for wholesalers in Nassau. The boats also carry passengers to and from the Out Islands at low fares, but be forewarned that the schedules of arrivals and departures are approximate (phone: 322-2049). A cautionary note: Potter's Cay is a fine place to take pictures, but vendors may put up a fuss unless you ask permission to photograph them. If you've just bought something, however, they're far more inclined to pose.

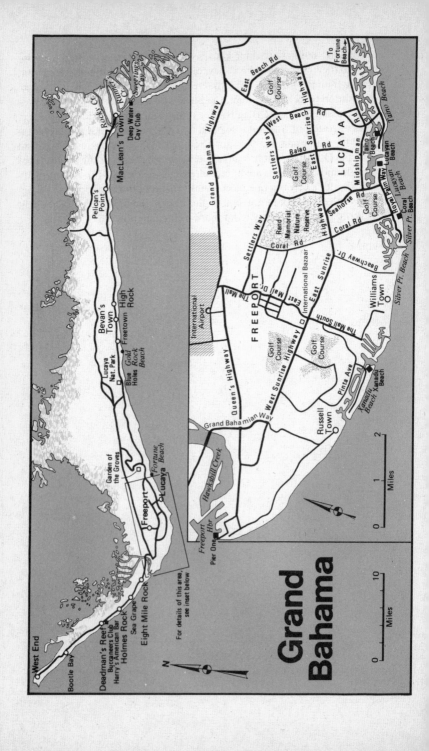

Grand Bahama

West End
Bootie Bay
Deadman's Reef
Buccaneers Club
Harry's American Bar
Holmes Rock
Sea Grape
Eight Mile Rock

Freeport
Lucaya
Fortune Beach
Garden of the Groves
Lucaya Nat. Park
Blue Holes Beach
Gold Rock Beach
Freetown
High Rock
Bevan's Town
Pelican's Point
MacLean's Town
Deep Water Cay Club
Sweeting's Cay
Runner's Cay
Rocky Cr.

For details of this area, see inset below

N

0   10
Miles

Inset

Grand Bahama Highway
East Beach Rd
Golf Course
Fortune Beach
To Fortune Beach
West Beach Rd
Taino Beach
Settlers Way
Balao Rd
East Sunrise Highway
Golf Course
Taino Beach
LUCAYA
Midshipman
Royal Palm Way
Lucayan Beach
Coral Beach
Seahorse Rd
Rand Memorial Nature Reserve
Coral Rd
Golf Course
Silver Pt. Beach
Settlers Way
Coral Rd
Beachway Dr.
FREEPORT
International Bazaar
East Sunrise Highway
Mall Dr.
The Mall
East
Williams Town
International Airport
The Mall South
Golf Course
Golf Course
Pinta Ave
West Sunrise Highway
Xanadu Beach
Queen's Highway
Russell Town
Grand Bahamian Way
Hawksbill Creek
Freeport Hbr
Pier One

N

0   1   2
Miles

Grand Bahama

Just 55 miles off the coast of Florida, Grand Bahama is the fourth-largest island in the Bahamian chain. Its population has exploded since the twin developments of Freeport and Lucaya were launched here in the 1950s and early 1960s, but for many years it was sparsely settled. Its original inhabitants were the Siboney, a Stone Age people from Cuba closely related to the Arawak; they were later displaced by the Lucaya, who migrated to the Bahamas sometime around AD 1000. Many of the Lucaya were carried off as slaves shortly after Columbus landed in the Bahamas in 1492; others were wiped out by war and disease, and Grand Bahama remained virtually uninhabited for the next 300 years, except for a few marauding pirates and a Tory enclave or two.

The island's name comes from the Spanish *gran bajamar* (great shallows), referring to the treacherously shallow waters that claimed scores of galleons navigating the Caribbean route during the 17th century. Pirates pillaged many of these wrecks, but they didn't make off with everything. Divers are still discovering vast fortunes here: In 1964, more than $1 million worth of jewels and doubloons were dredged up from a wreck in an area east of Freeport now called Treasure Reef.

The first permanent settlers arrived here during the 19th century. Some were pro-British American Loyalists who had tried their hands at farming cotton and sisal on the Out Islands but had to abandon their farms after the thin soil gave out. Most of the settlers on Grand Bahama made a living diving for sponges, catching spiny lobster and conch, and cutting timber. (Unlike most Bahamian isles, Grand Bahama has an ample supply of fresh water, which accounts for the lush forests—many now thinned by overcutting—in the island's interior.)

During the American Civil War, a number of settlers abandoned their farms here and moved to Nassau to cash in on the lucrative blockade-running trade. The island's economy picked up during Prohibition, when rum-runners found Grand Bahama a convenient conduit for Miami-bound contraband. Lumber companies from the Abacos moved here in the mid-1940s and sold pine to shipbuilders in North and South America. In the 1980s, Colombian drugs were funneled through here to Miami, but the US/Bahamian customs blockade has choked off most of that trade.

Today, tourism is the biggest industry on the island, thanks to a project launched in the mid-1950s by Virginia financier Wallace Groves. In 1955, Groves, who had run a timber concern on the island since the 1940s, made a proposal to the Bahamian government to build a tax-free city—the modern town of Freeport—near the south coast of the island. (A port in name only, it's actually 5 miles inland.) In exchange, Groves was granted exclusive development rights and tax exemptions. The complex was initially a failure, but in 1963, in a bid to revive the island's moribund economy, Groves built Lucaya, a large beach resort 5 miles southeast of Freeport. Lucaya's first class hotels, gambling casinos, and golf courses attracted new investors and soon turned Freeport's fortunes around. Between 1963 and 1967, investment in Grand Bahama more than trebled—as did its population. Growth controls were imposed a few years later, however, and since then the island's economy has expanded at a less breakneck pace.

Most people who visit the island make a beeline for the clean white beaches at Lucaya or the glitzy casinos in both Lucaya and Freeport, but those who want a break from the tourist spots can find plenty of quiet hideaways. The two moped/bicycle tours described here skirt the south shore of the island to the east and west of Lucaya. The shorter of the two driving tours leads to the historic old town of West End; the longer tour, which takes about three hours each way, winds up at some of the old settlements on the eastern end of the island.

The best way to travel between Freeport and Lucaya is by bus ($1 each way) or by taxi, though many of the sights can be reached on foot or by bike. To see the old communities in the east and west of the island, it's best to rent a car, as buses ramble along at a tortoise-slow pace (for car and bike rental and taxi information, see "Getting Around" in *Bahamas,* THE ISLANDS). It's a good idea to lock your car, both when driving around the island and when you get out to sightsee, and any valuables should be kept out of sight (or, better yet, left at your hotel).

GRAND BAHAMA BY BIKE OR MOPED

In the Lucaya area, the roads are good and the terrain is pancake-flat. Lovely Taino Beach is just under 3 miles from the hotels along Lucayan Beach. To get there, take Seahorse Road out of Lucaya toward Freeport and turn right onto Midshipman Road. Follow it for about a mile as it skirts the Bell Channel marina and then turn right again onto West Beach Road. Turn right at the *Stoned Crab* sign and follow the road to Taino Beach, a long, narrow stretch of white sand dotted with palm-frond umbrellas. On the beach is the *Surfside* restaurant (phone: 373-1814), serving native dishes. Nearby is the *Stoned Crab,* a popular seafood restaurant open for dinner only (see "Eating Out" in *Bahamas,* THE ISLANDS).

If it's a Wednesday evening, you can experience a real Bahamian beach party at *Outriggers* restaurant in Smith's Point, less than a mile away (see "Eating Out" in *Bahamas,* THE ISLANDS). To get there, go back to West Beach Road and turn right. On the next paved street (there's no sign), take another right and follow the road to *Outriggers.*

To reach the thick white sands of Fortune Beach, considered one of the island's best, return to Midshipman Road and head east. About 2 miles farther, turn right onto Doubloon Road, then right again at Spanish Main Drive, following the sign for the *Club Caribe* restaurant. A few miles down

Spanish Main Drive is "New Millionaires' Row," a cluster of beachfront houses belonging to Grand Bahama's most well-heeled citizens. If you have time, ride a little ways past the turnoff to Fortune Beach and take a peek at these luxurious mansions. Then, turn around and take a right on the packed dirt road which leads to Fortune Beach. The beach extends for miles and is flanked along its entire length by cedar pines, sea grape, and casuarina trees. Both locals and tourists hang out here on weekends at *Le Beach Shack* (phone: 373-4525), where lively music blares from a set of powerful speakers. Diners are handed a crayon at the entrance and urged to "be creative"; plenty of them have been, judging from the colorful graffiti on the walls and ceiling. The atmosphere is a little more sedate at *Club Caribe* next door (phone: 373-6866).

GRAND BAHAMA BY CAR

WEST END It's a leisurely 45-minute drive from Freeport or Lucaya to West End, the oldest settlement on the island. The route along the West Sunrise Highway and Queen's Highway is easy to navigate and well paved, and it meanders through several small towns along the way. From Freeport's *International Bazaar,* take West Sunrise Highway past the *Regency Theatre,* where the *Freeport Players Guild* puts on several productions a year (phone: 352-5533). Continue straight into the area known as Hawksbill, a residential community. The industrial section of the island is just ahead, recognizable by the large Uniroyal Chemical Plant, Syntex Corporation, and BORCO oil refinery signs. At the end of the road, turn left onto Queen's Highway to get to Freeport Harbour. Just before the entrance to the cruise ship berths is the turnoff to *Pier One* restaurant, where you can sit at a table on the terrace, throw chunks of fish and bread to seagulls hovering nearby, and watch cruise ships sail into the harbor. Seagulls aren't the only ones to get fed around here, either: Every night the restaurant stages two shark feedings. At 8 and again at 9 PM, about a dozen hungry sharks congregate in the well-lit water of the harbor to receive their free meal. (Also see "Eating Out" in *Bahamas,* THE ISLANDS.)

Return to Queen's Highway, turn right at the Freeport Power Company's black, three-story container (cheerfully adorned with a huge, yellow smiley face), and follow the road to West Sunrise Highway heading toward Freeport. At the first traffic light, turn left onto Grand Bahamian Way. You'll travel over a bridge at Hawksbill Creek, continuing toward the northwestern end of the island. This road is lined with casuarina trees. Along the shoreline are several mounds of conch shells (feel free to take a couple). Turn right on the beach road at the "Eight Mile Rock" sign and continue past the pastel-colored concrete homes and smaller wooden shacks, several with large satellite dishes adorning their front yards (look on your right for one with a Bahamian woman painted on it). Near here is a "boiling hole," where tidal pressure causes the salt water to bubble like water in a teakettle. (There are no signs, so ask a local for directions to the pool.) The hole is actually an inlet to a vast system of underground caves.

The beach road passes Hanna Hill and Holmes Rock and eventually leads to the village of Deadman's Reef. Don't let the name scare you off: This town is home to one of the island's better beachside dining and sunset-watching spots, the *Buccaneer Club* (see "Eating Out" in *Bahamas,* THE ISLANDS). Divers can explore the cays just off the reef; bring your own equipment, since there are no dive shops here.

As you head farther west, the villages become more sparsely populated, and the pastel homes give way to thick, green shrubs and low trees. At a sign welcoming visitors to "West End, The Home of Hospitality," turn right. Just before West End on this road is the *Chicken Nest* (phone: 346-6440), a beige building with beer posters lining the outside walls. Inside, the place features the island's best conch salad, as well as a pool table, a dartboard, and a jukebox.

West End's original inhabitants were Lucaya Indians, who lived in palm-frond huts and caught bonefish off the coast. Today, the village, featuring gaily painted wooden homes intermingled with more modern concrete houses, has the quaint, quiet atmosphere of an old resort town in the off-season. The community is only a shadow of what it was during the glory days of Prohibition, when the population hit 1,700 and the short piers were crowded with rum boats ready to make a quick nighttime run over to the coves along Florida's Biscayne Bay. A generation ago, the town was dominated by the *Grand Bahama* hotel, a resort in the Canadian Jack Tar chain. The resort closed in 1989, however, and at press time new owners were still being sought. The village once again relies on fishing for its livelihood; commerce has dwindled to the small *Harbour* hotel (phone: 346-6432), a couple of bars, and a few souvenir shops. Diagonally across the street from the *Harbour* hotel is *Mary Magdalene Church,* built of stone and wood in 1893. Farther up the road is a ghost town of windowless blue buildings—the former staff quarters for both the *Grand Bahama* and the town's abandoned lumber mill. Along the shore here are more conch shells (again, help yourself). The sea is shallow here, with bonefish flats stretching for several miles along the coastline. Bonefishing enthusiasts can hire Bonefish Folley (phone: 346-6233), a local who knows the waters well, as a fishing guide.

Now retrace the route and turn left onto Queen's Highway. At the *Freeport International Airport,* turn right onto Mall Road and then turn left onto Settler's Way. On Settler's Way is the *Rand Memorial Nature Centre,* a 100-acre nature preserve with 130 species of Bahamian plants, including a dozen varieties of orchid. A 2,000-foot trail ends at a sunken pool surrounded by flowering plants. Guided tours are offered twice daily. The center is closed weekends; admission charge (phone: 352-5438).

To get back to Freeport or Lucaya, turn left on Settler's Way after exiting the nature center and take another left on Coral Road to reach East Sunrise Highway. Turn right for Freeport, left for Lucaya.

EAST END Before leaving on this driving tour to the East End settlement, make sure you have a full tank of gas (gas stations are a bit scarce) and pack a bathing suit, a change of clothes, sneakers, sunscreen, mosquito repellent, and a picnic lunch (there are few restaurants here). Plan to spend a leisurely day, as the drive takes between two and three hours each way.

From the Port Lucaya area, take Seahorse Road out of town and turn right on Midshipman Road. From Freeport, take East Sunrise Highway, bear right on Seahorse, and turn left onto Midshipman Road. About 8 miles down the road, turn left onto Magellan Drive. This road leads to the *Garden of the Groves,* a 12-acre patch of land that boasts more than 5,000 varieties of flowers, other plants, and trees. The garden is named after Georgette and Wallace Groves, Freeport's founders, who donated the park to the island. Stroll along the paths past the various flora, streams, ponds, and small waterfalls that tumble into reflecting pools. A lovely, serene grotto here is popular for island weddings. Just inside the entrance is the *Grand Bahama Museum,* with exhibits of seashells, marine life, Lucaya Indian artifacts, and *junkanoo* costumes. The garden and museum are closed Wednesdays; admission charge to the museum (phone: 352-4045, garden; 373-5668, museum).

Return to Midshipman Road and turn right onto a well-paved road flanked by a seemingly infinite number of spindly trees known as Caribbean pines. The green undergrowth is comprised of palmetto bushes and agave or century plants. Keep a sharp lookout for a white stone marker about 10 miles along the road: This indicates the entrance to *Lucaya National Park.* An ecotourist's delight, this 40-acre park has marked trails that ramble through all five of the ecosystems found on this island: pine forests, ming trees (better known as prickly trees), mangroves, wetland coppice, and sand dunes dotted with sea grape and casuarina trees. (Be careful not to touch the giant poisonwood trees along the swamp of the wetland coppice, as they are cousins of poison ivy.) One trail leads to Ben's Cave, where the bones of several Lucaya Indians have been discovered in six feet of water. The cave is part of an elaborate underground cavern reputed to be the largest explored underwater cave system in the world. Another trail leading to the sand dunes—which at 20 feet are among the highest dunes on the island— also goes to Gold Rock, a pristine beach awash with white coral sand and fronted by shallow translucent waters. It's perfect for sunning, swimming, and picnicking. If you face the sea and look off to the left, you'll see the rock that gave this beach and the creek its name.

From the park, take a left turn and travel about 10 miles to the village of High Rock, passing an abandoned American missile-tracking station. Contrary to its name, there are no high rocks here; there are, however, miles and miles of picture-perfect beaches. If your timing is good, you may see the local fishermen returning with their catch. Just down the street is a tiny building that houses the *High Rock Public Library*—arguably the smallest library on the island. A few doors up the street, next to the Baptist church, is the *Ocean View* restaurant, a good place for a cold drink, a seafood lunch, and a game of dominoes (no phone).

The road gets rougher over the next 10 miles, especially near the rusting hulk of the *Burma Oil Depot,* which was abandoned some 20 years ago. About 3 miles past the depot, at the second of two tight bends, a road branches off to the right and leads to a sandbar lapped by clear waters—a secluded spot for a swim. Perhaps the finest beach on the island is 2 miles down the road, at Pelican's Point. You can hire fishing boats here at the little *Beach Lodge* hotel (phone: 359-4989).

The road passes a saltwater pool at Rocky Creek and ends at MacLean's Town, which is famous throughout the islands for its annual *Columbus Day* conch-cracking competition—the participants vie to be the first to crack and clean 25 conchs. From here, take a short water-taxi ride to the exclusive *Deep Water Cay* lodge across Runner's Creek. Bonefish are plentiful in the flats offshore, and the beach is scattered with pretty shells. Snorkelers frequent the reefs off nearby Sweetings Cay. To return to Freeport or Lucaya, either retrace the above route or hop onto the Grand Bahama Highway.

Bimini

Encompassing only 9 square miles, tiny Bimini is actually two islands, with a sprinkling of islets and cays thrown in for good measure. Skinny North Bimini is the more developed, while broader South Bimini is largely deserted. A quarter-mile-wide channel separates the two main isles, and a ferry shunts back and forth between them. Despite their occasional brushes with infamy and fame, the islands have retained a homey quality. The glitz and glamour of Nassau are lacking here, but tourists who are looking for a good quiet spot to dive or fish won't be disappointed.

Arawak Indians were probably the first to settle Bimini, followed in the early 19th century by Seminole slaves fleeing Southern plantations. The islands also have attracted all manner of visitors and temporary residents over the centuries. Spanish explorer Juan Ponce de León, heeding rumors that Bimini possessed fabulous riches, landed here in 1512, but found nothing worth writing home about. During the 17th and 18th centuries, rabble-rousers and miscreants of all stripes found the place appealing. Pirate Henry Morgan had a stronghold here in the late 1600s, and Bahamian sea captains ran supplies from here to the Southern states during the American Civil War. Rumrunners plied a brisk trade between Bimini and southern Florida during Prohibition days, and the many recent plane wrecks off the coast near the airport on North Bimini are testimony to the many failed drug runs between Colombia and Miami.

While some visitors take the sea route to Bimini—several cruise ships call here, and it's 12 hours or so by sailboat from southeast Florida, given favorable winds—most of the tourists who stop here come by plane. In addition to private charters, visitors may take *Chalk's* seaplanes from Ft. Lauderdale, Miami, or Paradise Island (phone: 347-3024; 800-4-CHALKS). Launched by Floridian Arthur Burns Chalk more than 70 years ago, the charter bills itself as the "oldest continuously operated airline in the world." Al Capone flew to Bimini on *Chalk's,* and so did deposed Cuban dictator Gerardo Machado y Morales, who fled his homeland under a hail of gunfire on a chartered *Chalk's* plane in 1933. The airline, which fell on hard times in the 1980s, was rescued by an American from Ft. Lauderdale. *Island Air* (phone: 305-359-9942 in Florida) also offers service from Ft. Lauderdale to Bimini on Mondays, Wednesdays, Fridays, and Sundays.

Once on North Bimini, it's impractical to rent a car; the distances are short, and visitors can get everywhere they need to go by walking, cycling, or taking a taxi. The two main settlements on North Bimini—Alice Town and Bailey Town—are only a 10-minute walk apart, and most natives commute by moped or bus. The walking tour described here takes tourists to the main sights in Alice Town; the cycling (or moped, for those who pre-

145

Bimini

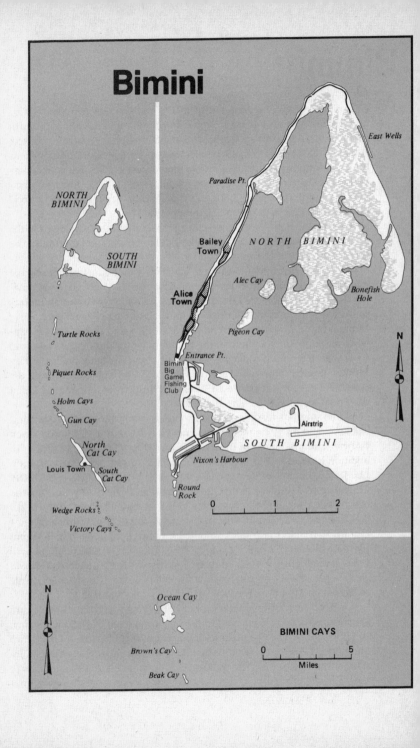

East Wells

NORTH BIMINI

SOUTH BIMINI

Paradise Pt.

NORTH BIMINI

Bailey Town

Alec Cay

Bonefish Hole

Alice Town

Pigeon Cay

N

Turtle Rocks

Entrance Pt.

Bimini Big Game Fishing Club

Piquet Rocks

Holm Cays

Gun Cay

Airstrip

SOUTH BIMINI

North Cat Cay

Louis Town

South Cat Cay

Nixon's Harbour

Wedge Rocks

Round Rock

Victory Cays

0   1   2

N

Ocean Cay

Brown's Cay

BIMINI CAYS

0   5

Beak Cay

Miles

fer) tour that follows begins at Alice Town and stops at some of the fine beaches to the northeast of town.

A BIMINI WALK

The tour described here takes an hour or so, depending on how quickly you want to ramble. From the airport you can take a taxi along the King's Highway to the tourist hotels outside Alice Town or, if you're on the island for the day and not weighed down with luggage, just head into town on foot. Alice Town is a small, hot, dusty little place, comfortably frayed at the edges and a little tatty. The Mercedes Benzes that used to cruise up and down the street here during the prime cocaine-running days of the 1980s have mostly disappeared. There are more bars than shops in Alice Town, just as there are on the rest of Bimini, but the locals, a friendly and patriotic lot, don't seem to mind that in the least.

Down the street is a private home surrounded by a verdant garden shaded by coconut palms. The house is built on the site of the *Bimini Bay Rod and Gun Club,* a hotel and casino destroyed in a hurricane in 1926. Next on the right, past *Brown's* hotel, is the *Fisherman's Paradise* restaurant (phone: 347-3220), which serves the local special of boiled fish and grits for breakfast as well as fresh lunch specials of lobster, grouper, snapper, and conch. Across the street is *Bimini Undersea Adventures* (phone: 347-3089; 800-327-8150), which takes divers to wrecks offshore and to the forests of black coral off the Bimini Wall.

Near the center of town stands the imposing limestone *Customs Hall,* painted white and candy-pink. (The police department, courthouse, and library once housed here have since been moved to other offices, but there is still a customs office in the building.) The *Perfume Bar* (no phone) near the *Customs Hall* has tropical fragrances from the *Perfume Factory* in Freeport and several imported brands, and the small, touristy straw market across the road sells baskets and trinkets made of shells. The path just beyond the market to the left soon leads to the island's main beach on the eastern strand. Next on the left is *Captain Bob's Conch Hall of Fame* (phone: 347-3260), where you can chat with owner Bob Smith, one of the island's finest deep-sea fishermen, over a bacon-and-egg breakfast. (In spite of its name, there is no hall of fame here, just some faded photographs of prizewinning catches on the walls.) The Royal Bank of Canada is next door, near *Sawyer's Scooters* (no phone), where mopeds can be rented. Opposite is the *Red Lion* bar and restaurant (phone: 347-3259), which serves good, inexpensive seafood dishes—and can turn rowdy at night.

Up the gentle hill to the left, the highest point on North Bimini, is the *Bimini Blue Water,* a small, pleasant hotel whose windows look out on the sea on both sides of the island. Its popular restaurant (phone: 347-3166) serves moderately priced native dishes. The hotel's marina and dockside pool are directly across the street, and fishing and diving tours are available. Next door is the *Blue Marlin Cottage,* the whitewashed limestone bungalow that Ernest Hemingway built for himself in the mid-1930s. Now a private home, it is said to look much as it did when the author lived here. It stands next to the *Compleat Angler* hotel (phone: 347-3122 or 347-3128), where Hemingway lived before the cottage was finished. Now home to Bimini's most famous bar, it's a classic two-story colonial building surrounded by shady verandahs, with dark varnished wooden floors and wooden paneling inside. Visitors can wander through the rooms and examine the memorabilia on the walls—there are newspaper clippings and pictures of a 785-pound mako shark and a 514-pound tuna that Hemingway caught years ago (there's no admission charge to the exhibits). Whirring ceiling fans mute the noise from the courtyard bar, where tourists sit around a twisted almond tree drinking Bahama Mamas, munching on conch fritters, and listening to a calypso band.

No one leaves Bimini without becoming an expert on Hemingway lore. After a couple of days here, tourists know all about the years Hemingway lived on the island (1934 to 1937), the novels he wrote here (*To Have and Have Not* and *Islands in the Stream,* the latter set on Bimini), his notorious bouts of drinking and carousing, the fishing expeditions in which Hemingway used a machine gun to kill sharks attacking his catch, and his famous boxing matches. Several men tried to capture Hemingway's $250 boxing purse; none succeeded.

Just northwest of the *Angler,* past a clutch of tourist shops, is the *Bimini Big Game Fishing Club* (phone: 347-3391). Owned by Bacardi, it's the poshest resort on the island (non-guests may stop here for drinks). Separated from the hoi polloi by a concrete wall and a high fence, the hotel is surrounded by coconut palms and flowering shrubs. It's particularly busy from March through September, when the big fishing tournaments are held here.

For those who can afford it, the game fishing off Bimini is among the finest in the world. Plenty of records have been set here; fishermen have netted 1,800-pound bluefin tuna, and a blue marlin can weigh up to half a ton and fight on the line for a solid eight hours or more. Those who can't afford to spend $500 to $700 a day on deep-sea fishing can bonefish in the shallows for less than half that price. Although netting a bonefish is a challenge, the fish make excellent eating. Locals "snap" them to align the bones in one direction and then grill them whole. Tourists who are lucky enough to catch one can probably coax a local into cooking it for them. Follow the high road (on the other side of the island) back to Alice Town.

BIMINI BY BIKE

The rest of North Bimini, which is just 2 miles long and a quarter of a mile wide, is explored easily by bike or moped. This tour starts at the *Bimini Big Game Fishing Club* (see above); just opposite is the home of Captain William C. Francis, a.k.a. Bonefish Bill, a lanky man with close-cropped graying hair who can spot a bonefish at 100 yards. Fishing trips with Captain Francis can be arranged through the *Bimini Big Game Fishing Club*. Novices who go out fishing with him can expect a stern rebuke if they fail to follow his instructions. Nearby is the *Bimini Breeze* bar and restaurant (phone: 347-3511), a cool haven that serves seafood and native dishes. West of here the King's Highway hugs the coast, passing scattered homes along the way. Fishermen clean and sell their catch along the beachside docks, and women tend the vegetable plots outside their brightly painted wooden homes, or hang laundry from the lines strung along the front porch. The road skirts by the *Bimini All-Age School*, where you may see kids in maroon-edged gray uniforms playing basketball in the yard.

Farther on past the power station is Bailey Town, a quiet native settlement. Small wooden and concrete-block houses stand next to the road. The settlement soon comes to an abrupt end, and the road cuts through a forest of slender pines. About a quarter of a mile beyond the town, the road ends at a dock by the entrance to two large private home developments. (A private road continues north and east of here for about 2½ miles to the tip of the island.)

The chief attractions off the northeast shore of the island are the curious ruins that some archaeologists say may be the remnants of the lost continent of Atlantis. (It's a farfetched claim, but the site is by any definition mysterious.) The ruins, which lie under 15 feet of water, can't be seen clearly from shore, but you can hire a boat and dive or snorkel near the site. Hundreds of stone blocks, each about four feet wide and two feet thick, are packed together in a sort of causeway that stretches for a hundred yards or so. Archaeologists haven't figured out what the structure was for, but they do know that the blocks are fashioned from a sedimentary rock not native to Bimini.

Nearby are some secluded coves sheltered by weathered limestone rocks—the perfect place for a picnic and an afternoon swim or snorkel. Hidden among the pines is a small cemetery where some of the headstones are more than 150 years old. Just past the cemetery a road branches off to the right; follow it to the east shore road, and take this road back in the direction of Alice Town. You will soon come upon two picturesque churches, *Our Lady of St. Stephen's* and *Wesley Methodist*. Services are often held during the week at midday, as well as on Sunday mornings; they're a pleasant retreat from the hot sun, and visitors are welcome. Farther down is the *Bimini Blue Water* hotel (see above) and the main beach on the island (it's the same beach that can be reached by the path from the center of Alice Town). A wide, steep-sloped swath of white sand that's popular with locals and tourists alike, it's just the place to rest after a Bimini bike tour.

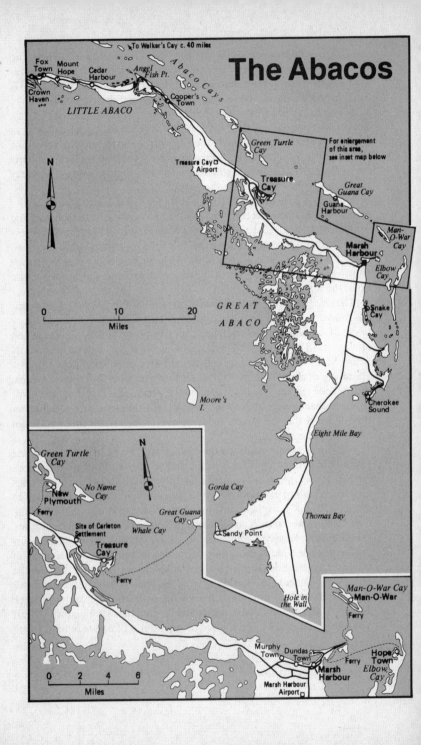

The Abacos

To Walker's Cay c. 40 miles

Fox Town
Mount Hope
Cedar Harbour
Crown Haven
LITTLE ABACO

Angel Fish Pt.

Abaco Cays

Cooper's Town

N

Treasure Cay Airport

Green Turtle Cay

For enlargement of this area, see inset map below

Treasure Cay

Great Guana Cay

Guana Harbour

Man-O-War Cay

Marsh Harbour

Elbow Cay

0   10   20
Miles

GREAT ABACO

Snake Cay

Moore's I.

Cherokee Sound

Eight Mile Bay

N

Green Turtle Cay

No Name Cay

New Plymouth
Ferry

Site of Carleton Settlement

Treasure Cay

Great Guana Cay

Gorda Cay

Whale Cay

Ferry

Sandy Point

Thomas Bay

Hole in the Wall

Man-O-War Cay
Man-O-War
Ferry

Murphy Town
Dundas Town
Ferry

Hope Town
Elbow Cay

Marsh Harbour

Marsh Harbour Airport

0   2   4   6
Miles

The Abacos

This boomerang-shaped archipelago, 130 miles long and roughly 15 miles wide, is just east of Grand Bahama and a quick hop from Miami and Ft. Lauderdale. Also referred to as Abaco, the Abacos comprise several islands and cays: Great and Little Abacos, Elbow Cay, Man-O-War Cay, Great Guana Cay, Treasure Cay, Green Turtle Cay, Spanish Cay, and Walker's Cay. The islands are special for many reasons. Nowhere else in the Bahamas does the colonial past seem as close as it does here on these palm-fringed cays with their pretty New England–style fishing villages. And the gin-clear seas off the coast are said to be among the finest sailing and fishing waters in the world.

Juan Ponce de León called here in 1513 during his search for the fountain of youth, but he found nothing more than a few bands of Lucaya Indians. Pirates hid out in the coves along the Abacos coast, for the reefs and shoals offshore were perfect wrecking grounds. More than 500 galleons, many laden with treasure, sank in the waters off the Abacos.

Tories from New England, New York, and the Carolinas put down roots here after the American Revolution, and many of the island's 10,000-odd permanent residents trace their ancestry back to them. The Loyalists settled at Carleton, near Treasure Cay in the central Abacos, but their farms soon failed, and the town was razed by a hurricane. In the late 18th century Carleton was abandoned, and the settlers tramped 18 miles south to Elizabeth Harbour. There, with the help of compatriots from Harbour Island near Eleuthera, they founded a farming and fishing community that eventually became Marsh Harbour. Other settlers colonized many of the small cays. Over the years, the Abaconians established a formidable reputation as shipbuilders, and their fast dinghies, smacks, and sloops were prized throughout the western Atlantic. Prosperous and conservative, they remained fiercely loyal to the Crown. Their descendants demonstrated that same loyalty by making several attempts to block the Bahamian independence movement in the 1970s. When their attempts failed and the Bahamas became an independent member of the British Commonwealth, they tried to secede and found their own nation. That plan failed, too, and forever divided the loyalties of the natives. Some left the Abacos, but most stayed.

Marsh Harbour is still the most important settlement in the Abacos, and it's easily reached by regular *Bahamasair* flights from Nassau and Freeport (phone: 327-8451), as well as by international flights from Miami, Ft. Lauderdale, West Palm Beach, and Orlando on *American Eagle* (phone: 800-433-7300), *Gulfstream/United* (phone: 800-992-8532; 305-871-1200 in Florida), *Island Express* (phone: 305-359-0380 in Florida), and *USAir Express* (phone: 800-622-1015). Most visitors to the Abacos stop first at Marsh

Harbour, spend a day or two seeing the sights and stocking up on provisions, and then take off for the fishing and diving spots on the smaller cays.

Marsh Harbour is at the crook of the bend in the Abacos chain, just opposite the aptly named Elbow Cay. From *Marsh Harbour Airport,* it's a 10-minute drive north to the town proper, which is situated on a broad spit of land on the eastern side of the island. To reach the main harbor, where the old town is, pass the large shopping center, and at the only traffic light on the Abacos, turn right onto Elizabeth Drive, which leads to the wharf.

ABACOS WALKS

About 3,000 people live year-round in Marsh Harbour on Great Abaco, and though it's the third-largest town in the Bahamas, it's hardly a metropolis. Most of the sights around town can be strolled in a leisurely half hour or less. Begin at the old harbor, where hundreds of boats bob up and down in the clear blue water. Here visitors can rent a sloop with crew or without.

The waterfront is dominated by the saffron-yellow *Conch Inn,* a sprawling colony of bungalows with its own 60-slip marina. Its bar and dockside restaurant are favorite local gathering spots (phone: 367-4000). *Dive Abaco* (phone: 367-2787), one of the largest scuba and snorkeling centers in the Abacos, is part of the complex. Nearby are several good restaurants, including *Mangoes,* which has a good bar (phone: 367-2366), and *Wally's* (phone: 367-2074), in a lovely pink-and-white colonial building. Bicycles can be rented at the apartments called *Abaco Towns by the Sea* (phone: 367-2227). Nearby *Marsh Harbour Exporters and Importers* (phone: 367-2697) sells cleaned frozen fish at bargain prices to tourists heading home.

There is little development between this point and the newer harbor on the south side of the spit, about a quarter of a mile away. The southern area, popularly known as Marsh Town, has been developed over the past decade or so. Marsh Town is dominated by the *Great Abaco Beach* hotel, which has expanded its full-service *Boat Harbour Marina* (phone: 367-2736) to 160 slips. The hotel is set back from the water, surrounded by coconut palms; you can dine on local specialties at its *Island Oasis Bar and Grill* (phone: 367-2871). *Seahorse Boat Rentals* on the waterfront (phone: 367-2513) rents boats, bicycles, snorkeling and fishing gear, and windsurfers; or try *Rich's Rentals* (Marsh Harbour; phone: 367-2742). For fine views, follow Harbour Road east for a mile and a half or so, passing the settlements of Pond Bay, Pelican Shores, Fanny Bay, and Upper Cut along the way.

North of Marsh Harbour, it's a pleasant 3-mile walk along Harbour Road to two quaint fishing villages, Dundas Town and Murphy Town. Explore the old clapboard and limestone churches and stop in at *Mother Merle's Fishnet* restaurant (phone: 367-2770) for a bite of broiled lobster or conch salad. On the way back, take a dip in the perfectly clear waters off the small beaches along the strand.

ABACOS BY CAR

Exploring Great Abaco by car used to require some grit and patience, but the roads have been repaved, making for more pleasant driving. Still, settlements are few and far between: Visitors with limited time may be better advised to spend their precious hours on the cays. Those who do drive are best off heading north, for that road leads to some spectacular beaches.

The 28-mile journey between Marsh Harbour and Treasure Cay is pretty uninspiring, hemmed in by monotonous stands of young pine. However, it's worth the drive to see the beach at Treasure Cay, one of the finest anywhere. The turnoff to the cay, which is linked by causeway to the mainland, is well marked. Coconut palms shade the dazzlingly white beach, which curves in a perfect 3-mile-long arc. Along the beach is *Treasure Cay* (phone: 367-2570), with some of the Abacos' best resort facilities.

From here, it's 25 miles to the northern end of Little Abaco. Just off the road a mile north of Treasure Cay, a brass plaque commemorates the spot where the island's early settlers founded the town of Carleton. A mile beyond it is the wharf where the ferries to Green Turtle Cay dock. *Treasure Cay Airport* is another mile or so to the north; the flights from there to Marsh Harbour take a mere 10 minutes.

Cooper's Town, a small fishing village 8 miles farther on, and the last town on Great Abaco, has received considerable attention recently; one of its own—Hubert A. Ingraham—was elected prime minister in 1992. There are good beaches nearby and farther on in Cedar Harbour on Little Abaco. Mount Hope, 5 miles away, is a slightly larger town, with a drugstore, a grocery, and *B. J.'s* restaurant (no phone). The *Zion Baptist Church* dominates Fox Town, the village 5 miles to the northwest, where there is a police station, a post office, and *Seaview* (phone: 365-2007), a good little seafood restaurant. Crown Haven, at the end of the line 2 miles on, has a barbershop, two rival churches, and the cheery *Black Room* bar and restaurant (no phone). The northern part of Little Abaco, accessible only by boat, stretches another 10 miles.

CRUISING THE CAYS

GREEN TURTLE CAY From Treasure Cay on Great Abaco, it's a short ferry ride to Green Turtle Cay, an old Tory stronghold that's definitely worth a visit. Water taxis run by the *Green Turtle Ferry Service* (phone: 365-4151) leave from the dock on Treasure Cay at 10:30 AM, 2 PM, and 4 PM, and they leave for Treasure Cay at 8 AM, 9:15 AM, 11:30 AM, 1:30 PM, and 3 PM. It's a 10-minute ride to the island; a round-trip ticket costs $16. On the way, the ferry cruises by New Plymouth Village on the south of the cay, a postcard-perfect fishing town. The ferry stops at New Plymouth after calling at the *Green Turtle Club*'s marina a mile farther north (phone: 365-4271).

New Plymouth (pop. 500) is the perfect place for a half-hour walking tour. This jumble of colorful saltbox houses overlooking Black Sound Harbour was settled in 1784. The Loyalists who founded the town established a prosperous boatbuilding industry here. Settlers also made a living catching turtles, diving for sponges, and shipping shark oil and sharkskins to traders in Baltimore and New York. Today the shipyards are closed, and many locals make a living catching lobster and crawfish. More than half of all the lobster exported from the Bahamas is caught in the waters nearby.

Directly opposite the ferry dock is King Street, which is barely 50 yards long. Stop for ice cream at homey *Laura's Kitchen* on King Street (phone: 365-4287), and continue on to bougainvillea-lined Parliament Street, the main thoroughfare. Directly in front of you, amid well-tended gardens, is the *Albert Lowe Museum,* named for one of the town's master boatbuilders. Models of several of the ships built by Lowe, who died in 1986, are displayed here, along with contemporary paintings by his son Alton. The rooms are filled with period furniture. The museum is closed Sundays; no admission charge (phone: 365-4094). Across the street is the *Loyalist Memorial Sculpture Garden,* landscaped in a Union Jack design and featuring bronze busts and clay sculptures of famous figures from Green Turtle Cay's past. It's open daily; no admission charge. If you turn left down Parliament Street, you will see the library, post office, customs hall, and the pink-and-white *Commissioner's Office.* On the left is the charming clapboard Methodist church, with a fine old mahogany altar and oil lamps lining the walls.

Farther on to the right is a well-maintained cemetery, and up the small hill past the local school is *Rooster's* bar and restaurant (phone: 365-4066), a rustic spot where you can enjoy simple native cooking, shoot a game of pool, and dance to live music in the evening. Continue on Hill Street for about a quarter of a mile until you reach a long, deserted crescent beach—the best place to swim in New Plymouth. Then follow Hill and Bay Streets back to the harbor, near the waterside *Wrecking Tree Bakery* (phone: 365-4263). Directly opposite the bakery is Victoria Street, home of *Miss Emily's Blue Bee* bar (phone: 365-4181), ostensibly the most famous bar in the Bahamas; the Goombay Smash—a drink made of rum and fruit that is a favorite throughout the islands—was invented here. The decor is touristy to the point of tackiness, with scruffy T-shirts hanging from the ceiling and hundreds of business cards plastered on the walls. Just down the street is the old jail, which apparently isn't used much, since the door has fallen off. Continue up to Parliament Street and make a right; then turn left onto Mission Street, passing some weatherbeaten homes; now make a right onto Crown Street, and head down the short road that branches off to the left and leads to a small dock.

Farther down Crown Street is the *Gospel Chapel,* a canary-yellow church known for its rousing revival meetings. Turn right on Walter Street, which leads back to Parliament Street. Walk down the street past the *Albert Lowe Museum* and the *Loyalist Memorial Sculpture Garden.* Opposite the garden, next to the former vacation home of British prime minister Neville Chamberlain, is the *New Plymouth Inn,* a good in-town hotel (see "Checking In" in *Bahamas,* THE ISLANDS). Near the end of Parliament Street is the

Ocean Blue Gallery (no phone), where paintings by more than 30 Bahamian artists are on display. From here it is a short walk along Bay Street to the dock, where you can hire a boat and dive for lobster and conch or try your luck fishing for grouper, yellowtail, or triggerfish.

ELBOW CAY Just east of Marsh Harbour off Great Abaco, Elbow Cay is one of the most visited islands in the Bahamas. Its main settlement, Hope Town, is a colonial fishing village of great charm. The island is reached by a 20-minute water taxi ride from *Albury's Ferry Service* in Marsh Harbour (phone: 367-3147 or 365-6010). The ferries leave daily at 10:30 AM and 4 PM; trips from the cay to Marsh Harbour are at 8 AM and 1:30 PM. The round-trip fare is $16. Before landing at Hope Town, the ferry calls briefly at the candy-striped lighthouse on the south end of the cay. Built in 1863 (and rebuilt in 1938), it stands 120 feet high, and its kerosene lamp still guides boats far out at sea. Visitors are allowed 10 minutes to scramble up the steep winding staircase to the observation deck to take in the panoramic view of the harbor and snap a photo or two.

The ferry pulls in at the lower public dock at the north end of Hope Town. There are two main north-south thoroughfares on the cay: "Up Along," the high road along the central spine of the island, and "Down Along," which parallels the harbor.

East of Up Along are long stretches of secluded beach, ideal for swimming and snorkeling. Along the way, stop in at *Captain Jack's* (phone: 366-0247) for a boilfish-and-johnnycake breakfast; at the *Wood Carvings* workshop (no phone) near the *St. James Methodist Church;* and at the *Wyannie Malone Museum,* which is dedicated to the memory of a widow with four children who arrived here around 1793. The museum, housed in a restored colonial building, gives a sense of what life on the island was once like. The rooms are filled with colonial furniture, and visitors can see the faded charts documenting the voyages of the Eleutherian Adventurers, who sailed here from Bermuda during the 17th century. There's also an Edison Talking Machine; old toys; a cistern; and a collection of handwoven linen. The museum is open daily; no admission charge (no phone). Beyond the museum is the *Hope Town Harbour Lodge* hotel, the best place to stay (see "Checking In" in *Bahamas,* THE ISLANDS). The road ends at the local cemetery.

The harbor road, Down Along—which runs for a mere 200 yards or so—is fronted by colonial saltbox houses overlooking the harbor. Along it are a handicrafts store, a dive shop, and the post office, commissioner's office, and police station.

MAN-O-WAR CAY This tiny island—barely a quarter of a mile long and as thin as a rail—is the capital of Abaco's modern boatbuilding industry. It's a 20-minute water taxi ride from *Albury's Ferry Service* at the dock in Marsh Harbour (phone: 367-3147 or 365-6010) to the cay. Boats leave daily from Great Abaco at 10:30 AM and 4 PM; trips from the cay are at 8 AM and 1:30 PM. The fare is $8; $12 round-trip. If you're on a different schedule than the regular boats, you can charter a ferry for $45. There's only a single small hotel here, the four-room *Schooner's Landing* (phone: 365-6072; fax: 365-6285), so most people just hop over for a couple of hours. Only 300 or so people live on the island, and the community is as sternly proper as the immaculately maintained clapboard homes surrounded by prim white picket fences. Many natives go to church three times a week—and twice on Sundays. Drinking is outlawed, and local women are barred from wearing shorts or bikinis; visiting women should observe this prohibition as well.

The harbor still bustles with the clamor of shipbuilders at work. *Albury's Sail Loft* (no phone) has an ample selection of clothes made from sailcloth, and *Joe's Studio* (no phone) sells nautical gifts. There are pleasant walks north and south of town along the shore, and the beach on the east side of the island offers superb swimming, snorkeling, and diving. Divers can explore the wreck of the Union gunboat USS *Adirondack,* which sank after hitting a reef six months after it was commissioned in 1862, and the wreck of the *San Jacinto,* which ran aground while chasing a blockade runner in 1865.

WALKER'S CAY The northernmost of the Abacos cays, Walker's Cay is reachable by private boat or chartered aircraft. Ponce de León is said to have landed here in 1513, and the island was later a refuge for criminals, from 17th-century pirates to Civil War–era raiders and rumrunners. Tourists have considerably improved its reputation. The island's fine resort, *Walker's Cay Club,* opened in the 1930s as a fishing club and was converted into a hotel in 1969 (see "Checking In" in *Bahamas,* THE ISLANDS). The dives off the nearby barrier reef are spectacular. Schools of queen triggerfish, Nassau grouper, blue chromis, and wide-eyed squirrelfish dart among the coral and the barnacle-encrusted wrecks offshore. Occasionally, the schools of minnows here can be so thick that divers a few feet apart lose sight of each other. Visitors can tour the tropical fish–breeding farm on the northwest side of the island. Deep-sea fishing tournaments are held here in the spring and summer.

GREAT GUANA CAY The home of the tiny *Guana Beach* resort and marina (see "Checking In" in *Bahamas,* THE ISLANDS), Great Guana Cay is accessible only by private charter boat or by a ferry that leaves twice daily from the *Conch Inn* on Marsh Harbour (the service is complimentary to hotel guests; non-guests pay $18 round-trip). The cay is a small spot of land lying between Green Turtle and Man-O-War Cays. Only about 80 people live here year-round, and there is nothing much in town aside from a few small shops, a schoolhouse, and an Anglican church. The main attractions are the beach (7 long miles of white sand fringed with coconut palms) and the excellent bonefishing and diving.

Andros

The biggest island in the Bahamas—140 miles long and 40 miles wide—Andros is surprisingly undeveloped, considering its proximity to Nassau and Miami. Much of the interior, known rather vaguely as "The Big Yard," is forested with dense stands of mahogany and pine, and the boggy marshes along the west coast, known straightforwardly as "The Mud," are even more impenetrable. Some of the best sights are offshore. The 120-mile barrier reef just off the east coast is the third-largest in the world and offers some spectacular dives.

Discovered by Columbus in 1492 and christened La Isla del Espíritu Santo (Island of the Holy Spirit), the island was later renamed for Sir Edmund Andros, a Governor of the Dominion of New England. (Modern Bahamians, anxious to repudiate their colonial roots, claim that the island is named after the Aegean isle of Andros.) Stories and legends have lent it a mysterious air. Islanders tell tales of giant octopus-like creatures called *lucas* that attack fishermen and divers. Children are warned to watch out for the *chickarnie,* a mythical red-eyed, three-toed bird said to roost in the dark forests in the interior. Ballads written in colonial times tell of the exploits of pirate Henry Morgan, who is said to have left a vast treasure in a cave off Morgan's Bluff on the northern tip of the island.

Andros has never been easy to explore, for it is broken up by labyrinthine lakes and channels. Water, in fact, is one of the main resources of the island. Unlike most Bahamian isles, Andros has large underground reservoirs of fresh water. These have helped to sustain the large forests on the island, making them less vulnerable to drought. (Timber has been a major export here since colonial times.) Today, Andros supplies Nassau with much of that city's potable water, shipped by barge. The island is also riddled with subterranean limestone caverns filled with sea water. When the roofs of these caves collapse, they expose clear, deep pools called blue holes.

While the interior of the island is largely inaccessible, there are some fine secluded beaches along the eastern shore. Twenty miles offshore lies the Andros barrier reef; the diving sites here are said to be among the best in the world. From the eastern edge of the reef, it's a sheer 6,000-foot drop to a narrow ocean trough called the Tongue of the Ocean (TOTO), named for its shape. Primitive fish—and submarines from the top-security US naval base on the east coast of Andros—cruise the depths of this 142-mile-long abyss. Cathedrals of elkhorn and staghorn coral tower in the crystal-clear water, where visibility can exceed 200 feet. Reef sharks, moray eels, eagle rays, and shoals of angelfish and friendly grouper feed nearby, and rare black coral clings to the precipice at the eastern edge of the reef. Coral also lines the submerged caverns underneath the island, which can be explored by diving through one of several blue holes.

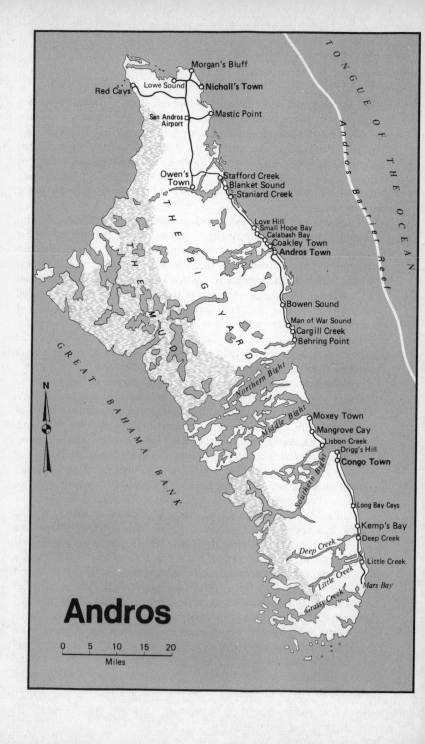

Morgan's Bluff
Lowe Sound
Nicholl's Town
Red Cays
San Andros
Airport
Mastic Point

Owen's
Town
Stafford Creek
Blanket Sound
Staniard Creek

Love Hill
Small Hope Bay
Calabash Bay
Coakley Town
Andros Town

Bowen Sound

Man of War Sound
Cargill Creek
Behring Point

TONGUE OF THE OCEAN

Andros Barrier Reef

THE BIG YARD

THE MUD

Northern Bight

Middle Bight

Moxey Town
Mangrove Cay
Lisbon Creek
Drigg's Hill
Congo Town

GREAT BAHAMA BANK

Southern Bight

Long Bay Cays

Kemp's Bay
Deep Creek

Deep Creek

Little Creek

Little Creek
Mars Bay

Grassy Creek

N

Andros

0   5   10   15   20
Miles

Sailing can be hazardous off the Andros reef—and on the Great Bahama Bank to the west—but sailfishing is popular here. The bonefishing off Andros is considered by many to be the best in the world, and there are marlin and bluefin tuna off the eastern shore. Bonefishing equipment, boats, and snorkeling gear can be rented at *Jolly Boy's Enterprises* in the town of Drigg's Hill (phone: 369-4767).

Most of the settlements in Andros are strung along the east coast, which is more salubrious than the marshy strands to the west. There are three main towns along the east coast: Nicholl's Town in North Andros, Andros Town in Central Andros, and Congo Town on South Andros (accessible only by boat). Planes fly regularly from Miami, Ft. Lauderdale, and Nassau to these towns, and mail boats call once a week at Nicholl's Town and Andros Town. It's not easy to get around, for rental cars are scarce and most of the roads, while paved, are poorly maintained. Travelers should plan ahead and decide where on the island they want to be based.

Andros Town is perhaps the most convenient spot for divers who want to explore the great reef. Seminole and Arawak Indians once lived in the area, and pirates anchored in the nearby coves during the 17th and 18th centuries. In the mid-1950s, A&P heir Huntington Hartford built the exclusive *Andros Yacht Club* here, with the financial backing of Swedish industrialist Axel Wenner-Gren. In its early years, the resort was enormously successful, but its second owner, American industrialist Louis Reynolds, lost interest in the project after his son and heir was killed by a plane propeller. The bank foreclosed on the hotel mortgage, and success passed Andros Town by. The village enjoyed a brief spell of fame in the fall of 1985, when Queen Elizabeth II stopped by for a visit. The recent completion of a few guesthouses and lodges may revive its fortunes as divers and fishermen discover the unspoiled reefs and fishing grounds. Places to stay include the government-operated *Lighthouse Yacht Club and Marina* and the casually comfortable *Coakley House,* a graceful villa located on two acres of land with its own dock not far from its parent establishment, the *Small Hope Bay Lodge,* whose diving facilities are available to guests of both hotels. (For details on all three properties, see "Checking In" in *Bahamas,* THE ISLANDS.)

The homey *Small Hope Bay Lodge* is really the best place to stay in the Andros Town area. It's located 3 miles north of Andros Town on Small Hope Bay, named for pirate Henry Morgan's proverbial claim that there was "small hope" that anyone would find his buried treasure. Dives can be arranged by the hotel—the reefs just off the bay are well worth exploring. There are also specialty dives into blue holes and coral caverns and guided "bush doctor" treks to see native plants, many of which have medicinal value. More than 50 varieties of orchid bloom in the forests here, and cranes, herons, egrets, and white crown pigeons can be spotted along ponds and creeks. Wild boars and four-foot-long iguanas live in the forests, as do many kinds of snakes—none of which, thankfully, is poisonous. South of Andros

Town are the villages of Cargill Creek and Behring Point, which both have good hotels, diving facilities, and bonefish flats. The best bonefishing on the island is said to be at Lowe Sound, just west of Nicholl's Town, which has good diving facilities and accommodations—try the *Green Windows Inn* (phone: 329-2515). Visitors with a taste for luxury can stay at the *Emerald Palms by the Sea* hotel in Congo Town on South Andros (see "Checking In" in *Bahamas,* THE ISLANDS). The beaches here are splendid, but the place is remote: the only way to reach Andros Town and the northern settlements from here is by boat.

ANDROS BY BIKE

The roads are fairly decent around Andros Town, and there is little traffic, so cycling is pleasant. Start from the *Small Hope Bay Lodge* (see above), which has sturdy bikes for rent. South of Small Hope Bay the road winds up and down the gentle hills along the eastern shore, passing several deserted beaches along the way. At Calabash Bay, with its tiny cluster of wooden houses, there is a pretty sickle-shaped beach and *Sampson's* restaurant and lounge (phone: 368-2615), which serves good native dishes. Next is Coakley Town, a tottery old village with a Catholic church and a couple of shops. Near *Coakley House* on the waterfront (see above) is the *Landmark* (phone: 368-2082), a restaurant with homey pine-paneled rooms, a balcony bar, and excellent Bahamian cooking. There's also a harborfront marina, another restaurant, and a disco. Cross the bridge over Fresh Creek into Andros Town; you'll see the flamingo-pink bungalows of the *Lighthouse Yacht Club and Marina* on the left (see above). Nearby is the *Androsia* factory, where visitors can watch batik cloth being dyed; there is also a gift shop on the premises. It's closed weekends (phone: 368-2020).

ANDROS BY CAR

Andros isn't an automobile-friendly place. New cars here have been known to rust through in two years, and most of the locals ride the bus or hitchhike. If bumps and ill-marked side roads don't bother you, though, you may want to devote a day or two to exploring the fine beaches and bonefishing flats up and down the east coast. Your hotel can usually arrange rental of a local's private car for a day or two. There are also two rental agencies: *Amklco* (Main St., Fresh Creek; phone: 368-2056) and *Berth Rent-a-Car* (Calabash Bay; phone: 368-2102).

NORTH OF ANDROS TOWN It's a 28-mile drive along a deserted paved road from Andros Town north to Nicholl's Town. The road, which parallels the water, is lined with thick stands of pine. Two miles past Small Hope Bay are the secluded beaches at Love Hill. Snorkelers should stop to explore the coral gardens just offshore. Eight miles farther on is the settlement of Staniard Creek. Turn right onto the wide paved road that leads to the village. The town has two picturesque churches, the *Zion Baptist Church* and the

Lighthouse Chapel, once brightly painted and now faded to a pale lemon and lime. The beach, which is shaded by coconut palms, is a good place for a swim, or you can hire a boat (contact *Jolly Boy's Enterprises,* based in Drigg's Hill—see above) to go out to the flats and try your luck at bonefishing.

Stafford Creek, about 5 miles on, past the *Forfar Field Station* marine science center, is popular for its good beaches and bonefishing. At the fork about 10 miles farther, a left turn leads to the *San Andros Airport,* which serves Nicholl's Town, and a right turn leads to Mastic Point, a fishing village with a gas station, grocery store, and church. Backtrack to the *San Andros Airport* to reach the northern tip of the island. There is a crossroads 5 miles north of the airport; the road straight ahead leads to the village of Morgan's Bluff. Henry Morgan is said to have hidden his pirate treasure in the cave on the hill overlooking the harbor. (Bring a flashlight if you wish to explore the cave, which opens up into a vast chilly gallery more than 300 feet high.)

A left turn at the crossroads leads to Lowe Sound, a straggly little town only one street wide. Coconut palms shade the road, and a dozen jetties jut out into the water, evidence of the thriving local fishing industry. The flats offshore are said to be the best bonefishing grounds in the world. *Kevin's* guesthouse (no phone) is comfortable, and *Big Josh* seafood restaurant and lounge next door is a good place for lunch (phone: 329-7517). Fifteen miles west of Lowe Sound, reachable by boat or a bumpy unpaved road, is Red Cays, populated by the descendants of black and Seminole slaves who escaped from Florida during the early 19th century. The villagers live much as their ancestors did, building palm-thatch houses, hunting fish, and practicing old religious rites. The community now earns a living selling straw baskets and mats; visitors can watch demonstrations at the crafts center in Lowe Sound.

A right turn at the crossroads north of the airport leads to Nicholl's Town, the main settlement on North Andros. (To reach the town, take a left off the main road onto an unmarked spur near a rocky bluff.) Seminole Indians once lived near this secluded spot, which is now dominated by the former *Andros Beach* hotel. The hotel was closed indefinitely at press time, though its marina is still in operation.

SOUTH OF ANDROS TOWN The road south hugs the coast for 25 miles, passing a handful of settlements before reaching the southern end of North Andros. There is a T-junction just past Andros Town. The road to the left leads to the *Atlantic Undersea Test and Evaluation Center (AUTEC),* one of several top-secret US/British naval-research centers along the east coast of the island. The road to the right passes through two small settlements, Bowen Sound and Man of War Sound, where the bonefishing is said to be good. A few miles south, at Cargill Creek, are two first-rate fishing camps: *Andros Island Bonefishing Club* (phone: 368-5167) and *Cargill Creek Lodge* (see

"Checking In" in *Bahamas,* THE ISLANDS). For information about both camps, contact the *PanAngling Travel Service* (phone: 800-533-4353; 312-263-0328 in Chicago). While neither is air conditioned, *Cargill Creek Lodge* is the newer and more comfortable of the two. Both have no-frills restaurants that serve homestyle lobster, conch, grouper, chicken, and ribs.

A few miles south, at Behring Point, is another popular fishing lodge, *Nottages Cottages* (see "Checking In" in *Bahamas,* THE ISLANDS). This spot, just above Northern Bight—the creek that separates North and Central Andros—is a favorite launching place for bonefishers setting off to explore the labyrinth of creeks and cays to the south. Bonefish weighing 12 pounds or more have been netted in these waters. South of Behring Point, driving isn't really an option. The settlements of Moxey Town and Mangrove Cay on Central Andros are reachable only by boat or water taxi; the latter crosses once in the morning and once in the afternoon. You can park your car right by the dock at Behring Point. Visitors who wish to reach the settlements on South Andros must take a water taxi to Lisbon Creek and a ferry to Drigg's Hill. At Lisbon Creek, snorkelers can explore a network of underwater caverns, and there is a spectacular dive from the blue hole on Linda Cay. Gear and dive trips are available from the island's only dive operator, which is affiliated with the *Small Hope Bay Lodge* (see above).

From the ferry stop at Drigg's Hill, take a taxi to Congo Town, the main settlement on South Andros. The road south of Congo Town becomes progressively more isolated—and bumpy—but it's worth the trip, for it leads to Long Bay Cays, possibly the finest coconut-palm beaches on all of Andros. There are also good beaches farther south at Kemp's Bay and at Mars Bay, the southernmost settlement, where the road ends.

Eleuthera

About 11,000 people live on Eleuthera, which is 110 miles long and, in many spots, only about a mile wide. The first permanent European settlement in the Bahamas took root here during the mid-17th century, and the island still has a strong colonial air. Its rolling green hills are dotted with ruined plantations and quaint pastel-hued villages, including Spanish Wells, just offshore, said to be the wealthiest town in the Bahamas. The deliciously deserted beaches and good offshore surfing and diving are the lures here.

It's best to explore the island by car rather than bicycle. While the terrain isn't too rugged (though there are a few rough patches, and a four-wheel-drive vehicle is a good idea), the distances warrant it. There are plenty of rental cars available on Eleuthera—just be sure to check the gas gauge and the location of the nearest gas station before setting out. Island rental companies are notorious for leaving very little gas in the tank. If you do decide to cycle, keep in mind that bikes and mopeds aren't permitted on ferries, and a lock is needed if you wish to leave your vehicle on the docks while island-hopping in the north. Also note: If you want to swim at one of the many stretches of beautiful, isolated beaches here, wear your bathing suit underneath your clothes, as most do not have changing facilities.

Perhaps the best way to see Eleuthera is to start at Governor's Harbour in the center of the island, head south, and then wander back to the historic spots in the north. Founded in 1648, Governor's Harbour is the heart of island life. (It's the technological capital, too, for it has the island's only traffic light.) The first colonists probably landed near here, on Cupid's Cay just off the western edge of the harbor. The settlers, staunch Puritans from Bermuda, were led by William Sayle, a former governor. They called themselves the Eleutherian Adventurers, after the Greek word for "freedom." After landing on Cupid's Cay, the group argued and split up, and Sayle led a large contingent to the northern part of the island, leaving a handful of dissenters behind. A causeway now links Governor's Harbour to the cay, where there is a quaint little community with two landmarks, the stately commissioner's house and the 19th-century *St. Patrick's Anglican Church*.

Though its beginnings were humble, Governor's Harbour became one of the busiest and wealthiest towns in the islands. Pineapple and citrus fruit were shipped from here to New York, Baltimore, and other ports on the Eastern seaboard during the second half of the 19th century. So sophisticated were its inhabitants that wealthy Nassau matrons came here to see the latest finery from London and New York. The style of those days still survives in the fancifully trimmed Victorian houses that line the side streets.

There are a few gift shops, a bank, and a couple of hotels and guesthouses in and around town, including the new *Hyatt Cape Eleuthera* resort,

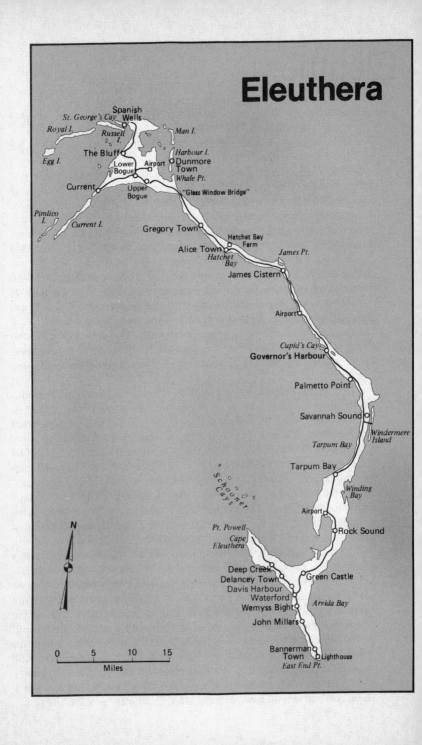

featuring 300 rooms and its own airstrip, and a *Club Med* on the Atlantic side (for details in both, see "Checking In" in *Bahamas,* THE ISLANDS). The *Club Med* resort is built on the site of the first hotel on the island, *French Leave,* which opened in the 1940s. It was said to have been the home of Mauritian Alfred de Marigny, who was accused—and later acquitted—of murdering Nassau millionaire Sir Harry Oakes in 1943. Nowadays the big event of the week is the arrival of the mail boat, which generally chugs in on Friday or Saturday.

ROUTE 1: SOUTH OF GOVERNOR'S HARBOUR

Head south out of town on the Queen's Highway; 5 miles down is Palmetto Point, where many wealthy American expatriates live. Just south of town is a sign marking the road that leads west to Ten Bay, where there is a small limestone cave and a beach.

It's 7 to 10 miles to the next settlement, the picturesque fishing village of Tarpum Bay. (The name is a corruption of "tarpon," a large fish that abounds in the flats offshore.) Take a stroll along the harbor in the late afternoon and watch the fishermen clean their catch. Several artists—most of them American expatriates—work and exhibit here, including Macmillan Hughes and Mal Flanders. Ramble down the streets lined with pastel houses, or climb to Hughes's "castle" on the hill; built by the artist himself, it's a quirky product of the Scotsman's imagination, and inside it he displays more of his artwork. Watch for a sign near the center of town indicating a sharp turn to the left; this leads back to the Queen's Highway, which continues south toward Rock Sound. Less than a mile outside Tarpum Bay, a road branches off to the left toward *Club Eleuthera* (phone: 334-4055), a small, all-inclusive resort catering to Italian charter groups. The beach and pool here are reserved for guests, but visitors are welcome to stop for a meal at the restaurant, one of the few on this end of the island.

Just north of Rock Sound on the right is the small airport where both domestic flights from Nassau and international flights from Florida touch down. The town, which was settled during the early 18th century, has a Bermudian feel, with narrow streets and prim pastel cottages. The place was originally called Wreck Sound, since most residents made a living by "wrecking"—scavenging cargo from ships that foundered on the rocks and shoals offshore. Today it's home to just over a thousand residents. Few outsiders came here until the early 1940s; one of the first was Arthur Vining Davis, chairman of the Aluminum Company of America, who built a winter home south of town.

Take a stroll through town, stopping in the boutiques along Front Street, which faces the placid waters of the bay. Just a block up Albury Lane, one of the first cross streets in town, is *Sammy's Place* (phone: 334-2121). Chef/owner Sammy Culmer established his redoubtable reputation at the swanky *Sofitel Cotton Bay Club*. The food here is homey and unpretentious: Try the conch fritters and peas and rice.

On the southeastern edge of town, past a cemetery and a schoolyard, is a geologic oddity that's worth a detour. It's a blue hole roughly 125 yards wide and at least 100 fathoms—that's 600 feet—deep. The pool is fed by sea water that seeps through the porous limestone bedrock. Visitors can swim here or throw bits of bread to the angelfish and schoolmasters that swim in the clear blue water. Fishing or removing oysters is prohibited.

South of the blue hole, the road hugs the western shore, and the rocky Schooner Cays seem to float just offshore. Terns and white crown pigeons wheel over the calm water. Just before the small farming community of Green Castle, a road branches off to the left to the *Sofitel Cotton Bay Club*. The resort, once a private club, was built in the late 1950s by Juan Trippe, the flamboyant founder of the late lamented *Pan American Airways*. Trippe flew in friends on the "Cotton Bay Special," a 727 Yankee Clipper, to play golf on the 18-hole course designed by Robert Trent Jones Sr. The large villa on the grounds was once the vacation home of American industrialist Edgar Kaiser. At press time, the resort was closed indefinitely, but was expected to reopen under new management. (Also see "Golf" and "Checking In" in *Bahamas,* THE ISLANDS.)

Just after Green Castle, a town founded in the 19th century by freed slaves, the island widens and splits into two forks. The road northwest leads to Davis Harbour, where boats are moored in a sheltered cove, and passes through the rustic fishing villages of Waterford, Delancey Town, and Deep Creek. The southeastern route winds through farming and fishing villages—including Wemyss Bight, John Millars, and Bannerman Town—to the *East End Point Lighthouse* at the southern end of the island.

ROUTE 2: NORTH OF GOVERNOR'S HARBOUR

The road north runs straight to the airport, about 10 miles from town (the airport was built for a US Navy base—now closed—on the eastern side of the island). In 3 or 4 more miles is the small village of James Cistern, named after a 19th-century governor who built a reservoir for Governor's Harbour. A few traditions still linger in this isolated town; notice the outdoor ovens made from a sand-and-limestone mixture called "tabby." Just past town the road skirts a series of cliffs, and the views are spectacular.

Huge silos loom in the distance on the way to Alice Town and Hatchet Bay; they are all that remain of a large dairy farm built in the mid-1930s by American Austin Levy. The farm was intended to be self-sufficient: Cattle were fed grain grown on Eleuthera, and their milk was processed here before it was shipped to Nassau. At the height of the farm's activity, just after World War II, a refrigerated ship laden with milk, butter, eggs, and poultry made daily trips from here to Nassau.

Signs just outside Alice Town point west toward Hatchet Bay Cave, which is worth a side trip. If you don't have a flashlight, a local guide will light the way for a small fee. The steps just past the narrow entrance of the cave were probably carved by farmers who came to gather nitrogen-rich bat guano to use as fertilizer. The half-mile-deep cave widens into a broad vaulted chamber just 10 or 15 yards from the entrance. Icicle-like stalactites and stalagmites grow here, and hanging from the walls are hundreds of leaf-nosed bats, so-called for the floppy appendages on their snouts.

About 3 miles beyond Alice Town is a fine 5-mile stretch of small beaches on the eastern side of the island. The surfing here is excellent, but the beaches can be tough to reach: Visitors may need a four-wheel-drive vehicle to negotiate the barely visible track (it's a little more than half a mile from the main road to the shore). Halfway along this stretch is Gregory Town, the pineapple capital of Eleuthera. Tourists who are on the islands the first weekend in June should stop by for the *Pineapple Festival,* which is celebrated with a pineapple-drink-mixing contest, lots of pineapple eating, and a "Pine-athlon" race, with contestants swimming half a mile, running 3 miles, and bicycling 4½ miles. Pirates hid out here in the 18th century and kept a lookout for ships from the high cliffs behind the harbor. After the buccaneers cleared out, many Loyalists, or Tories, moved here following the American Revolution. By the 20th century, the town looked like a Cornish fishing village. Today, pineapple growers and American and Canadian expatriates live in this picturesque town, and tourists fill the hotels during the winter. Stop by the *Thompson Bros. Supermarket* (phone: 335-5009), a family-run place that sells scrumptious homemade pineapple rum.

Five miles past Gregory Town the island narrows to a sliver just wide enough for a car to drive across. Sailors called the place the Glass Window Bridge, for they could "see through" the island from the rough waters of the Atlantic on one side to the calm blue-green waters of the Great Bahama Bank on the other. American artist Winslow Homer, who spent some time in Eleuthera after the Civil War, captured the scene in a painting.

Beyond the bridge the island widens, and the road meanders through the farming villages of Upper and Lower Bogue. The land here is marshy, or "boguey," as the natives say. The left turn past Lower Bogue leads to the prosperous little town of Current, which overlooks the tranquil waters to the west. Many of the houses here are built on pilings. The townsfolk are thought to be descendants of Lucaya Indians, who lived in the Bahamas in pre-Columbian times. More likely their ancestors were English settlers who occasionally intermarried with free blacks, a practice that was discouraged in other settlements.

Back on the main road, you'll soon come to a fork: The right-hand road leads to *North Eleuthera Airport* and the ferries to Harbour Island; the left winds to the dock for the ferries to Spanish Wells.

The road to the left leads first to The Bluff, a fishing village perched by a miniature harbor that was once a settlement for freed slaves. Citrus trees grow in neat rows near the road. Signs past the turnoff to The Bluff point the way to Preacher's Cave; the well-marked track meanders about a mile to the site. Inside, the ceiling arches 100 feet overhead, and sunlight filters in through fissures in the roof. It was here, on the lovely stretch of deserted beach that fronts the cave, that the main contingent of Eleutherian Adventurers came ashore in 1648. Since this is the windward side of the island, the water can be choppy, but it's a pleasant place for a picnic.

Back on the main road, it's a short drive to Gene's Bay, where the ferryboats to Spanish Wells dock at the eastern end of town. The ferries (passengers only; park your car at the dock) run about three times daily (except Sundays) and cost $5 per person one way. It takes just a couple of minutes to reach St. George's Cay and the settlement of Spanish Wells, which got its name from the Spanish galleons that used to take on fresh water here. Most of the residents of this hidebound seafaring town make a living catching spiny lobster; it's a lucrative business, apparently, for Spanish Wells is said to have the highest per capita income of any community in the Bahamas. Notice the not-so-subtle signs of wealth: the large brick homes on the western edge of town, the competing video rental shops, and the satellite dishes perched on top of homes. Red-roofed clapboard houses line the narrow streets in the eastern part of town, and towheaded locals eye visitors cautiously before they nod in greeting. (Note the fine straw hats worn by the men; they can be purchased locally.) It's a reticent, inbred, overwhelmingly white community—and has been for centuries. Before leaving, stop for a conch sandwich at *La Langousta* (phone: 333-4147), a dockside restaurant run by Walton Pinder and his Brazilian wife.

Return to Gene's Bay on the passenger ferry and then drive 10 minutes or so east on the main road to get to the Harbour Island ferry dock. Unlike Spanish Wells, Harbour Island is a tourist-oriented place, so the ferries here are bigger. It costs $3 per person, one way, to take the 10-minute trip to the dock at Dunmore Town (commonly called Harbour Island); the ferry does not run on Sundays. Guesthouses, hotels, and restaurants line the waterfront, and several more hotels face the blush-colored beach on the eastern side of the island. Visitors can hail a taxi to take a tour of the island, or they can rent mopeds at the shop on the inland end of the dock.

Harbour Island—or "Briland," as the locals say—was settled more than 300 years ago; it was the original capital of the Bahamas. Ramble slowly down the narrow, tree-lined streets. Some of the homes here are over 200 years old. A white cottage on Bay Street north of the dock displays a sign proclaiming it a Loyalist house built in 1792. Three fine old churches stand on Dunmore Street: Anglican *St. John's; Wesley Methodist,* built in 1840; and Catholic *St. Benedict's,* whose adjoining convent was built in 1922 to house the Sisters of Charity. From here, head for the beach on the Atlantic side for sun or a dip, or stroll by *Valentine's Yacht Club and Inn* on the waterfront (also see "Checking In" in *Bahamas,* THE ISLANDS). For more information on Harbour Island, see *Quintessential Bahamas and Turks & Caicos* in DIVERSIONS.

Cat Island

Few tourists—and not even many Bahamians—know much about Cat Island. Don't spread the word: It's one of the loveliest and most unspoiled of the Out Islands. It was named for English sea captain (and pirate, most likely) Arthur Catt, who also lent his name to Arthur's Town, a village at the north end of the island. The isle was known for years as San Salvador, for it was long believed to be where Columbus first landed in the New World. This notion was officially debunked in 1892, when a panel of experts, relying on descriptions from Columbus's long-lost journal and other sources, decided that the *Pinta* had really landed on Watling's Island to the southeast. In 1926, Watling's Island was renamed San Salvador, and Cat Island received its humble new name.

This gossamer-thin isle, 48 miles long and less than a mile wide in places, is fertile by Bahamian standards, and most of its inhabitants farm for a living. Cat Island pineapples and tomatoes are particularly famous; potatoes, melons, peas, and beans are also raised here. The isle once had the reputation of being wild and untamed, for more Arawak Indians lived here than on any island in the Bahamian archipelago when Columbus arrived. The Indians are long gone, but vestiges of old colonial traditions remain. Some farmers still clear the land with machetes and till with grub hoes, as they've done for centuries, and women still bake bread in outdoor ovens. Talisman-like "duppies"—bottles or cans filled with earth, hair, and fingernails—protect country homes. (The duppies are a remnant of obeah, the voodoo-like black magic once practiced by slaves and free blacks.) Some of the old folks still know how to dance an English waltz or quadrille, and traditional rake-and-scrape bands still play at weddings and parties.

Most visitors land on the island at the little airport in Arthur's Town. Only a few hundred people live here, but it's one of the most important settlements on the island. (The town's history is recounted in the autobiography of its most famous resident, actor Sidney Poitier.) A grassy square stands in the center of town, and there's a school off to one side. To the north, across the harbor, stand the tumbledown remains of the original settlement; nearby is the town's hot nightspot, *Lovers Boulevard* (no phone), which calls itself a "disco and satellite lounge" because of the satellite dish on the roof.

It's hard to get lost on Cat Island, for one paved road runs from north to south, and the villages are strung along it like beads on a necklace. Most of the towns line the western shore, where the waters are calmer. The island widens at both ends, and the geography there is slightly more complicated, but it's still easy to find your way around. The best way to see the island is to start at Arthur's Town and head south. Although it's possible to ride a bike or moped, be forewarned that the roads can be rough in spots. Anglers

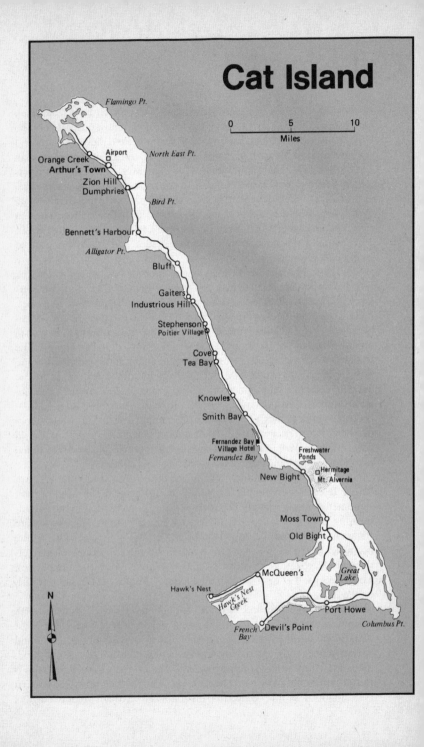

Cat Island

Flamingo Pt.

0   5   10
Miles

Orange Creek
Arthur's Town
Airport
North East Pt.
Zion Hill
Dumphries

Bird Pt.

Bennett's Harbour

Alligator Pt.
Bluff

Gaiters
Industrious Hill

Stephenson
Poitier Village

Cove
Tea Bay

Knowles

Smith Bay

Fernandez Bay
Village Hotel
Fernandez Bay

Freshwater
Ponds

Hermitage
Mt. Alvernia

New Bight

Moss Town

Old Bight

McQueen's

*Great
Lake*

Hawk's Nest

*Hawk's Nest
Creek*

Port Howe

Columbus Pt.

*French
Bay*

Devil's Point

N

may want to start with a detour to Orange Creek, the only settlement north of Arthur's Town, where the bonefishing in the flats offshore is particularly good. (Rental of bicycles, mopeds, and fishing gear can be arranged through your hotel.)

Just south of Arthur's Town is the tiny community of Zion Hill, where you may see women sitting on their porches plaiting palm fronds. A mile farther south, just beyond the village of Dumphries, is Bennett's Harbour, with its lovely half-mile-long waterfront. One of the island's oldest towns, it was founded in the 1830s by Governor James Carmichael Smyth, who designated it a settlement for blacks freed from slave ships. East of town beyond Thurston Hill is Bird Point, which overlooks the Atlantic (ask for directions; the trail is faint and unmarked). Wrens, blackbirds, egrets, and several kinds of heron nest in the shrubs beside the path; near the shore are some natural salt ponds, called salinas, which were worked commercially about 50 years ago and are now abandoned. Visitors may still see an islander raking salt here now and then. Back on the main road, past Alligator Point to the west, is Bluff, a derelict old town that was once a wealthy settlement when cotton was king.

For the next 25 miles or so, the road winds through several small farming villages. Near Gaiter's Settlement, huge limestone caves riddle the cliffs on the western shore, but you need a boat to explore them. The women of Industrious Hill are known for their palm-frond plaiting, while Stephenson is famous for its rooftop ornaments called "prettys." Just below Stephenson is a tiny community called Poitier Village, where almost everyone claims to be related to Sidney Poitier.

The next few communities—Sawyer, Cove, Tea Bay, Bachelor's—are unpretentious little towns where farmers tend their crops of sweet potatoes, onions, and pigeon peas. Next is Knowles, which is big enough to have a gas station and a primary school, the only one in the central part of the island. (High school students travel south to Old Bight, the biggest town in these parts, for classes.) Smith Bay is somewhat larger, with several churches, a clinic, and a government packing house, from which produce is shipped to Nassau. During the busiest months of the year, as many as eight cargo boats sail from here each week.

Next comes Fernandez Bay, whose fine beach is still relatively undiscovered. On the beach is the *Fernandez Bay Village* hotel, run by the Armbristers, one of the oldest families on the island; it has several villas, a grocery store, nightly beachside dinner buffets featuring traditional island dishes and a bonfire, and one of Cat Island's few telephones. (Also see "Checking In" in *Bahamas,* THE ISLANDS.)

The freshwater ponds just east of here are home to the Cat Island turtle, a rare species possibly stranded here at the end of the last Ice Age. (It's also possible that Lucaya Indians brought the turtles here from South America.) Years ago, the Lucaya caught the turtles, which they called "peter," with a hook and line baited with fruit. Cat Islanders still prize them for their meat.

Three miles south of Fernandez Bay is New Bight, a large town by island standards; the commissioner's office, police department, and post office are located here. The good local food served at the *Bluebird* restaurant (no phone) on the main road attracts patrons from all over the island.

New Bight is the gateway to the *Hermitage,* a religious retreat atop Mt. Alvernia. Park the car; the footpath to the retreat begins in the center of town near the commissioner's office. The climb is arduous but short, for the mountain, the highest spot in the Bahamas, is only 206 feet high. The summit affords a panoramic view of the deep blue Atlantic to the east and the calm azure waters to the west. The climb to the chapel, bell tower, and tiny house—all hand-hewn from native rock—is marked by the stations of the cross.

The *Hermitage* is the handiwork of Father Jerome, born John Hawkes, who came to the Bahamas in 1911 as an Anglican missionary and later converted to Catholicism. An architect by training, he designed and built several churches in the Bahamas, including Anglican *St. Paul's* and Catholic *St. Peter's* in Clarence Town on Long Island and the *Monastery of St. Augustine* on New Providence. When he retired in 1939, he was granted permission to build the Alvernia retreat. His grave—he died in 1956 at the age of 80—is in a cave just below the *Hermitage.*

Five miles south of New Bight, on the way to Old Bight, is the small village of Moss Town, named for the Spanish moss that hangs from the trees on this part of the island. Here in the south the island broadens to its greatest width: nearly 15 miles. The island's only major crossroads is just north of Old Bight. The left (east) fork skirts Old Bight and a pond called Great Lake and continues to the historic town of Port Howe. The right (west) fork cuts through the center of Old Bight and heads toward the south shore. From there it meanders west to Devil's Point, McQueen's, and Hawk's Nest.

The east road to Point Howe skirts Columbus Point on the southeastern tip of the island. About a mile before Point Howe, a dirt track branches off and leads to the point, but the terrain is rough and the last couple of miles must be traversed on foot. It's worth the walk, for the views from the point, where steep cliffs sweep down to the ocean, are spectacular. Back on the main road heading toward the town of Port Howe, the terrain is open and flat, and pineapple plants flourish in the rich red soil.

Port Howe is hardly a port—its harbor is fringed with treacherous reefs and shallow waters. Some say that the village's name may have been deliberately misleading. The town's early residents, many of whom made a living by scavenging shipwrecks, apparently decided to increase their business with a little false advertising. Legend says that they hung lanterns from the trees to exaggerate the size of the "port," beckoning hapless sailors to shore.

Just west of Port Howe stand the ruins of what was once the 2,000-acre *Richman Hill–Newfield* plantation. Owned for many years by the Armbrister family, it is now overgrown and crumbling, though visitors can still see the remnants of the slave quarters and the large octagonal house that overlooked the ocean. A few of the walls that surrounded the elaborate gardens still stand, and the once-lovely pools are filled with stagnant water. Locals say that gold and jewels salvaged from nearby shipwrecks are buried here.

Between Port Howe and Devil's Point the road skirts a series of 200-foot cliffs, affording the homes perched near them breathtaking views. Five miles offshore is Tartar Bank, where locals fish. For another fine view, continue straight past the turnoff to McQueen's to reach Devil's Point on the southwestern tip of the island. An old island saying has it that here "cork did sink and iron float"—a reference, most likely, to the meeting of the rough Atlantic waters and the calm western seas rather than to a preternatural event.

Follow the main road north to McQueen's, a tradition-bound farming community of palmetto-frond thatch houses where women still make their own baskets and bake in outdoor ovens. Near the town is Hawk's Nest Creek, a bird sanctuary where great blue herons nest. From here, turn around and retrace the route to Arthur's Town; to skip the loop around Great Lake, bear left at the fork.

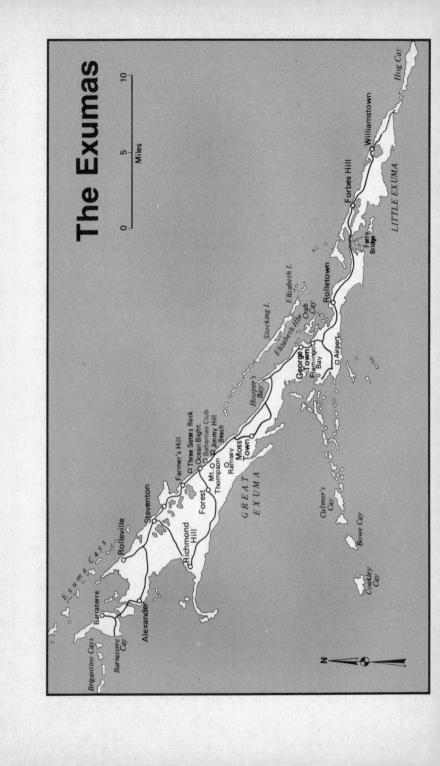

The Exumas

This 100-mile-long string of stepping-stone islands and cays is one of the great finds in the Out Islands. The Exumas, 365 in all, are sparsely populated; only 3,539 people live here year-round, most of them on Great and Little Exuma, the largest islands in the chain. Some of the best sailing waters in the Bahamas are here, and there are fine dives off 5,000-foot-deep Exuma Sound to the east. The shallow pools just offshore, whose colors range from jade to celadon to opal, are superb for bathing and bonefishing.

Although the islands are still largely unsullied by tourism, Great Exuma's tourist population is sure to increase by leaps and bounds after the first casino in the Out Islands opens at the new *Bahamas Club.* Construction was under way at press time and is expected to take a total of five to eight years, though the resort is slated to open for business this year. Plans are also in the works for a new water-purification system and a wildlife sanctuary on the island.

Lucaya Indians are believed to have lived on this archipelago before the Spanish carried them off as slaves during the 16th century. In the 17th century, salt rakers came to the Exumas by the hundreds, as did pirates seeking a haven for their booty. The islands later became a refuge for a handful of Loyalists fleeing the newly independent United States. Cotton and salt were the main sources of wealth throughout the 18th century, and many slaves were brought here to labor on the plantations and salinas. Eventually, though, both industries failed.

Much of the land here was granted by the Crown in the late 18th century to Lord John Rolle, who according to some accounts gave his plantations to his slaves after they were freed in 1834. Some say Rolle's gesture was genuinely magnanimous, while cynics claim he had no choice; in any case, the slaves eventually prevailed, and many took Rolle's name. To this day, most of the arable land on the Exumas cannot be sold; instead, it is passed down from generation to generation in island families, many of which still bear the name Rolle. Islanders still tend their small fruit and vegetable plots and husband their goats and sheep as they have for centuries. Farmers sell their onions, tomatoes, mangoes, avocados, and pineapples to the hotels on the islands, or ship them by mail boat to Nassau. Fishing and tourism are the mainstays of the modern economy.

Many Exuma cays are reachable only by boat or chartered plane. Staniel Cay north of Great Exuma has good sailing and fishing; divers can explore the grotto where parts of the James Bond movie *Thunderball* were filmed. (At low tide you can snorkel into the cave.) Overnighters can stay at the *Staniel Cay Yacht Club,* which caters to private pilots and yachting folk (see "Checking In" in *Bahamas,* THE ISLANDS). North of Staniel Cay, off the western shore between Conch Cut and Wax Cay Cut, is the *Exuma Land*

and Sea Park, a 200-square-mile reserve—reachable only by boat—where delicate coral gardens grow only a few feet below the surface of the water.

About a thousand people live in the Exumas' capital, George Town, which is the liveliest spot in the islands. Situated on deep Elizabeth Harbour on Great Exuma, it is reachable by *Bahamasair,* which makes daily trips between Nassau and Freeport and the airport 9 miles south of town, or by *American Eagle,* which flies daily from Miami. Tourists with relaxed schedules can reach the Exumas on the *Grand Master,* the mail boat that ferries supplies to the islands; it leaves Nassau each Tuesday and docks in Elizabeth Harbour the following morning. (The boat, which returns to Nassau each Thursday, takes only a limited number of passengers, so inquire at your hotel or call 393-1041 well in advance.) For three days each April, the harbor here is filled with sloops racing in the *Out Island Regatta,* one of the grand events of the year. Fishing boats from across the islands also come here in April to compete for the "Best in the Bahamas" title.

GREAT EXUMA ON FOOT

Small, historic George Town is an ideal place for a leisurely stroll; visitors can see all the main sights in half an hour or so. Start in the center of town on the Queen's Highway at *Club Peace and Plenty,* named for the English trading ship that brought Lord Rolle to the Exumas in 1783. The hotel, opened in 1955 by a grandnephew of Florida railroad/real-estate baron Henry Flagler, is built around the remains of an old sponge warehouse and market (see "Checking In" in *Bahamas,* THE ISLANDS). Opposite it is the *Peace and Plenty Boutique* (phone: 336-2551), selling Androsia batik prints; the *Sandpiper* (phone: 336-2604), for original hand-silk-screened clothing; and *Exuma Fantasea* (phone: 336-3483), a diving and water sports operation that also rents Boston whalers to fishing enthusiasts.

Up the Queen's Highway to the north is *St. Andrew's,* a lovely Presbyterian church with a high gabled roof, Norman arch doorways, and smart blue trim. Local theater productions are staged in the community center next door. Just up the road, the town peters out and the countryside begins.

South of *Club Peace and Plenty* on Queen's Highway, amid well-tended gardens, is the pink *Government Building,* modeled after *Government House* in Nassau. The post office and customs and police departments are inside. Just beyond it, opposite a park and a small straw market set up under a spreading banyan tree, is the *Two Turtles Inn,* a rustic hotel (with a popular outdoor bar) centered around a stone courtyard overlooking the harbor. The staff there will arrange diving tours and boating, and there are bicycles and scooters for rent (also see "Checking In" in *Bahamas,* THE ISLANDS).

Down to the right, near the local supermarket, is the delightful Mediterranean-style *Town Café* (phone: 336-2194). It's the best place in town for breakfast, and it serves decent lunches as well. Farther down on the left is *Gemelli's* (no phone), the local pizza hangout, and *Exuma Transport* (phone: 336-2101), the best place on the island to hire a car. Owner Sam Gray also runs *Sam's Place* (phone: 336-2579), a good seafood restaurant a stone's throw away. Sit on the balcony and munch on a conch salad as you watch the boats dock in the harbor. There are a few more shops overlooking nearby Victoria Pond.

After lunch, walk back toward the center of town to *Club Peace and Plenty,* where the ferries to Stocking Island dock. Ferries head to the island, which is just a mile offshore, at 10 AM and 1 PM. The crossing is free for hotel guests; otherwise the round-trip fare is $8 per person. On Stocking Island you can hunt for sand dollars and conch shells on the beach at low tide or relax over a barbecue (weekends only) at the beachside bar and grill. Divers can explore the Mystery Cave beneath the island or the 90-foot-deep blue hole called Angel Fish. (For more information on Stocking Island, see *Quintessential Bahamas and Turks & Caicos* in DIVERSIONS.)

GREAT EXUMA BY BIKE OR SCOOTER

The best route begins at George Town and follows the Queen's Highway north along the east coast of Great Exuma for 8 miles or so to Ocean Bight, stopping at the secluded beaches along the way. About 2 miles north of George Town is the *Peace and Plenty Beach Inn,* a trio of buildings built right on Bonefish Bay (see "Checking In" in *Bahamas,* THE ISLANDS). A few miles farther on, past *Exuma Straw Work* (no phone), which sells local handicrafts, is the turnoff to sheltered Hooper's Bay. Many of the villas here are surrounded by well-tended gardens of bougainvillea, pink and yellow hibiscus, birds of paradise, and amaryllis. Many pleasant beaches line the shore. Farther north, beyond the small village of Ramsey, is Jimmy Hill, famous for its long-deserted beach. Just to the north at Mt. Thompson is a picturesque Seventh-Day Adventist church, from which craggy Three Sisters Rock is visible just offshore. The tour ends at Ocean Bight a mile up the road. The tenor of this sleepy fishing village is expected to change considerably in the coming years with the opening of the new *Bahamas Club,* the sprawling residential and resort complex that will boast the Out Islands' first casino.

THE EXUMAS BY CAR

NORTH OF GEORGE TOWN It's a pleasant half-day drive from George Town to the tip of Great Exuma 30 miles to the northwest. The route along the Queen's Highway winds by the ruins of several old plantations, many of which are still being farmed. Boats are for hire in several of the small fishing villages along the way, and some of the finest beaches on the island are just a few hundred yards from the road. Eight miles north of George Town, a road—Pindling Drive—branches off to Moss Town, a farming village on the west side of the island. Its brightly painted houses contrast with the weather-beaten hues of the *St. John the Baptist Church* and a small Anglican chapel, which look as if they have survived many a storm. North of the village the road bends east to join the main coastal route.

A few miles on, past another secluded beach, are three of Lord Rolle's old plantations: *Farmer's Hill, Roker's Point,* and *Steventon.* Fields of cotton used to blanket the hillsides here until blights and chenille bugs destroyed the crops during the early 19th century. The grand plantation houses are gone, leaving only a scattering of wooden buildings painted in hues of green, yellow, and red. The descendants of the slaves who labored here more than a century ago still live nearby, tending their plots of corn, pigeon peas, and sweet onions. The taciturnity of the villagers is probably due more to shyness than animosity. If you ask, they'll be glad to point the way to the best beaches.

Rolleville, one of the largest and oldest settlements on the island, is a somnolent village with a few thatch houses and the whitewashed *Church of God of Prophecy.* The beaches here are well worth the trip. Stop by the *Hilltop Tavern* (phone: 345-6006) for a plate of grouper fingers and a chat with the owner, Kermit Rolle, a fine storyteller who knows the island well.

Past Rolleville, the road turns to dirt, leading after a bumpy mile or so to a perfect crescent beach. Heading back south, about 5 miles past Rolleville, there is a paved road off to the right with a sign pointing toward Alexander. This road leads past Alexander to Barraterre, a small cay linked to Great Exuma by a causeway, and one of the few spots that can be visited on the marshy western strand. Goats graze on the fields surrounding Alexander, another old settlement founded on the site of an 18th-century cotton plantation. Turn left at the *Mt. Sania Baptist Church;* the causeway is just ahead, past *Smith's Food Supplies* and the post office. Barraterre is a pretty fishing village with three landmarks: the Baptist church; *Ryann's Variety Store* (no phone), selling exemplary straw baskets; and the *Fisherman's Inn* (phone: 355-5017), with good barbecue, two rooms for rent, plus dancing to reggae and calypso music at night. The beach is fine for a short stroll, and you can watch the fishermen haul in their daily catch of grouper, conch, and bonefish.

SOUTH OF GEORGE TOWN From George Town south to Little Exuma, the road runs for 15 miles along the east coast, passing through several picturesque fishing villages. A half mile south of George Town is Flamingo Bay, where a cluster of private luxury villas overlooks the clear waters of the sound from a high promontory. Just beyond the bay, a wide paved road forks off to the right and leads to the old airport, where drug enforcement agencies float an Aerostat barrage balloon a mile above their station to intercept signals from drug-running vessels.

The next settlement, Rolletown, doesn't appear to have changed a whit over the past 50 years. Turn left into the village and right at the top of the hill to find the cemetery, where the tombs of 18th-century settler Captain Alexander McKay and his wife and child lie. McKay immigrated to the

Exumas from Scotland in 1789 and was granted 400 acres of farmland by the Crown. His wife and child died in 1792—the tombs give no explanation for their fate—and McKay died less than a year later.

Up ahead is the former *Blue Hole* café, which was bought by the owner of *Club Peace and Plenty.* The two-story clapboard building will become part of a hotel called the *Peace and Plenty Bonefish Lodge.* At press time, the lodge was still under construction, but was slated for completion this year. A fleet of skiffs for bonefishing in the miles of wading flats just offshore is available under the direction of Captain Bob Hyde (phone: 345-5555).

About 7½ miles south of George Town, the road crosses Ferry Bridge to Little Exuma Island. Just past the bridge, watch for a hand-painted sign on the left proclaiming "Tara, Home of the Shark Lady." (The sign just above it announces that the Tropic of Cancer runs right through the Shark Lady's home.) Ms. Gloria Patience, who is in her 70s, named her home after the *Gone With the Wind* plantation and greets visitors with a bone-crushing handshake, strengthened, no doubt, by years of wrestling sharks into her fishing boat. She claims to have caught more than 2,000; the biggest, she says, was an 18-foot tiger shark, and the meanest was a hammerhead that battered her boat to bits. Ms. Patience, miraculously, has never been hurt. She still motors out each day to bait and check her lines. When she's not regaling visitors with stories, she's hawking her shark steaks, shark's-tooth necklaces, shell mobiles, ancient green glass bottles, and the seascapes painted by her husband. After visiting the Shark Lady, proceed a few more miles toward Forbes Hill and look for a sign on your left for *La Shante* (phone: 345-4136), a club where you can have lunch and enjoy a swim at a stunning crescent-shape beach. *La Shante* also has three pleasant rooms, with private bath and cable TV.

Forbes Hill—a clutch of colorful old houses—is the last stop before Williamstown, which is dominated by the tall spire of *St. Mary Magdalene Church.* Look for the salt marker obelisk by Williamstown. It's shaped like a Grecian pillar and was placed there to show ships at sea that salt was available on the island. Williamstown is also the site of the old *Hermitage Plantation,* where cotton was grown in the days of slavery. Semi-intact slave huts can be seen on the grounds and visitors can ramble through the ruins of the plantation greathouse.

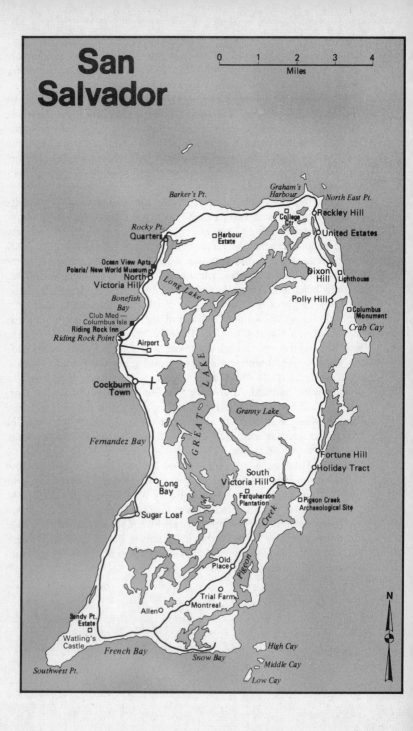

San Salvador

0   1   2   3   4
Miles

Barker's Pt.

Graham's
Harbour

North East Pt.

College
Ctr

Reckley Hill

Rocky Pt.
Quarters

Harbour
Estate

United Estates

Ocean View Apts.
Polaris/ New World Museum
North
Victoria Hill

Long Lake

Dixon
Hill

Lighthouse

Bonefish
Bay

Polly Hill

Columbus
Monument

Club Med —
Columbus Isle
Riding Rock Inn
Riding Rock Point

Airport

Crab Cay

Cockburn
Town

GREAT LAKE

Granny Lake

Fernandez Bay

Fortune Hill
Holiday Tract

Long
Bay

South
Victoria Hill

Sugar Loaf

Farquharson
Plantation

Pigeon Creek
Archaeological Site

Pigeon Creek

Old
Place

Trial Farm
Montreal

Sandy Pt.
Estate

Allen

Watling's
Castle

French Bay

Snow Bay

High Cay

Middle Cay

Low Cay

Southwest Pt.

N

San Salvador

The fame of this little knob of coralline limestone, about 12 miles long and 6 miles wide, is well out of proportion to its size. Though the facts are still disputed, most historians believe this is where Christopher Columbus first landed in 1492. Columbus called his first landfall San Salvador, but confusion arose later as to which isle he had actually visited first. Throughout early colonial times, this one was known as Watling's Island, after a buccaneer who lived here in fine style. During the late 19th century, scholars declared Watling's Island the original San Salvador, based in part on descriptions in Columbus's recently discovered journal of his first voyage. In 1926, the island was officially renamed, thanks in large measure to the lobbying of Chrysostom Schreiner, a Benedictine missionary who lived here for many years.

Similar in shape and geography to the isle of Grand Turk (which some historians believe could have been Columbus's first landfall), San Salvador is tiny enough to be toured in a day. Many visitors come to explore the reefs and wall off Riding Rock Point, which has some of the best shallow-water diving spots in the Bahamas. The interior of the island, which is flat and largely unpopulated, is riddled with brackish lakes. Many of the lakes are linked by small canals dug by settlers who found it easier to get around by boat than over land.

Most of the sights on San Salvador, including the lighthouse at Dixon Hill and the ruins of the old plantations to the south, are best reached by car or moped; rentals of vehicles, as well as fishing equipment, can be arranged by hotels. The roads are generally well maintained, but in the southeast they can be rutted and tough to negotiate on two wheels. The main road that skirts the perimeter of the island—it's about 35 miles around—is called the Queen's Highway, but neither it nor any of the side roads branching off it is marked. If you're unsure of a turn, don't hesitate to ask for help. Most of the 500 or so people who live here were born on the island and know it like the back of their hands. If you want to swim or snorkel, wear your bathing suit underneath your clothes, as you can't count on the availability of changing facilities at beaches.

SAN SALVADOR ON FOOT

Walkers can take several short strolls along the west coast from the *Riding Rock Inn* (see "Checking In" in *Bahamas,* THE ISLANDS). Heading north on the highway from the inn, it's a 15-minute walk to the beach at Bonefish Bay, where the swimming is excellent and the bonefishing is not bad either. On the way, the road skirts the old *Pan American* building; it was used as a tracking station during the early days of the US space program in the

1960s, was then a school, and is now part of the luxurious *Club Med—Columbus Isle* resort (see "Checking In" in *Bahamas,* THE ISLANDS).

South of the inn, it's a 20-minute walk along the Queen's Highway to Cockburn Town, the island's capital; you'll pass a dive shop and a tiny marina on the way. East of the inn, across the Queen's Highway, there is a short marked trail to an old observation tower in the interior of the island. The tower overlooks Long Lake, a finger of Great Lake, the largest on the island.

SAN SALVADOR BY MOPED OR CAR

If you choose to drive, head north on the Queen's Highway from the *Riding Rock Inn* (see above). Just past Bonefish Bay is the small community of North Victoria Hill. The large estate on the beach, called *Polaris-by-the-Sea,* is owned by Ruth Durlacher Wolper, widow of Hollywood producer David Wolper. On the estate is the *New World Museum,* which houses pre-Columbian artifacts and a few objects thought to have been left by early Spanish explorers. Many of the artifacts displayed here were found at the *Palmetto Grove* archaeological site on the beach just north of the estate. If you want to visit the museum, contact Mervin Benson (phone: 331-2126); there's an admission charge. Next to the museum is *Club Arawak* (phone: 331-2126), a snack bar and occasional nightspot, and nearby are the *Ocean View Apartments* (phone: 331-2676), the only guest accommodations on the island besides the *Riding Rock Inn* and *Club Med.*

Just north of North Victoria Hill and south of Rocky Point is the village of Quarters; still standing here are the ruins of the old slave quarters of *Harbour Estate,* a plantation owned by Loyalist Burton Williams. The grave of Benedictine missionary Chrysostom Schreiner is somewhere on the property. His coffin reputedly lies directly atop that of Burton Williams—because, it is said, it was too difficult to dig a new grave in the hard rock. Nearby are the ruins of the *Columbus* hotel, which was built in the 1930s by entrepreneur Sir Harry Oakes and leased to Britain's Royal Air Force during World War II. Just beyond is the *Palmetto Grove* archaeological site—it's easy to miss, because virtually everything unearthed here has been carted away.

The road rounds the northwest corner of the island and parallels the broad sweep of Graham's Harbour. Some scholars maintain that Columbus was referring to this harbor when he described an anchorage on San Salvador large enough to shelter "all the ships of Christendom." (Take a dip here if you like; the beach is narrow but long, and the water is calm.) Scores of dinghies—or "smack boats," as Bahamians call them—race here every *Discovery Day* (October 12).

The road rambles on to North East Point and turns south toward Reckley Hill, where the Pratt family has lived for several generations. The US Coast Guard signal station that stands here was shut down more than 10 years ago. South of Reckley Hill is United Estates, the second-largest town on the island. Known to locals as UE, it's hardly a town at all—just a few houses and chapels scattered on a scrubby plain. Some locals say the village was named sometime in the 19th century by poor blacks imitating the pretentious speech of white foreigners.

Just down the road is Dixon Hill, where one of the world's last kerosene-powered lighthouses stands on a rise 163 feet above the ocean. Built by the British in the late 19th century and remodeled in 1930, the 72-foot-tall lighthouse emits a double flash every 10 seconds; the 400,000-candlepower beam can be seen by ships up to 19 miles out to sea. It's a demanding task to operate it: Every hour, the keeper pumps kerosene to the giant wick that fuels the lamp, and every two hours he pulls the weights that keep the beacon rotating. If she's around, Marcia, the keeper's daughter, will be glad to give visitors a brief, free tour.

The observation deck near the top of the lighthouse commands a fine view of the coast and the saltwater lakes that fleck the interior of the island. To the southeast is the town of Polly Hill, which sprang up around an old plantation. Beyond it is Crab Cay, where, in 1891, the *Chicago Herald* erected a marker commemorating the 400th anniversary of Columbus's voyage to the New World. (The connection seems tenuous, but there *is* a reason: Chicago was the site of the *1892 World's Fair,* which was called the *Columbian Exposition.*) The site the *Herald* picked was probably not where Columbus landed, however. The reefs just offshore are treacherous, and written records seem to show that after Columbus sighted land, he sailed to the western coast to come ashore. Nonetheless, the monument on Crab Cay declares incontrovertibly: "On this spot Christopher Columbus first set foot on the soil of the New World. Erected by the *Chicago Herald,* June 15, 1891." There is no road to the marker, but if the tide is low and the wind calm, you can park by the side of the road and slog across to the cay along East Beach, which fronts the lighthouse. It's a 2-mile trek to the spot where a small footpath leads from the beach to the worn limestone monument on the point.

Past Polly Hill the Queen's Highway skirts the western shore of a large lake. It's a desolate stretch of land; there are few birds here on the windward side of the island, and vegetation is sparse, except for a scattering of wild cotton and sisal plants and a pomegranate bush here and there. Three miles down are Fortune Hill and Holiday Tract, two modern villages established near old plantation sites. Just south of them, about a mile off the highway on a rough unmarked track, is the excavated archaeological site of *Pigeon Creek.* The artifacts, which are displayed at the *San Salvador Museum* in Cockburn Town, show that the spot was occupied by Arawak Indians for several generations.

Past the site the road follows the western shore of Pigeon Creek, which is actually an estuary. In colonial times cargo boats chugged up and down this 4-mile stretch of water, ferrying goods from ports to settlements in the center of the island. One of the largest of these was *Farquharson Plantation,* which lies west of the Queen's Highway near the modern village of South

Victoria Hill. The plantation has been carefully excavated, and the objects unearthed, including the estate journal for 1831–32, offer some indication of what life here must have been like. The 2,000-acre estate, only a small part of which was arable, was owned by Charles Farquharson, a magistrate for Watling's Island. About 55 slaves worked on the farm during the time the journal was written; of them, just over a dozen labored in the fields, raising cotton, corn, livestock, citrus fruit, and lignum vitae trees. Farquharson purchased flour, cloth, rum, and furniture; the farm was otherwise self-sufficient. Vegetables and pumpkins were raised for the household, and homegrown sage, catnip, and castor beans were used to treat minor ailments. The family subsisted on chickens, turkeys, and bonefish caught in nearby coves, and horses and mules were bred to work in the fields. The journal doesn't describe relations between master and slave, but in 1834, just a few years after it was written, emancipation was proclaimed, and life on the farm must have changed drastically.

Past the plantation, the road winds through what was once a bustling farm region, where the villages of Old Place, Breezy Hill, Trial Farm, Montreal, and Allen flourished a century ago. The settlements are now almost entirely abandoned, and the place has a ghostly feel. The road curves west near Blackwood Bay, and just to the left stand the ruins of an old church. Built in the early 20th century, it is called *Belmont Church* by the locals, for it stands on the ruins of an old estate called *Bell Mount.* The side road east of the church, which locals call Columbus Landing Road, skirts the south shore of the island and veers north toward the mouth of Pigeon Creek. The view along the coast is breathtaking, and the beach at Snow Bay on the east coast is snowdrift-white and virtually deserted.

Past French Bay, the main road turns north, and just to the left is *Sandy Point Estate.* The pirate John Watling was said to have lived here in the 17th century, and the place was known for years as *Watling's Castle.* (Despite the pious-sounding name of his ship, the *Most Holy Trinity,* Watling was as ruthless as they came.) Archaeologists maintain that the ruins here are the remnants of a plantation built during the early 19th century on land owned by Bud Cade Matthews, believed to have been a Loyalist who fled America during the Revolution. Unlike many other plantations on the island, *Sandy Point* prospered, remaining a working farm until 1925. In recent years, much of the property has been subdivided for homes and sold. A derelict tower still stands on the estate, and can be reached by the road just west of the dock. Lookouts who manned the tower searched the horizon for ships bringing goods from Nassau. If the ships crashed on the reefs offshore—a welcome event to those watching from here—they were scavenged.

To reach Southwest Point at the tip of the island, take Sandcliff Road, which branches off the Queen's Highway just north of the plantation. The road curves south to the point and then loops back to rejoin the highway just south of the plantation. Near the point—it's not marked, but is fairly easy to find—is a limestone cave called Dripping Rock, with an old well inside. Fruit trees—limes, mangoes, and sour oranges—flourish near the shore, and there is a secluded beach just north of the cave.

Heading back north along Queen's Highway, with the calm sea waters off to the west, you'll pass the abandoned settlement of Black Rock before reaching the area known as Sugar Loaf, which takes its name from a rocky outcropping just offshore. The paved road that forks to the left leads past the abandoned settlement of Strown Landing to the secluded cove at Sugar Loaf Beach.

Two miles farther north, near the tumbledown town of Long Bay, stand two monuments. The larger of the two, a stark, modernistic structure of dark gray stone designed by architects Pedro Alvarado and Antonio Vilchis, was built in 1968 by the organizers of the Mexico City *Olympic Games*. The ship carrying the *Olympic* flame from Greece to Mexico stopped here, and the monument's torch was lit. The flame is rekindled each *Discovery Day* with great fanfare. Just north of the *Olympic* monument stands a cross erected in 1956, flanked by flags of several nations; it is a tribute to—and a plea for—world unity.

Head toward Cockburn Town, past wild sisal plants that wave in the breeze on the island side of the road. The plants have spiky, dark green leaves and yellow or white blossoms crowning stems that shoot up to 25 feet in the air. Two varieties grow here: the smaller silk sisal, used to make bags and baskets, and the larger black or manila sisal, which was woven into rope. The sisal industry flourished here in the late 1890s and early 1900s, but once production picked up in the Philippines after the Spanish-American War, Bahamian growers were wiped out.

On the south edge of town, overlooking the shore, is a small Catholic cemetery. A wooden cross commemorates the mass celebrated there on January 25, 1891—the first on the island since 1492. The oldest marked grave belongs to W. Morrah Savage, a lighthouse inspector with the Royal Navy who died in 1885.

Nearby is the public dock, where the mail boat that brings supplies from Nassau calls each week. Across the highway from the dock is First Avenue, the main street of the neatly laid-out Cockburn Town (it's pronounced as one word, *Ko*-burn-town). Named for Sir Francis Cockburn, Governor of the Bahamas from 1837 to 1844, it's the administrative capital of the island.

Most of the sights worth seeing are crowded into the first few blocks of First Avenue. The *San Salvador Public Library* stands on one corner of the intersection of First Avenue and Queen's Highway. A pub, the *Ocean View Club* (phone: 331-2676), stands just opposite—stop in for a Kalik beer. Most afternoons, an ancient "straw woman" sits under an almond tree, plaiting her bags and baskets. Across the street in the old telegraph building is the *San Salvador Gift Shop* (phone: 331-2191), run by Iris Fernander. Nearby is the *Harlem Square Club* (phone: 331-2777), Marcus Jones's spacious bar; with a little prodding, he'll talk about his world travels. Across the street is the *Three Ships* restaurant (phone: 331-2787), run by Jones's wife, Faith; aside from the *Riding Rock Inn,* it's the only place on the island where you can get boiled fish and grits for breakfast (reservations necessary for dinner). Next door is Jake Jones's grocery store; up the block, on Carey Street, is *St. Augustine's Anglican Church,* which was consecrated in 1888.

Along the Queen's Highway north of the dock stand the commissioner's house, the *Holy Saviour Catholic Church*—Christopher Columbus is immortalized in a ceramic tile imbedded in the stucco façade—and the *San Salvador Museum.* The building that houses the museum dates from the mid-19th century; it once served as jail, courtroom, and commissioner's office. There are now exhibits on the island's Lucaya settlements—including artifacts from *Palmetto Grove, Pigeon Creek,* and *Long Bay*—and on Columbus's voyage here. Photographs and mementos from various colonial estates are displayed in the second-floor gallery. To arrange a visit, see Iris Fernander at the gift shop in downtown Cockburn or call her brother Clifford (phone: 331-2676); there's an admission charge.

Turks & Caicos

Of the eight main islands in the Turks and Caicos, seven are inhabited (only East Caicos remains unpopulated): Grand Turk and Salt Cay in the Turks archipelago and the Caicos Islands of South, Middle (Grand), and North Caicos; Pine Cay; and Providenciales (commonly called Provo). About 14,000 people, including part-time residents, live on these islands, more than half of them on Provo and Grand Turk. For the most part, the islands are as flat and dry as the Arizona desert—the highest hill in the entire colony, on Grand Turk, is only 163 feet tall, and the Turks and Caicos receive an average of only 26 inches of rain a year. Vegetation is sparse; there's little besides stands of windswept pine and palmetto and several varieties of cactus (including the red-topped Turk's head, for which the Turks Islands are named). Some of the islands were once forested, but salt rakers cleared the land to make room for their pans. Few crops are grown, except on the Caicos, where island residents raise small plots of corn and pigeon peas.

Until about 30 years ago, salt continued to be the mainstay of the economy; now shellfish—and tourists—are the big money-makers. Haiti and Florida are the main consumers of Turks and Caicos conch, and most of the spiny lobsters caught here end up on American tables. The big hope for the future is tourism. The British government has encouraged the development of the colony's tourist industry, which it hopes will bring the islanders closer to self-sufficiency. Provo, in the Caicos group, is the most developed for tourists, and the building boom in progress there is not unlike the boom on Grand Bahama in the 1950s and early 1960s. But with a little luck and some good planning, the development in the Turks and Caicos should not spoil the pristine beauty of the place completely. Locals have banded together to protect the reefs that ring the islands, and even on Provo you can still find some lovely secluded spots—once you get past the bulldozers and the earth-moving equipment.

In addition to scheduled flights (see GETTING READY TO GO and "Getting Around" in *Turks & Caicos,* THE ISLANDS), several charters shuttle back and forth among the smaller isles and cays. Visitors can even hop over for the day to one of the uninhabited isles such as West Caicos, where amenities are few but the swimming and diving are great. If you do plan to visit some of the more remote spots, make arrangements carefully. If you charter a boat or a plane to one of the unpopulated isles, be very specific about when you want to be picked up. Bring a map and plenty of sunscreen, carry your own food and water, and make sure someone at your hotel knows where you're going and when you plan to return.

Here, then, are brief descriptions of the seven inhabited Turks and Caicos Islands—Grand Turk and Salt Cay in the Turks; and Middle, North,

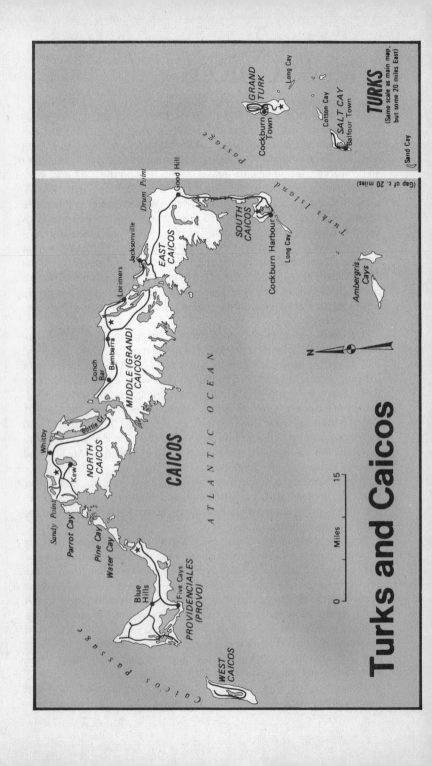

Turks and Caicos

ATLANTIC OCEAN

CAICOS

Caicos Passage

WEST CAICOS

PROVIDENCIALES (PROVO)

Blue Hills

Five Cays

Water Cay

Pine Cay

Parrot Cay

Sandy Point

Kew

NORTH CAICOS

Whitby

Bottle Cr.

Conch Bar

Bambarra

MIDDLE (GRAND) CAICOS

Lorimers

Jacksonville

EAST CAICOS

Drum Point

Good Hill

SOUTH CAICOS

Cockburn Harbour

Long Cay

Turks Island Passage

Ambergris Cays

(Gap of c. 20 miles)

GRAND TURK

Long Cay

Cockburn Town

TURKS
(Same scale as main map, but some 20 miles East)

Cotton Cay

SALT CAY

Balfour Town

Sand Cay

N

0   Miles   15

and South Caicos, Pine Cay, and Providenciales in the Caicos. You can see
the major sights on some in a day or less; others deserve a bit more time.
We also take you on a walking tour through historic Cockburn Town on
Grand Turk and on a driving tour across Provo. For hotel addresses and
phone numbers not listed here, see "Checking In" in *Turks & Caicos,* THE
ISLANDS.

GRAND TURK

Grand Turk's 9 square miles hold around 6,000 of the colony's 14,000 people. The island boasts a high school, a small hospital, international banks,
and an airport with a 7,000-foot airstrip. Like most of the Turks and Caicos,
the scenery is hardly worth writing home about. The land is flat, dry, and
covered with old salinas and scrub. The great treasures are offshore. Coral
reefs protect a good deal of the island, and divers have a choice of spectacular wall-diving sites.

Juan Ponce de León paid a call here in 1512, and some historians claim
that this is where Columbus first sighted land in 1492. Once the center of
the now-defunct salt industry, Grand Turk is the islands' administrative
center, and Cockburn Town is its major settlement. The town, a dusty,
sleepy little village, has a Bermudian look to it; if you're looking for nightlife,
this is definitely *not* the place. Until recently, donkey carts still rattled along
the harbor road, known as Front Street (its official name is Duke Street).
The donkeys still roam the island, but the carriages that once transported
visitors have disappeared. Don't despair: The town is small enough to be
explored on foot.

A GRAND TURK WALK

Start at the *Kittina* hotel, the oldest and largest resort on the island, which
stands right on the beach at the south end of town. Walk north up Front
Street past the *Salt Raker Inn,* a comfy Bermuda-style hostelry where the
locals stop for a beer and a little gossip. Just up the road is the *Turks Head
Inn,* housed in an 18th-century building that's been designated a historic
landmark. In the center of town, up the red brick sidewalk, is the Victorian-
era library. The *Cable and Wireless Building* is on the waterfront; it's cheaper
to call long-distance here than from the hotels. Nearby, on the same street,
are two banks, several government offices, and the town's only non-hotel
restaurant, the *Poop Deck* (no phone), which usually runs out of the daily
special by 2 PM.

Also near the center of town is *Blue Water Divers* (Front St.; phone:
62432), where you can rent all the diving equipment you need. Nearby is
the former *Guinep Lodge,* a historic home that now houses the *Turks and
Caicos National Museum* (Front St.; phone: 62160). It has an excellent
exhibit on the Molasses Reef wreck, the oldest shipwreck ever recovered
from these waters (the ship sank ca. 1512). The museum is closed Saturday

afternoons and Sundays; there's an admission charge. Past the museum the road doglegs around an old salt pond called North Salina. The road west of the pond leads to the *Guanahani Beach* hotel on near-perfect Pillory Beach, where you can stop for a swim and a rum cooler. Locals maintain that Columbus landed somewhere along this shore in 1492. The town's abandoned icehouse, in operation as recently as the 1940s, is nearby.

Follow the same road back toward town; it soon runs into Pond Street, which skirts the back of town. Nearby are several more salinas, a scattering of pastel-colored homes, and some very old warehouses. *Her Majesty's Prison* is on Pond Street, and across the salina is a 19th-century Methodist church, one of the oldest in the colony. Colonel Murray Hill, on the eastern side of mile-wide Grand Turk, is the highest point on the island and a favorite rendezvous for lovers.

If you'd like to continue your explorations, hire a cab through your hotel and visit the island's outlying sights: old *St. Thomas Anglican Church;* Governor's Beach, near *Waterloo,* the governor's stately 19th-century home; the lighthouse and the deserted naval station; and the missile-tracking station (where John Glenn was debriefed after splashing down near Grand Turk after completing his 1962 Mercury space mission). All are open to the public during daylight hours; none charges admission.

SALT CAY

Nine miles from Grand Turk, accessible by boat and only five minutes away by air, this 3½-square-mile island is shaped like a slice of pie pointed south. At the tip the surf is rough, but the east side is indented with quiet bays and inlets, and the beach that stretches across its wide northern end is as white and peaceful and perfect as a beach can get, though a few small hotels now dot its edge. Windswept and quaint, Balfour Town boasts relics of the island's whaling and salt-raking days. The windmills here haven't operated since 1971, and the abandoned salt flats look like skating rinks melting in the sun. Locals talk of reviving the saltworks to show tourists how they once were run. There is one dive outfit on the island (*Porpoise Divers;* phone: 66927), and the Talbot brothers will be glad to take you fishing. Contact them through the district commissioner's office (phone: 66985). In late winter and early spring, humpback whales swim up the Turks Passage off the west coast on the way to their spawning grounds. They sometimes can be spotted from the beach near the *Windmills* hotel.

MIDDLE (GRAND) CAICOS

Reached by ferry from North Caicos or by air from Provo, Middle (or Grand) Caicos is the largest of the group, though only 400 people live here year-round. The island has recently been spruced up, with 10 miles of repaved road and an extended and renovated airstrip. Just a few places on the island offer lodging: *Eagle's Rest Villas,* with eight two-bedroom, two-bath units (six of them recently built) featuring living rooms, fully equipped kitchens, and cable TV; the much more rustic and inexpensive four-room *Maria Taylor's Guest House* (phone: 63322); *Arthur's Guest House* (phone: 66100), with two guestrooms; and Annie Taylor's *Sea View Guest House* (phone: 66117), with four rooms available in an air conditioned house with two bathrooms, a kitchen, a dining room, and a living area with a TV set. The secluded beach near Mudjin Harbour is exceptionally beautiful, and there are extraordinary limestone caves along the cliff-edged northern coast. It's worth the trouble to find the caves, if only to see the reflections of the stalactites and stalagmites in the clear saltwater pools. Taxi driver Cardinal Arthur (phone: 66107 or 66100) offers cave tours. For more than a decade, groups of American archaeologists have been coming to Middle Caicos to explore the caves and ruins near Bambarra and Lorimers. Bambarra was settled by survivors of the Spanish slave ship *Gambia,* which was shipwrecked offshore in 1842. Most of the slaves were Bombarras from the Niger River Valley in West Africa, hence the town's name. Archaeologists also come to hunt for Lucaya Indian artifacts and to explore the ruins of Loyalist plantations along Benjie Ridge.

NORTH CAICOS

One of the most verdant of the islands, relatively speaking, North Caicos is best known for its 6-mile beach and excellent bonefishing. Its 1,600 permanent residents live in four tiny villages: Bottle Creek on the island's eastern edge, Kew and Whitby in the center, and Sandy Point in the northwest. Near Kew stand the recently excavated ruins of *Wade's Green Plantation.* On the island's many nature reserves and sanctuaries, visitors can see West Indian whistling ducks, ospreys, grebes, and flocks of flamingos, which look from a distance like billowing pink clouds. At the *West Indian Mariculture Crab Farm,* between Whitby and Bottle Creek, you can learn how Caribbean king crabs are nurtured from tiny eggs to hefty adults; special tours and boat trips are available. The farm is open daily; no admission charge (phone: 67213). Fine out-island hideaways are available to vacationers at *Pelican Beach, Prospect of Whitby, Joanne's Bed and Breakfast* (phone/fax: 67301), and *Ocean Beach* condos.

PINE CAY

One of the chain of islets that links North Caicos and Provo, Pine Cay is quietly notable for the *Meridian Club* resort, the social center for a residential enclave of some 25 homes that occupies this 800-acre private island. The club is exclusive, but not in a class-conscious sense, though some of its guests may be listed in the Social Register. It's special for its devotion to uncomplicated relaxation and to preserving the peace and beauty of the island. Pine Cay's shimmering 2-mile beach is lovely for sunning, swimming, strolling, and snorkeling, and there are several hiking trails and nature walks for visitors looking to do some exploring. The resort offers regular boat trips to small, deserted islands nearby: Fort George Cay, where the remains of cannons from an 18th-century British fort are visible just off-shore, is worth a visit, and Water Cay and Little Water Cay are excellent for shelling.

PROVO

Green, hilly Provo is one of the largest of the Turks and Caicos Islands (37½ square miles) and the most sophisticated from the standpoint of tourism. It lies near the western edge of the Caicos chain, just east of uninhabited West Caicos. About 3,500 people live here year-round, and tourists and part-time residents swell the ranks considerably.

The scenery on Provo isn't remarkable; most of the island is covered with scrub and stunted trees, and there is little in the way of natural beauty aside from the nature reserve at Crab Pond. The 12-mile-long beach along the north coast near Grace Bay is very fine, though, and it is there that the island's big resorts, including the *Grace Bay Club,* the *Ramada Turquoise Reef* resort and casino, and the *Club Med Turkoise,* are located.

Also on the east end, near the slips where the ferry to the neighboring Caicos Islands docks, is the *Island Sea Centre* and its conch-breeding farm (phone: 65849). Here, conch eggs are nurtured in geodesic domes and fed farm-raised algae until they're large enough to be transplanted to seabed nurseries. The research project is sponsored in part by the University of Miami and *PRIDE (Prevention of Reefs and Islands from Degradation and Exploitation),* the Provo-based nonprofit environmental organization dedicated to preserving the pristine waters and delicate coral reefs of the Turks and Caicos. Formerly open to the public, the center, along with its snack bar and gift shop, was destroyed in an arson fire in 1993 and is not expected to reopen to tourists for at least another year or two. The farm supplies conch to Haiti, the Bahamas, and Florida, as well as to local residents and restaurants.

PROVO BY CAR

Visitors who don't mind dusty, unmarked roads can rent a car (a four-wheel-drive vehicle is recommended to reach the beaches on the north and west coasts) and visit other spots on the island. The main road, the Leeward Highway, runs east to west along a 100-foot ridge not far from the north shore. Take a map, since few of the roads and settlements are marked. Heading west from the conch farm, past the turnoff to the big resorts on Grace Bay and the settlement of Kingston, is Richmond Hills, site of a ruined Loyalist plantation and now an enclave of modern homes. Beyond it is the road to Turtle Cove on the north shore, where the *Erebus Inn* overlooks the blue-green water of the bay. If you're hungry, stop by the inn's excellent *La Crêperie* restaurant. The *Turtle Cove Inn,* with its restaurant, *Jimmy's,* and the *Turtle Cove Landing* shopping center are nearby. (For details about *La Crêperie* and *Jimmy's,* see "Eating Out" in *Turks & Caicos,* THE ISLANDS.)

Back on the main road, located in the shopping and commercial development known unimaginatively as *Central Square,* is the lively California-style Mexican restaurant *Hey José* (see "Eating Out" in *Turks & Caicos,* THE ISLANDS). A little farther down on the right is *Cheshire Hall,* another Loyalist plantation that dates from the 1790s. The ruins here are more accessible than those at Richmond Hills, and you can poke around the remaining foundation stones and imagine what the place was like a couple of hundred years ago. About a mile farther on, where five roads converge, is the area known as "downtown," a soulless place with an assortment of modern shopping centers, banks, offices, and modest eateries.

Fishermen should take the south fork out of downtown, which leads to the excellent bonefishing flats on Chalk Sound. On the way, the road passes near the South Dock Harbour, where the big freighters dock; the *Mariner Inn* on Sapodilla Hill (some of the rocks up the hill behind the inn are carved with the initials of sailors who were shipwrecked here over the years); and a few secluded beaches.

The road leading directly west from downtown dead-ends at the airport; the northwest fork from the intersection here leads to the decent beach at Thompson Cove point on the north coast and wanders through the settlement of Blue Hills. The town is said to have been founded by the surviving passengers of a French ship that was dashed against the reefs here early in the 17th century. In early August, the residents of Blue Hills celebrate *Emancipation Day* with a *Carnival*-like parade. About 3 miles down the road is Wheeland, a small settlement with a couple of restaurants and nightclubs that offer live entertainment a few times each week. The pavement ends after Wheeland; you'll need a four-wheel-drive vehicle to reach the lovely, secluded beaches on the north and west coasts and the Crab Pond nature reserve in the interior.

SOUTH CAICOS

Some 22 miles west of Grand Turk, across the Turks Passage, South Caicos is anchored behind a sweep of coral reefs that offer an enormous variety of dives. The little town, Cockburn Harbour, is friendly but not much to look at. The only buildings of historic interest are the 18th-century *Commissioner's House* and the warehouses of the old saltworks. The focal point of the community is Cockburn Harbour itself, the best natural harbor in the Turks and Caicos and the islands' fishing capital. Anglers bring in their catch of conch and lobster here, and every May the bay is filled with sloops and smacks competing in the *Commonwealth Regatta.* Wild horses graze on the scrub on the eastern part of the island. There is a 7,500-foot airstrip, where *Turks and Caicos Airways (TCA)* flights and a steady stream of private craft touch down.

Index